Cannabis Cultivation

A Complete Grower's Guide

Mel Thomas

Green Candy Press

Cannabis Cultivation
A Complete Grower's Guide, 3rd Edition
By Mel Thomas

Published by Green Candy Press
San Francisco, CA
www.greencandypress.com

Copyright © 2012 Mel Thomas
ISBN 978-1-931160-83-4

Cover leaf image © iStockPhoto

Interior and back cover photographs © 420Clones.com, Allele Seeds Research, AlphaKronik Genes, Alpine Seeds, Apothecary Genetics, ASG Seeds, Austrian Toker, Autofem Seeds, BC Bud Depot, BC Northern Lights, Bomba Seeds, Bubble Man, Cabin Fever Seed Breeders, Cannanetics, Ch9 Female Seeds, D.T. Gonzales, David Strange, Dinafem Seeds, Don't Panic Organix, Dr. Atomic Seeds, Dr. Canem & Company, Dr. Greenthumb Seeds, Dr. Underground, Dutch Passion, Ed Borg, Emerald Triangle Seed Co., Emily Blunt, Eva Female Seeds, Finest Medicinal Seeds, Freebie, Gage Green Genetics, Garry Von Billen, GBI, Genetics Gone Madd, Giorgio Alvarezzo, GotBuds?, Growl LED, Grubbycup Stash, Hannah S., Hero Seeds, Holy Smoke Seeds, Homegrown Fantaseeds, HortiLab Seeds, HydroFarm, HydroHuts, HydroPlex, iStockPhoto, Kannabia Seeds, Karmaceuticals LLC, Kiwi Seeds, Larry Utley, M. Heinrich, Magus Genetics, Mandala Seeds, Mel Thomas, MG Imaging, MMJars, mmjclones.org, Mosca Seeds, Mr. Nice Seeds, Mystic Artist, MzJill, Noel van Shaik, No Mercy Supply, OG Genetics, OGA Seeds, Original Seeds, Peak Seeds, Paradise Seeds, Paulo Ferreira, Pedro A., Pepper Design, Pitt Bully Seeds, Poor White Farmer Seeds, Project Skunkenstein, PureBred Growers, Red Star Farms, RYKA Imaging, Sativa Steph, Sativa Tim, Sensi Seeds, Shantibaba, Short Stuff Seeds, Sinsemilla Nursery, SinsemillaWorks!, Skip C., Soma Seeds, Spacekracker, Spliff Seeds, Stealth Grow Lights, Subcool, Team Green Avengers, TH Seeds, The Joint Doctor, The Potfather, TrimPro, Weado, Weed.co.za, Weed World, Wizards of Oz.

Printed in China by 1010 Printing International Limited
Massively Distributed by P.G.W.

Dedicated to the thousands of men and women serving
prison sentences for cannabis.

"Education is an admirable thing."
Oscar Wilde. 1854-1900.

DRUGS RING SMASHED

FOUR men were expected to appear before ████████████tes today in connection with a multi-million pound drug factory found when armed police raided a disused warehouse.

The men were arrested and brought to ████████████following raids on properties in ████████████ ████ where another drug factory was discovered.

Th████████████ women were also arrested during Operation Vortex which involved 31 officers from ████████████along with police from ████████████ the Metropolitan police and the South West Regional Crime Squad.

The four faced questioning in relation to a large scale cannabis factory found in ████████████ in November last year.

Detective Inspector ████████████ of ████████████police said, "the search and arrest phase of Operation Vortex went very well with all the suspects arrested and the seizure of a large volume of exhibits and documents along with varying amounts of drugs, notably the live factory of more than 600 plants in ████████████.

But ████████████said "the factory discovered in ████████████ ████last year had a far larger capacity than the one found yesterday. Hydroponics factories can produce £1 million street value of drugs per year and make huge profits for criminals who run them.

However they also demand much equipment, electricity and power, which is usually obtained dishonestly."

FACTORY-Police uncovered a cannabis manufacturing plant in ████████████

Detective Ins████████████

paid £45,000 in cash warehouse in a quiet street in ████████████ The gang installed sophisticated growing equipment, including dehumidifiers, powerful lights and irrigation systems.

'Tardis'

The 475 square metre warehouse was code-████████████March 13. Another man after being found with a small amount of cannabis and released. The remaining prisoners will be dealt with by police in the

'factory for cannabis'

Contents

With this book and just a little effort, you could be growing your own buds within a few weeks!

Foreword

I've been in jail and I am a little bored.
Tom Horne. 1904.

The author of this book was a notorious European cannabis cultivator based in London. Code-named "Mr. Big" by detectives, he was eventually arrested after a covert operation involving four separate police forces and charged with conspiring to produce $3.5 million worth of skunk cannabis. The trial judge called him "A horticultural expert involved in a resolute and successful attempt to produce cannabis on a commercial scale."

On November 29, police searched the author's premises. They discovered that a large area within the premises had been concealed behind a secret door and contained a sophisticated hydroponic growing environment with dehumidifiers, lighting and irrigation facilities. The environment was professionally wired-in, bypassing the metered supply. The growing area was 200 feet by 30 feet, enabling six crops per year of 660 pounds of cannabis to be produced. 'Skunk' cannabis is priced at 27 cents per ounce – potentially $2.5 million per year, or at a wholesale cost, ranging from $6,160 per pound - $840,000. Based on the amount of equipment found at the premises, it is estimated that electricity valued at $37,128 had been used. Aggravating features of the case were the very high value of cannabis produced from the two factories, and the highly professional operation for the large-scale production of a controlled drug.

The author and his co-accused were sentenced to more than 14 years between them and ordered to pay over $210,000 in fines or serve an additional three years without parole. Convicted of producing cannabis, "Mr. Big" was held as a category 'A' prisoner on a maximum-security wing in one of Europe's most secure jails. This book was conceived in that prison.

Update 2011. A few people have asked me about the case and the press cuttings. I was arrested in the United Kingdom in 1996. In those days you could buy a warehouse in the North of England for US $70,000 cash and that's why we went there. The depositions implicated me in cannabis production and

Don't Panic Organix produces some incredible strains, such as Funxtaz Get Rite, bred by Eddie Funxta for medical patients.

other offences. I was sentenced by His Honor Judge Julian Hall in the U.K. Google him. He is well-known for his leniency toward pedophiles, remarking that a 10-year-old rape victim was dressed "provocatively" and freeing another pedophile, telling him to buy his six-year-old victim a new bicycle. He was not so obliging with me and I received 5 years imprisonment, amongst other things, and he also seized my house. I served the category A part of my sentence in Woodhill prison, Milton Keynes, U.K. I make no excuses. I did it for the money, but my motivation was sincere. Prohibition is ridiculous. Who has the right to stop you growing or using cannabis? It is not a drug; it's a plant. Put it in the Earth and it grows. Drugs are powders, needles and nasty tablets, not ancient and sacred herbs...

Shiva Bless

The dark green colors on this plant indicate a strong indica background.

1. The Cannabis Plant

I know the grass beyond the door, the sweet keen smell.
Dante Rossetti. 1828–1882.

The name Hemp comes from the Old English word hænep and is the common name for plants of the entire genus C.sativa, although the term now usually refers only to cannabis strains cultivated for fiber and not drug crops. Cannabis is a hardy plant that grows in both temperate and tropical conditions throughout the world and can thrive in diverse and sometimes challenging environments. Botanists can't agree as to which family cannabis belongs; initially it was classified one of the Nettle family (Urticaceae), although this was based more on visual characteristics than biology. It was later reclassified into the Fig family (Moraceae). However, this is still causing disagreement, so in view of its uniqueness, cannabis is now classified Cannabaceae along with the genus of hop plants. When dating pollen samples it is difficult to establish the difference between hemp and hops, its botanical relative. In most studies, hemp and hops are not separated from each other. Instead, they are reported as hops/hemp or Cannabaceae. Cannabis can grow in height from one to four metres (3 to 15ft), depending on variety and

The direct sunlight that this outdoor grow receives has led to fantastic growth.

1

growing conditions. It is classified as an herbaceous annual. "Herbaceous" simply means the plant is an herb and "annual" refers to its life cycle, meaning the plant grows, reproduces and dies in one season. It is an heliotropic plant, preferring direct sunlight and open spaces, and so grows poorly in shaded areas.

Because of its importance as a crop, cannabis has been transported and grown in many diverse regions, apart from areas of extreme cold or humidity, and was introduced worldwide by our ancestors. It was almost certainly the Scythians who introduced hemp into China but it is widely accepted that the Chinese were the first to domesticate the native Asian plant, or at least document its use. Its centre was in present-day northern China where there is a continuous record of its use from Neolithic times to the present day. Cannabis is believed to have been introduced into Northern Europe by The Vikings. The Spaniards took it to Mexico and Peru, the French to Canada and the English to North America, where it was revered as a valuable fiber crop. Cultivars dispersed so widely from their natural habitat over such a long period and subjected to constant human selection for set characteristics tend to hybridize, and frequently become so altered that they barely resemble the original plant. Unlike other cultivars, cannabis remains true and thrives in the wild despite its long history as a major crop plant. There are three distinct varieties of cannabis that are grown for their Tetrahydrocannabinol or THC content: Cannabis sativa, Cannabis indica and Cannabis ruderalis.

This bud is in the early flowering stage. Soon its trichomes will be full of THC.

Cannabis sativa

These plants are characterized by long thin flowers and spiky leaves. They originate from equatorial regions where the growing season is hotter. They are not generally used for outdoor cultivation in colder climates, although some hybrids can produce good yields in such conditions. Cannabis sativa produces more of a high than Cannabis indica buds do.

Cannabis indica

These plants originated in the Hindu-kush areas of Central Asia, where the weather is changeable and growing conditions can be harsh. Hardy plants, they mature early and are characterized by broad, short leaves and heavy, tight flowers. Cannabis indica varieties are ideal for both indoor and outdoor cultivation in cooler climates.

Cannabis ruderalis

Cannabis ruderalis is a variety of cannabis that grows wild in parts of Eastern Europe and Russia. It is characterized by its early flowering, with some plants starting irrespective of the photo-period. Cannabis ruderalis is ideal for cultivation in cooler climates and areas where conditions are harsh. There are Dutch hybrid varieties available that combine Cannabis ruderalis and Cannabis indica.

Greenhouses can contain both indica and sativa crops, but remember, space is an issue as sativas tend to be much leggier plants.

This healthy bud is from a sativa-indica hybrid that demonstrates positive traits from both parent strains.

3

This bushy female plant is an indica-dominant hybrid.

Cannabis is dioecious, which means the plant is either male (staminate) or female (pistillate), although genetically unstable hermaphrodites with both male and female flowers do occur. Sexual reproduction is carried out by the female flower in the ovaries at the base of the pistils, containing the female germ cells. Fertilization occurs when male pollen unites with female ovules.

Cannabis regulates its development and flower production by measuring the length of daylight falling onto its leaves. It produces a light-sensitive hormone called phytochrome that is responsible for altering the plant from vegetative growth into flowering when it reaches a critical level. Cannabis plants change from the vegetative state into the flowering cycle when they receive 12 hours of uninterrupted darkness. They will respond to this change no matter where they are grown, even under artificial lighting. Cultivators can use this response to their advantage by controlling the plants' day lengths, either by changing the lighting cycles or by covering outdoor and greenhouse plants. Plants that are grown under lighting are given 18 to 24 hours of daylight to keep them in the vegetative stage. Plants given 24 hours of daylight will grow 25% faster. There is no requirement for them to sleep; however, the grower needs to calculate the cost in terms of electricity used. If there is a problem with consuming excessive amounts then the cycle should be run at 18 hours for best results. Cuttings under fluorescents respond better to 24 hours of daylight.

Only the female flower produces buds, and there is no difference in the potency of plants that are flowered at different ages, younger plants just yield less. Once the flowering cycle has been induced a young plant will have the same THC content as an older one.

THC, also known as tetrahydrocannabinol or delta-9-tetrahydrocannabinol is the name given to the cannabinoids, found in cannabis plants, which are unique to the species. They are not found anywhere else and although we can synthesize them in a laboratory, we have still not found a synthetic equal to THC. These cannabinoids are actually made up of several different but related chemicals with similar effects. They are known as CBN, THCV, CBV and CBDV. There is also one chemical – labeled CBD – that is known to block the psychoactive effect of the others. Some plants will have all sets of chemicals in their make-up, and there are several different versions of THC found in differing plants, so in practice we label these all as THC. THC production is known to increase in cannabis plants grown at higher altitudes and is thought to have some function in protecting the plant from ultra violet radiation. THC also exhibits antibiotic properties, suggesting a role in protecting the plant from mold or disease. Some suggest that THC has a function in repelling herbivores and insects. This may be the case; however, as an insect repellent it is fairly inept. It can also be argued that many herbivores actively seek out cannabis plants, which should not have evolved toxins that reward animals for eating them, and humans should not have developed a reward mechanism within the brain for THC.

Barracuda from Dr. Canem & Company Seeds is a dazzling outdoor strain.

In 1988, Allyn Howlett, a researcher at St. Louis University Medical School, discovered a specific receptor for THC in the human brain. These are a type of nerve cell that THC binds to on a molecular level, causing it to activate. The receptors are found throughout the brain, but are clustered in regions responsible for

The dark red pistils indicate that this plant is ready for harvest. Its trichomes will be packed full of THC.

thought, memory, movement and emotion. Interestingly, these receptors are not found in the brain stem that controls involuntary functions such as breathing and blood circulation. This explains the low toxicity of THC and why no overdose has ever been recorded. No one has ever died as a direct result of ingesting THC, nor have there been any instances of brain receptor damage through cannabis use. THC stimulates the specialist receptors, but unlike alcohol and other drugs, cannabis chemicals do not wear out the receptors that they stimulate.

One estimate of THC's lethal dosage for humans indicates that roughly 1500 pounds of cannabis would have to be smoked within 15 minutes (approx). to cause death. Studies indicate that the effective dose of THC is at least 1000 times lower than the estimated lethal dose. Heroin, by contrast, has a therapeutic ratio of 6:1, alcohol is not far behind with a level of 10:1 and cocaine is rated at 15:1.[1.1] If you wanted to make 1500 pounds of cannabis lethal to humans you would be better advised dropping it on them.

In order to recognize delta-9-tetrahydrocannabinol the brain must in theory produce its own version of the chemical, perhaps to regulate pain management, appetite, or even thought and emotions. Raphael Mechoulam discov-

A beautiful plant from Dinafem Seeds in Spain. This female flower is just about ready to harvest.

ered the brain's own endogenous cannabin in 1992. He named it Anandamide, which means 'inner bliss' in Sanskrit. The cannabis plant produces a complex chemical very similar to one that we naturally produce ourselves.

The THC drug is principally contained in multicellular structures on the surface of the flower heads and smaller leaves called stalked capitate trichome glands. These appear as tiny, translucent, mushroom-like structures that are visible through a magnifying glass. The heads of these structures contain oil that is secreted as a sticky resin and that contains high levels of THC.

Trichomes laden with THC resin adorn this gorgeous plant.

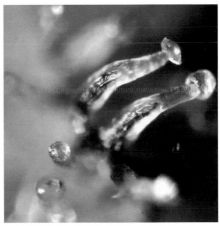

These trichomes on Alpine Seeds' Strawberry are filled with extremely potent resin.

The glands are not the only multicellular structures on the plant's surface. Bulbous glands, also known as sessile glands, are found on some of the leaves and contain low levels of cannabinoids. The other structures to look out for are unicellular hairs that actually look like short hairs, and cystolith hairs, which appear pointed under the magnifying glass and contain calcium carbonate deposits. Neither of these two structures contain any cannabinoids.

The male develops small clusters of white flowers that release pollen before dropping from the plant. The male dies shortly after the flowers drop. Male plants have low quantities of THC and are usually removed from the crop to avoid the pollination of the females. Once a female has been pollinated all her efforts go into seed production, which is not what marijuana producers want. By leaving the female unpollinated you get thicker, more resinous buds whose weight is composed of flower material, not seeds. The Spanish word for seedless is "Sinsemilla," and this is what gives these harvests their name.

Thick stems like these can support large harvests of ganja.

In order to ensure an all-female crop, most cultivators take cuttings from a known female and grow genetically identical clones as opposed to seedlings. If you have a crop of seedlings you can identify the females once flowering has started by their small white hair-like pistils emerging from bulbous pods at every branch union. The males produce small green balls that will develop into flowers.

The structure of the cannabis plant stem is of interest to cultivators. Directly underneath the green bark are two layers responsible for the transportation of water and nutrients between the leaves and the plant. The leaves are basically sugar factories where sunlight is collected and used in the production of energy. Sugars and phosphatides are produced by combining this energy with carbon dioxide from the atmosphere and nutrients from the soil. The layer directly beneath the outer bark is called the phloem and its tissues are used by the plant to conduct food processed in the leaves back down into the plant itself. Beneath this there is another layer called the xylem, a tissue responsible for conducting water and nutrients back up to the leaves to be used in the production of sugars.

We can use the structure of the plant stem to our advantage when carrying out asexual propagation. It is possible to reduce the stress to the mother plant and cuttings by using a technique known as air layering. This method involves creating a clone, complete with roots that are still attached to the parent plant. We do this with a little careful surgery on the clone site: cutting into the phloem and disrupting the flow of nutrients away from the selected area, while leaving the xylem intact and still feeding the newly developing clone. When the drain of food back into the mother is shut off, the clone is able to utilize it in the production of new roots. The clone will be a complete genetic copy of the mother, inheriting all of the same characteristics.

Cannabis inherits its characteristics from its parent plants. When sexual reproduction takes place, male and female germ cells join together. Every plant cell contains chromosomes that hold genetic information. Each pair of chromosomes contains two genes for each characteristic: cannabis plants have 10 pairs of chromosomes, making a total of 20. Plants that contain these normal sets of chromosomes are called diploid. Abnormal numbers of chromosomes within one plant cell are generally referred to as polyploid plants.

Footnotes:
1.1 http://en.wikipedia.org/wiki/Tetrahydrocannabinol

Grape Stomper from the experts at Gage Green Genetics is a highly reliable strain with a great reputation.

2. Choosing Your Location

A man may learn wisdom, even from a foe.
Aristophanes. 380 BC.

This grower chose a remote outdoor location for his garden so that his plants were safe, secure and healthy.

Artificial environments, known as grow rooms, offer the cannabis grower a safer alternative to outdoor cultivation, with the benefit of year-round consistent crops. Grow rooms can be built in a variety of locations and can vary in size from small cupboards to warehouse-sized marijuana farms. Your location needs to be secure and free of extremes of temperature or dampness, and requires a supply of water and electricity. Successful grow rooms can be built in both commercial and residential premises.

Residential

- Spare rooms (bedrooms are ideal)
- Attics and lofts (although these can suffer from excessive heat during the summer months)
- Cellars (damp can become a problem in some cellars and basements)
- Cupboards and closets
- Outhouses and sheds (including greenhouses)
- Garages
- Mobile homes (including trailers and campers with access to power)
- Apartments

Commercial

- Industrial units
- Warehouses
- Office blocks (provided they are secure)
- Agricultural buildings (such as barns and poultry units)
- Lock-up garages (power can sometimes be a problem in these setups)
- Retail units (unused areas including living accommodation)
- Horticultural units
- Containers (these can be buried but dampness can become a problem in underground setups)

The location and size of the grow room is determined by the crop that you want to produce. Cultivators interested in growing enough for their own consumption need only a small amount of space in which to grow their plants; a cupboard setup using low-wattage lighting can provide all they need. Those wanting to cultivate on a commercial scale will require premises where they can farm with rows of 1000-watt high-pressure sodium lights and automated hydroponics.

Having decided on the location, you can set about building an artificial environment in which to grow. All setups, regardless of size, have the same basic requirements.

- Light of the correct spectrum
- Water at the correct temperature
- Nutrients in the correct balance
- Air rich in carbon dioxide and well circulated
- Humidity and temperature within the correct range

To achieve this artificial environment you will supply light to the plants using horticultural lighting purchased from specialist retailers, control the air, humidity and temperature with heaters, dehumidifiers, fans and carbon dioxide emitters, and deliver nutrients to the plants from fertilizers.

A DIY garden made from a large tupperware bin can produce enough buds to supply you for months.

Good reflector hoods and a good reflective wall covering can help increase yield.

The walls of this grow room are covered in highly reflective material to maximize light efficiency.

Preparing the Grow Room

Before installing the artificial environment, the grow room needs to be prepared. It is important to seal all windows and doors to prevent light contamination from outside. In residential locations, windows should be prepared by first hanging a net curtain or Venetian blind. Thin plywood is then sprayed with matte black paint and secured over the whole of the window opening from the inside. Finally, tape along the edges with masking tape to ensure that the window is lightproof. When windows are viewed from the outside they appear black, so the board creates an optical illusion behind the net or blinds that is difficult to detect, even close up. The room appears as if it is empty and unlit.

Atmospheric controllers help maintain optimum humidity and temperature in your grow room.

If you are not using carbon dioxide emitters, and providing that it is not a downstairs or neighbor-facing window where odors may be detected, vents can be built into the plywood screen. However, you must ensure that you leave the window slightly open. Bend ducting twice through 90° to prevent light from escaping. If it's not possible to fix a vent into the window opening, use two lengths of ducting run from the best point of entry to give you an inlet and outlet vent, positioned at opposite ends of the room. The vents can be bathroom extractor fans, although these may be a little noisy for some setups. Silent-running extractors can be purchased and are definitely worth the additional cost.

Clean the grow room thoroughly, wiping down all surfaces with a diluted disinfectant or 5% bleach solution, then paint the walls white. Light distribution in a grow room is greatly increased by making all surfaces and walls reflective. White paint is up to 75% efficient at reflecting light from its surface. Mylar sheeting, available at most hydroponic suppliers, is a massive 95% efficient at reflecting light and can be used to cover the wall surfaces, or hung on a framework to make an enclosed, reflective tent. Alternatives to paint or Mylar sheeting are white plastic sheeting or aluminum foil. Use aluminum foil

Office desk fans are ideal for air circulation.

Green Planet provides great nutrients for all types of growers.

Soil conditions can be improved by using additives like perlite, vermiculite, and natural peat moss.

with the shiny side facing the wall to avoid hot spots. Mirrors should not be used as reflectors because they soak up light instead of bouncing it back onto the growing plants.

During daylight, shut the door to the grow room and stand in the darkened room – this way you will see any light that is not blocked out effectively and you can remedy the situation. Remember that light coming into the grow area will ruin your flowering cycle, and light shining out from the grow room can compromise your security. Areas to watch out for are leaks around windows and doors and cracks in the floors or brickwork. Use aluminum or duct tape to seal leaks.

This grower is using a multi-level system to maximize production in his grow space.

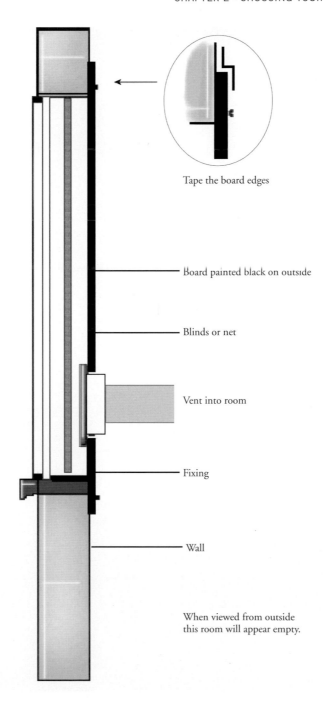

Tape the board edges

Board painted black on outside

Blinds or net

Vent into room

Fixing

Wall

When viewed from outside
this room will appear empty.

Mako Haze from Kiwi Seeds is a great all-around plant offering a stunning high.

3. Security

Three can keep a secret, if two of them are dead.
Benjamin Franklin. 1706 - 1790.

Whatever your requirements, the location of your grow room must be secret. If you're cultivating on a small scale at home, you must keep knowledge of your grow room confined to a "need to know" basis. If you have a larger setup away from home, you should take steps to avoid being followed.

Learning a few basic counter surveillance techniques can help keep you one step ahead of the authorities. If you live in a city or large town, keep authorities off your track as you move to and from your grow room by using public transportation (boarding buses and trains at the last possible moment) and by entering busy department stores and leaving by fire exits. Try to find routes that involve crossing pedestrian bridges or using underground pedestrian tunnels where anyone following you is channeled and forced into showing himself. Constantly change your route.

If you have to drive to your grow room, take a route that involves moving through traffic lights and one way streets. Try to time your crossings as the lights change and make obvious diversions that a tailing vehicle can't copy without being noticed. Surveillance teams will use four or more vehicles to follow you, including motorcycles, so always try to be what the police term "surveillance aware." Find an area away from your home location where you can pull over and physically check the underbody of your vehicle, as modern tracking devices can be placed underneath and held in position by a series of small magnets. These devices have a range of over six miles and are regularly used on police operations, along with satellite tracking systems that have unlimited range. Tracking devices emit a signal that allows them to be located with hand-held devices that can be purchased from specialist suppliers. Or, have your vehicle swept by a reputable company to detect and eliminate eavesdropping and surveillance devices.

If you use a cell phone, leave it at home whenever you visit your grow room. Even when switched off, cell phones emit a pulse signal, powered by their own internal battery, which is intended to link the phone to the nearest

This discreet hatch can be opened for access to your clandestine grow room.

The hatch opens to reveal a secret grow operation.

transmitter. The pulse signal can also provide the phone company with details of your movements that the police can and do use, both in surveillance operations and in court cases. It is very tempting to take pictures of your plants, but be extremely cautious when using your cell phone's digital camera application. The latest iPhones for example have a built in GPS function that will record the exact location where the image is taken. This GPS facility is extremely invasive and will also track your move-

Your cell phone can be used not only to track your movements, but also as evidence against you in a court of law. Leave it at home when you visit your grow site.

ments in real time on the built in 'maps' application.

You should also avoid contacting associates on your cell phone or land line. Telephone tapping is used by police both legally, with the relevant court orders, and illegally. Most telephone surveillance is never mentioned in court cases and is used purely to collate information on you, so never discuss anything on your telephone. Cell phones are very easy to tap into and text/voice messaging services are even easier because your number can simply be cloned onto a laptop facility where messages can be recorded and saved.

Part of police procedure is to link surveillance targets by the numbers that they telephone. The dates and times are noted and listed, which then helps the police intelligence teams to build a picture of your associates. They will produce this information in any subsequent court cases to link defendants. Use public pay phones when you need to contact someone, but be aware that surveillance teams are trained to wait near the pay phone, even lining up while you are using it, so that they can be next to use the phone and to verify your call. They dial a specially established number that is constantly being changed, and an operator tells them all the connections that have been made from that phone. Although the police get the numbers, they can't record the conversation: by doubling back on yourself and watching for people who use the pay phone or phone booth after you, you can frustrate their efforts. A friend of mine showed me statements a police surveillance team had made about him. One officer wrote, "I waited outside of the phone booth, Smith finished his call and then left the booth, he held the door open for me and said, 'There's

Beware of leaving fingerprints on any plastic bags you use while growing.

Fingerprints can be used to incriminate you in court, so wear a pair of gloves while you work.

still credit left mate.' I waited, then verified all the calls he had made from that booth." Unaware he was under surveillance; my friend had left credit on the phone for the surveillance officer who used it to check all the phone numbers he had called.

Voice activated recording equipment is used throughout Europe and North America. By recording and analyzing your speech patterns, then loading this information into the computer program, the telephone company can intercept your call. Keyword activation is also in use and flags specific words that you may use over the phone, such as 'drugs' or 'cannabis.' Be aware that listening devices are routinely placed into suspected cannabis dealers' houses, often illegally, and the information gathered is collated and acted upon. Since the terrorist attacks of 9/11 the security services have been given unprecedented powers to carry out intrusive surveillance on any citizen they choose to target. Avoid leaving fingerprints in your garden or on any equipment. This is not as relevant for small home producers, but anyone working on a larger scale should always wear gloves. The first thing police scenes-of-crime officers do when a cannabis factory has been discovered is to fingerprint every surface. Beware of bringing equipment into the grow room that you have handled away from the area, and do not touch any plastic bags you use to package and distribute dried marijuana: that's how they identify growers.

Remove all identification that can link your lights and equipment to any horticultural suppliers or the police will take statements from them. Not all will cooperate, but on my last conviction, statements from a U.K. hydroponics and cannabis seed supplier gave police details of every purchase I had made going back 18 months. The company and the drug squad then searched the company's computer database to see if any of the defendants' names appeared

Do not keep any records that can implicate you in illegal activities.

on their mailing list. U.K. police officers even traveled to Holland to speak to a major horticultural lighting manufacturer based there, as they had found several of their lights in our possession.

Police investigation teams will search for any paperwork that can be linked to you. Never keep written records of telephone numbers, addresses or even your crop's progress. Any financial dealings you have written down will be called "deal lists" and used to calculate how much you have profited from your cultivation. Your profit is used against you at court appearances and can result in higher fines for smaller growers, and longer terms of imprisonment for larger producers. If you are subject to asset seizures these lists will be used to increase the amount you must pay.

Avoiding Detection of Odor and Heat

The distinctive odor that cannabis plants produce when they're growing can easily be contained within the growing area. The smell will not permeate through walls; however, vents can be a concern, so try to position your ventilation ducts so that they do not allow odors to be detected.

Place filters over the vents to prevent any pungent smells from escaping. Carbon filters work well; however, although the activated charcoal can last up to 12 months, you should replace them much earlier. Ionizers have some effect on controlling odors in smaller setups, and work by emitting negative ions into the grow area. Air purifiers that combine powerful ion emissions with multistage, odor absorbing carbon filters can be purchased and are ideal for smaller grow rooms. Ozone generators can also be used to remove odors from your grow area and they are effective; however, many growers avoid them due to the health risk that ozone (O_3) can pose. Ozone molecules quickly break down once released, typically within 30 seconds; however, once the odors have been destroyed O_3 can easily build up in the room.

You can build an ozone generator yourself using a high voltage neon sign transformer, but ensure that you place this near an external exhaust fan and only consider using one when other methods prove to be ineffective. I was convicted of running a warehouse-sized cannabis factory that was located in the heart of a residential area for over two years and there was never any smell detected. All we did was install carbon filters over the exhaust fans and replace them regularly.

Police forces now use helicopters equipped with thermal imaging cameras that identify unusual sources of heat. When flown over grow room locations, they can cause problems for the cultivator; however, they are not as effective when used in daylight hours and anyone running a larger setup should have the light cycle adjusted to take advantage of this. Locate larger farms in industrial areas where manufacturing occurs or, alternatively, cultivate in rural areas where flights don't take place. Smaller cultivators need not worry about heat sources unless the grow room is located in a roof space or upstairs room, as the imager is not that sensitive. Windows can be a problem and if you have excessive heat in the room these become very noticeable on the thermal imager. Survival blankets, also known as space blankets can help in containing the heat and many growers use them to cover window openings and walls, however, they will struggle to totally eliminate the heat signature and should only be used in conjunction with good ventilation and/or air conditioning. Try to position your vents near, or in, chimney breasts or heating exhaust flues,

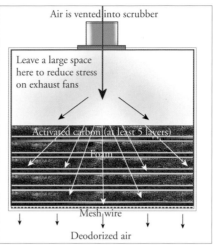

Air is vented into scrubber

Leave a large space here to reduce stress on exhaust fans

Activated carbon (at least 5 layers)

Foam

Mesh wire

Deodorized air

The extractor system in Sinsemilla Nursery's export grow room keeps the garden from overheating. Sinsemilla Nursery also does consultation services for growers.

To make a carbon air filter just place 20mm layers of foam between at least five 250mm layers of carbon and use mesh wire to support the bottom layer. Replace the carbon every three or four months.

The survival blanket on the walls provides insulation and prevents heat loss.

This fan vents directly from the lamp area to remove the excess heat generated by the bulbs.

where the heat would naturally occur. Many growers try to locate larger grows in basement areas where it is easier to dissipate the heat. If you must use a roof space try to take adequate precautions against the heat signature by insulating the space with heat reflecting material and using well positioned vents. Excessive heat build-up can be a particular problem during winter months if you have snowfall in your area, you do not want to be the only house with no snow on the roof. Once a potential grow has been identified by the helicopter, authorities will further investigate using hand held thermal imagers and in some respects these are more of a problem to the grower than the helicopter based systems. These devices give every police officer the ability to detect your grow room's heat emissions.

The authorities don't like to release figures but the percentage of grow rooms detected solely by thermal imaging cameras is small; the majority of seizures are made by police acting on information from informants. In most instances the thermal imagers are only deployed after information has been received about a potential cannabis factory, as helicopter flights are expensive

Keeping your grow as discreet as possible means you can enjoy dank nugs like these in the privacy of your own home!

to fund and better deployed elsewhere. However, most electrical companies use helicopters to inspect their power lines, and many of these are also fitted with thermal imaging cameras. The authorities now subcontract surveillance work out to these companies and they will deploy their thermal image cameras on behalf of the police.

Viuda Blanca from Spain's Pitt Bully Seeds is a great strain.

4. Electricity and Lighting Systems

Stolen sweets are best.
Cibber. 1671-1757.

The massive lamps above this hydroponic garden require extensive ventilation to prevent heat from building up.

Vegetative plants grow well under good lamps with reflector hoods and a fan for air circulation.

Electricity companies monitor their customers' bills and if there is a sharp rise in consumption they will contact you, usually quite innocently, to ask why. They may even want to check to see if the meter is faulty. Power companies are not so much concerned with how much electricity you are using, but rather how much you are using relative to past usage, so any significant increase or decrease will trigger a flag in the power company's billing software. In the case of a marked reduction they may wish to swap the meter over and check its calibration. If they still suspect something, they may put a meter-checking device on the line upstream from your house for a few weeks, which will identify any discrepancies.

Large numbers of HID lamps switching on at the same time will cause what is referred to as a 'spike' that can be monitored by the electricity company, and there have been reports of law enforcement officers identifying cannabis factories through this surge. If you are only using a small number of HID lamps this should not present a problem, but in larger setups try to stagger the startups of banks of ballasts or consider using generators. Smaller setups using fluorescent lights, LEDs or small high-pressure sodiums will not make a marked impression on consumption, but a larger rotation setup with more than six 1,000-watt lamps will spin the meter dials.

Some enterprising outlaws bypass their electricity meters so that a false reading is given to the electric company. Others have been known to attach modified transformers to the outside two cables entering the meter box, causing the dials to spin backwards. Companies are aware of these moves and are bringing out ever more sophisticated systems, but even digital card and key meters can be bypassed. However, hacking an electricity meter will not stop power spikes; you will still be drawing the same electricity, it just doesn't register on your meter. New digital systems can now measure electricity use at the substation transformer, without needing a home meter. These

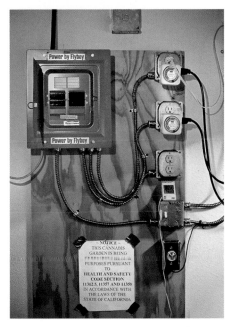

This complex wiring system required a professional electrician to complete.

have been specifically designed to put an end to electricity theft as metering at the transformer eliminates the ability for thieves to bypass or manipulate conventional meters. This technology is new and not universally installed. At present it is only cost effective to install meter-free systems on newly built housing estates. Electricity theft will increase the severity of any punishment, should your grow room be discovered, and there have been instances of cannabis grows being discovered because of the power theft.

Electricity can kill you if you don't know what you are doing!

The combination of electricity and water that you find in grow room environments is potentially lethal, so mount all fittings off the floor and away from water storage tanks. Install circuit breakers into your setup to shut the system down if you develop a problem. If you are unsure about any wiring, consult a qualified electrician. With careful management, it is possible to run a grow room that doesn't attract the curiosity of the electric company. You can run a stealthy unit of several 400-watt lamps that will cost no more than running a few extra electric heaters in your house. It would take concerted pressure from the police to make a power company go looking for these minor increases in consumer bills. The company doesn't need to be tied up in court testifying,

Good growers monitor the temperature of their garden very carefully due to the excess heat produced by HID lamps which can hamper growth and cause mold.

losing both money and man-hours with no benefit to shareholders. The bottom line is the power company wants your bill to go up, that's why they're in business. Growers can cut non-grow room electricity consumption by switching to gas for household heating and cooking appliances. Computers, air conditioning, water heaters and electric kettles all use a lot of power so moderate their use, purchase a kettle that is heated on the gas cooker and install energy saving light bulbs throughout the house, turn down the thermostat on your water heater and don't use a microwave oven (that's as much as 1500 watts), wash dishes by hand and ensure no lights or electrical appliances are left on unnecessarily.

Generators

It is possible to go 'off grid' and run your grow room on a fuel-powered electrical generator. The size of generator required is obviously governed by the number of lights, extractors and other electrical equipment you will be running, and you therefore need to calculate the grow room's total power consumption. Always purchase a generator that produces significantly more wattage than your grow room needs, in order to avoid any strain on the engine, and provide a buffer. It is always better to run two smaller generators side by side, or supplement one machine with your household power, as generators require regular maintenance and can suffer breakdowns.

Exhaust fumes are toxic and must be vented outside. This is best done by extending the original exhaust upwards and out of the grow area, using larger bore metal piping. Tape any connections in your exhaust extension with 'exhaust repair tape,' available from car accessory outlets. All generators are noisy and even so-called silent running units are audible, but units can be muffled by placing them in a sound proof enclosure.

Fuel costs are the main consideration for the grower, and there are two basic types of generator available:

Gasoline

These are quieter than diesel powered generators and are comparatively inexpensive to purchase, but expensive to run. They are useful in compact setups, or as an additional power source for larger grow rooms that are drawing too much electricity. After selecting the correct wattage for your grow, check how long the machine will run on a full fuel tank. This will give you some idea of the daily running costs. It is possible to have gasoline generators converted to run on propane, which is cleaner and also a source of CO_2 that can be utilized in the grow area, but these fumes should still not be inhaled.

Diesel

These generators are noisy, but reliable and cheaper to run than gas engines. If you are thinking of powering a larger grow room 'off grid' then you will need to acquire a diesel generator. Purchase larger generators second hand and have them serviced by a local dealer. Those used by film companies to power outdoor shoots are ideal and very quiet, but generators used to power lighting and construction work are more readily available and are just as reliable, although these do tend to be noisy. Your local electricity company will also have powerful diesel generators that are used during power failures and maintenance work, and these are sometimes available on the second hand market, but they are also noisy. Do not contact the electricity company to ask for these second hand generators. Source them through craigslist or a reputable second hand dealer. The main benefit of diesel generators is that they can be run on low cost fuels such as biodiesel, some heating oils, or paraffin (kerosene) heating oil mixed with a small amount of lubricating engine oil (generally 2 pints of oil to 5 gallons of heating oil). Fresh vegetable oil can also be used as a fuel, but it is too viscous in its original state so is mixed 50/50 with diesel oil; or you can simply add 1 pint of methylated spirit (methanol) to 4 gallons of cooking oil. This will power a diesel engine, but less efficiently than biodiesel, which is a refined fuel made from vegetable oils or animal fats. Check online for information regarding good fuel mixes for your specific brand of generator, as there is some variation between different makes and models.

The concept of using vegetable oil as an engine fuel dates back to 1895 when Dr. Rudolf Diesel developed the first diesel engine, which was powered by peanut oil. Henry Ford further developed the engine to run on hemp oil, which would be particularly apt for powering cannabis grows. It is easy to make your own biodiesel from discarded vegetable oil, obtained from fast food outlets. Cooking oil should be separated into glycerine and esters (biodiesel). However, it is a time consuming process and although you can simply filter it and add methylated spirit, it is more efficient when processed with methanol (CH_3OH) and caustic soda or lye ($NaOH$). Methanol and caustic soda combine to form a mixture known as sodium methoxide ($Na+ CH_3O-$), which is very caustic. If you do try making refined biodiesel yourself ensure that you wear a proper respirator, chemical resistant gloves, and use eye protection.

Making refined biodiesel from waste cooking oil

Caution:
- Do not inhale any processing chemical vapors.
- Always have a hose running and wear the correct protective equipment.
- If any chemicals splash onto your skin, wash immediately with water.
- Only use glass, enamel or steel containers.

Requirements:
- Powerful electric drill with paint or plaster mixing attachment.
- Mixing container (steel oil drum).
- Heat source (don't use an open flame).
- Thermometer.
- Respirator.
- Chemical-resistant gloves.
- Eye protection.

- Emergency running water in case of splashes, as methanol burns painlessly.

1. The vegetable oil should be filtered if it contains food particles or other foreign matter; use a double layer of cheesecloth in a funnel. You may have to warm the oil to 95 °F to ensure that it runs freely.
2. Once the oil has been filtered it is placed into the mixing container and heated to 212 °F to boil off any water.
3. Mix the caustic soda (or Lye) and methanol to form sodium methoxide that is then added to the oil. Experiment with small, measured amounts of the caustic soda, methanol and oil mixture in a glass, screw top jar, shaking gently until it is dissolved. If the glycerine and esters separate you have the correct mix; the semi-liquid glycerine has a dark brown colour and the biodiesel is a honey colour. If they don't separate, add more caustic soda/Lye.

Once you have the correct mix you then scale the quantities up to get the required amount for your larger drum. An approximate guide is:
- Vegetable oil = 5 gallons
- Methanol = 1 gallon
- Caustic soda or Lye (variable) = 127.7 grams (4.3 oz)

4. Immediately add the sodium methoxide to the oil in your steel drum and mix with the drill/mixing attachment for a minimum of one hour. After mixing is complete allow the mixture to settle for at least 8 hours . The heavier glycerine will sink to the bottom of the container leaving the biodiesel (esters) on top.
5. The biodiesel can then be pumped off and the glycerine drained or left to solidify. You can leave the glycerine to settle for 4 weeks by which time the remaining methanol will have evaporated off and the glycerine can then be composted.
6. The biodiesel should be allowed to stand for at least 24 hours before it is again heated to 212 °F to remove any remaining water.
7. The biodiesel then needs to sit for a further 7 days to allow any soap residues to settle. The fuel is then pumped off the top and filtered again. You can use cheesecloth in a funnel but for final filtering it is best to use a car or marine fuel filter. Badly filtered biodiesel can clog your generator's fuel filters.

Sweet Tooth 4 from the masters at Alpine Seeds is a fantastic indoor strain with a sweet and fruity aroma.

Visually examine your newly made biodiesel; it should look like clear, light brown vegetable oil. Check the pH; it should be neutral (pH 7). It is now ready to be used as an environmentally friendly engine fuel.

Biodiesel cleans off fossil fuel films that coat the interior parts of older diesel engines so when first switching to biodiesel, take care to regularly check and change your generator's fuel filters.

Alternative Energy Sources

Solar Energy

Photovoltaic (PV) solar cells directly convert sunlight into electricity. The simplest photovoltaic cells power watches and calculators, while more complex systems can be used to generate electricity for a single building or, in larger numbers, for power plants that also use 'concentrating solar power systems,' which use the sun's heat to generate electricity. The sunlight is collected and focused with mirrors to create a high-intensity heat source. This produces steam or mechanical power to run a generator that creates electricity. Solar panels convert sunlight directly into electricity with an efficiency of about 13%. The

Jillybean from Subcool, MzJill and Team Green Avengers is a delicious strain that offers an upbeat and happy high.

earth's surface receives close to 1,000 watts per square yard of energy from the sun. Solar panels can convert these 1,000 watts into about 130 watts of electricity per square yard of solar panel surface. Since solar panels are usually mounted in a fixed position, the sun does not always strike them straight on and you can't count on getting the full 130 watts all day. Early in the morning and later in the day solar panels have a much-reduced output. As a rule you can get the equivalent of about 42% of maximum output per 12-hours of sunlight, and less on cloudy days.

The main drawbacks to using solar panels are the purchase and installation cost; you require two hundred and fifty Kevlar backed, 12 inch square, 3w-12v solar panels with 250 diodes wired in series, one with each panel, to produce 750 watts. You also require sunlight to create the power and systems rely on DC batteries so that energy produced during the day can be stored. The electricity produced by a photovoltaic module must be run through an inverter to convert it from DC to AC power. When considering a photovoltaic system, you should be concerned with the AC output. That is, how much energy is coming out of the inverter and into your grow system.

Alternating Current
(AC) is a flow of electricity that constantly changes direction between positive and negative.

Direct Current
(DC) flows continuously in one direction. Direct-coupled systems need no electrical storage because they only operate during daylight hours, which limits their usefulness, and solar panels are not recommended as a sole power supply, even if you only run LEDs or compact fluorescent lights. However, if you are thinking of investing in solar power for your home, they are a cost effective addition to your power supply, and, if combined with utility grid power, can significantly reduce your electricity bills. Most solar users are coupled to the utility grid and sell excess electricity back to the power companies. Stand-alone systems produce power independently of the grid. Hybrid systems combine solar energy with additional power sources such as wind or diesel generators, and these are a better option for remote growers.

Small Wind Energy Systems
Wind turbines are expensive and only suited for rural areas where planning restrictions may prohibit larger stand-alone applications. However, smaller wind

Santa Maria F8 from No Mercy Supply in Holland is one of the world's most celebrated strains.

turbines can be used in connection with utility grid power (also called 'grid-connected' systems).

A grid-connected wind turbine can reduce your consumption of utility-supplied electricity. If the turbine can't deliver the amount of energy you need, the utility makes up the difference. When the wind system produces more electricity than the household requires, the excess can be automatically sold back to the utility company.

The downside to wind power generation, apart from the initial installation cost, is that you need an average annual wind speed of at least 9 mph.

Light

This is one of the major factors that will affect your cannabis plant growth. Plants use a process known as photosynthesis to convert carbon dioxide into sugar, releasing oxygen back into the atmosphere as they carry out this chemical process. Although light appears white to the human eye, it is in fact a mixture of colors. Plants absorb the red, violet and blue spectrum, leaving green as the color we see; this indicates that green is the least absorbed of the color spectrum. Even though HID lights have leanings toward a particular end of the light spectrum (blues for metal halide, red for high pressure sodium), they emit light in the full visible spectrum in just the same way as a household light bulb. In general, plants respond to all light; however, they get the most benefit from various blue and red wavelengths. Consequently, they get the least benefit from greens and yellows as most of it is reflected back.

Light Coverage and Spacing

All indoor grows require a minimum 50 watts of HID (6,000 lumens per 1 sq ft) of illuminated area:

- A 250-watt HID will illuminate a 2' x 2' garden.
- A 400-watt HID will illuminate a 3' x 3' garden.
- A 600-watt HID will illuminate a 3.5' x 3.5' garden.
- A 1,000-watt HID will illuminate a 4' x 4' garden.

Uniform light distribution is better achieved using several lower wattage lamps than individual 1,000-watt lights. 3 x 600-watt HIDs will give better light distribution than 2 x 1,000-watt HIDs in the same grow area, despite having less intensity. Similarly, 2 x 400-watt lamps are better than 1x 1,000-watt.

Lamps are usually rated in watts and lumens, but this is not as accurate as the standard measure of energy known as Photosynthetic Available Radiation (PAR).

Photosynthetic Available Radiation (PAR)

This differs from lumens in that it is not a direct measure of energy. It is the standard measure of light available for photosynthesis and is expressed in photons. Photosynthesis takes place as plants absorb these photons. PAR measures lamp output between 400 and 700 nanometers (nm).

Watt (W)

This is the standard unit of power. 1 joule of energy per second corresponds

This garden is being grown under LEDs produced by GROWL LEDs which utilize blue and red wavelength light to maximize grow efficiency.

to a power of 1 watt. As a rule of thumb cannabis gardens require at least 50 watts per square foot.

Lumens

Lumens are the measure of light intensity and are relative to, but different from, wattage. They are based on what the human eye can see, rather than what a plant uses for photosynthesis. Indoor cannabis gardens require 3,000 to 9,000 lumens per square foot, and successful gardens receive at least 6,000 lumens per square foot. Lumen output is a measure of flux (light energy that a lamp emits). This peaks at around 550 nm, which is the green region of the light spectrum, and decreases at both the red and blue wavelengths. This means that two light sources emitting the same total amount of energy can have different lumen ratings. Light intensity diminishes rapidly as the distance

You can easily grow cannabis under a 70w lamp with a reflector hood like this.

from the bulb increases, a 400-watt HPS bulb initially emits 50,000 lumens at 1 foot but this falls to around 3,500 lumens at 4 feet away. Therefore you need to ensure that you hang a 400-watt HPS lamp at least 2 feet away from the canopy so that you are giving your plants 12,500 lumens, which is more than enough to promote heavy bud development.

> 1x 400-watt HPS
> 1ft distance = 50,000 lumens
> 2ft distance = 12,500 lumens
> 3ft distance = 5,555 lumens
> 4ft distance = 3,571 lumens
>
> 1x 600-watt HPS
> 1ft distance = 90,000 lumens
> 2ft distance = 22,500 lumens
> 3ft distance = 9,999 lumens
> 4ft distance = 6,428 lumens
>
> 1x 1000-watt HPS
> 1ft distance = 140,000 lumens
> 2ft distance = 35,000 lumens
> 3ft distance = 15,555 lumens
> 4ft distance = 9,999 lumens

Lux

This is a measure of illumination and refers to the light energy that reaches your growing surface. Lux is equivalent to lumens/m², but also takes into account reflector efficiency, glass barriers and your lamp's distance from the plants.

Color Temperature

Higher color temperature means more blue color, lower temperature means more red. Color temperature is expressed in degrees Kelvin

Color Rendering Index (CRI)

CRI measures how close to a color a light source makes objects appear. A perfect light source would have a CRI of 100. In general, the higher the CRI rating of a lamp, the truer the different colors will appear.

This can become a little confusing so simply ensure you use a minimum of 50 watts per square foot. The more light that cannabis

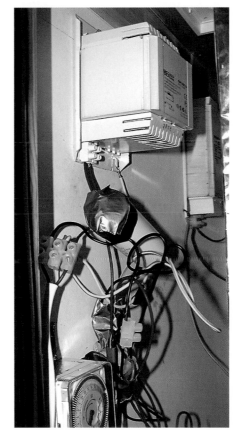

This ballast has been wired poorly. Good growers have well-organized electrical systems.

receives, the better it will grow, especially if you are releasing carbon dioxide (CO_2) into the room. Even under 1000-watt HID lamps, plants only receive 25% of the light available outside on a sunny day. Cannabis that is grown in low light levels will be tall with thin stems and sparse flowers. Lamps are hung as close as possible to the tops of your plants without scorching them: typically at about 18" with HID lamps. Test the temperature with the back of your hand, it should not feel uncomfortably hot.

The two main types of lights used for successful indoor cultivation are fluorescents and high intensity discharge (HID) lamps. Mercury vapor (MV) lamps can be used to cultivate cannabis plants but are extremely inefficient, producing only 8,000 lumens per 175 watts. In comparison, a high-pressure sodium lamp will emit 15,000 lumens per 150 watts. Plant growth is also slower under MV lamps due to the color spectrum they emit, which is poor compared to other lights that are available. Don't use halogen lamps to grow cannabis. In theory the PAR is good but they induce huge internode spacing, poor vegetative growth, and produce dangerous amounts of heat.

Lighting Systems

Fluorescent Lighting

Fluorescent lights are used primarily for growing cuttings or in small closet-type setups. They have reduced output compared to HID lights, but they are cheap to run. When using fluorescents in enclosed setups you must bear in mind that the heat-to-light ratio is higher than most metal halide lamps and that although they can be used for some mini and micro installations, they are not recommended.

When using fluorescents, use the cool white variety, which are rich in the blue spectrum of light and will produce bushy plants up to 15" high. They can be purchased from electrical wholesalers and retail outlets. It is relatively straightforward to build a system with several tubes attached to a plywood base that has been covered in reflective foil. Alternatively, the grower can purchase ready-made fluorescent modules that come housed in their own reflectors.

Fluorescents marketed as grow lights are available but are much less efficient than standard fluorescents and produce less light. High output fluorescent tubes are available in two foot and four foot lengths that give out a maximum of 24,000 lumens; however, they cost as much as high intensity discharge lamps, which are a better option.

Many cultivators make use of fluorescents as a low-cost addition to HID systems, using them to supplement the light supply. Fluorescents can be suspended above crops or hung between individual plants to boost growth.

High Intensity Discharge Lamps (HID)

HID lamps are the main choice of the indoor marijuana cultivator. They are cheap and efficient to run and provide the necessary light spectrum. Each light requires a ballast that comes ready-wired as a remote unit, with the light and reflector connected to it. In some Dutch lights the ballast is built into the light casing and these Poot lamps are the main choice for commercial nurseries that supply garden plants to the trade. Lamps are hung in rows above the greenhouse crops.

This lamp can provide enough light to support several decent cannabis plants.

Ballasts are used to power High Intensity Discharge Lamps and are available for sale online and at your hydroponics store.

These two HIDs with reflector hoods will grow a huge harvest.

45

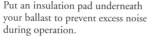
Put an insulation pad underneath your ballast to prevent excess noise during operation.

These lamps are air cooled because of the excess heat they produce.

Metal Halides (MH)

Metal halides (MH) produce a natural-looking light and are used by some cultivators during the vegetative growth phase. Once flowering is induced, the lights are replaced with high-pressure sodiums that are better suited for flowering. This is unnecessary as plants will grow efficiently under sodium lights for both the vegetative and flowering stages, and furthermore, the plants will have a shorter internodal length. MH lights are available in 175-, 200-, 400- and 1,000-watt sizes. The low wattage lamps are recommended when raising cuttings.

High Pressure Sodium (HPS)

HPS lights are more efficient than MH lamps, producing more light and less heat per watt of electricity consumed. The light produced is from the correct spectrum for flowering and still gives good results during the growth phase. Sodium lights are deficient in the blue spectrum and are therefore not used for raising cuttings, although adding fluorescents to the garden can compensate for this. The concentration of red and yellow light that HPSs emit promotes a higher flower-to-leaf ratio in growing plants than MH or fluorescents. HPS lights are available in 75-, 100-, 110-, 125-, 400-, 600- and 1,000-watt sizes. They can also be adapted from security lights: as long as they are high-pressure sodium, they are suitable for cultivating.

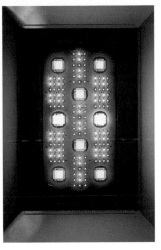

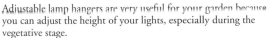
Adjustable lamp hangers are very useful for your garden because you can adjust the height of your lights, especially during the vegetative stage.

Stealth Grow Lights manufactures some of the best LEDs available.

Pulse Start Metal Halide

These digital bulbs are made in four unique Kelvin colors: 3k, 4k, 6.4k and 10k. The wattages range from 100 to 1,000. Basically, the unit rotates multiple lamps of different Kelvin temperatures over the plants, to provide full spectrum lighting. 1000-watt commercial grade bulbs were originally designed exclusively for large food production facilities, but are now widely available. The Commercial Grade bulbs come in three proprietary colors: 2.8k (fruiting/flowering), 5.7k (full spectrum) and 10k (ripening). However, the cost for this type of setup is still putting many growers off using them.

Son-T Agro

Son-T Agro lamps are HPS lamps available commercially for horticultural use. The manufacturers have added 30% more light in the blue spectrum to the bulb. They have a slight increase in output over standard HPS (typically around 6%) but have a 25% shorter life. You can buy lamps in the standard 250w to 1,000-watt range. If you already use HPS lamps you can purchase the Son-T Agro bulbs separately and they will be compatible with your system.

Compact Fluorescent Lamps (CFL)

These lights are also called 'Energy Saving Bulbs' and are available from all good hardware stores, but ensure that you don't confuse the advertised wattage with actual wattage: 100-watt CFLs only emit as much light as a 100-watt incandescent bulb and the actual wattage is between 10-30 watts. The 10-30-watt bulbs can be plugged into an incandescent (household light bulb) fixture but the 50-watt bulbs, which are preferred for compact cultivation setups, are made for outdoor use and require a different fitting.

The problem with CF bulbs is they don't project useful lumens any distance, so the 50 watts per square foot rule can't apply. You need to use as many of the smaller CFs as can be positioned around your plants, typically around 2 inches from the foliage. The larger wattage CF bulbs are designed for plant growth and come in the red and blue spectrum. These are useful for propagating, mother plants, small grows and additional lighting.

LED (Light-emitting diode)

At present HID lamps produce better crops, but LED lights do not consume much power, do not require ballasts, and produce a fraction of the heat of HID lamps, causing plants to transpire less. Early LED grow lamps used hundreds of fractional-watt LEDs and were not very effective, having only a single band of blue and red light. Newer LED grow lamps use automotive grade 6 watt LEDs and have shown 'similar' results to HID lamps, so are worth considering for smaller grows or as an addition to other lighting systems, however, they currently have similar limitations to CF lamps (see above). The technology is improving and advancements will hopefully produce lamps equal to, if not better than, HID lighting.

Sulfur Plasma

These are grow lights based on sulfur plasma technology. Currently they are very expensive and only available for research purposes, but they should be on the market around 2013. The lamp and magnetron unit is electrode-less and includes an evacuated quartz bulb partly backfilled with argon and sulfur, plus a magnetron, for exciting a ball of plasma within the bulb. Tests show that young cucumber plants grew more than 60% faster than those grown under HPS, and more than 120% better than those grown under compact fluorescents, with a marked increase in branching and larger leaves. The first results also showed that the young cucumber plants were 64% heavier than those grown under HPS (SON-T) light, at equal light strength. The lamps produce less than half the infrared heat per watt when compared to HPS or Metal Halide.

Metal Halide lamps produce natural-looking light and are often used during the vegetative growth phase.

Dank nug grown under GROWL LEDs.

GROWL LEDs are highly efficient and use a fraction of the power of HIDs.

Air cooled closet garden with reflector hood and reflective walls for increased light efficiency.

Other Types Of Lights

Light Emitting Plasma – LIFI

The LIFI Plasma light was not invented to grow plants and therefore the spectrum is lacking in red. However, companies are researching how to use metal halides within the plasma cell in order to create a better spectrum for plant growth. Others are experimenting with LEDs in an effort to correct the spectrum. If these trials prove successful the LIFI will become another suitable option for growers.

Mercury Vapour Lamps (MV)

These can be used to cultivate cannabis plants, but they are extremely inefficient, emitting a poor color spectrum and producing under half of the lumen output of HID lamps. Plants grown under MV light will exhibit poor growth, and give you very low yields.

Tungsten Halogen Lamps

Don't use halogen lamps to grow cannabis. In theory they emit the correct measure of light for photosynthesis (PAR), but they induce chronic stretching during vegetative growth, promote poor flowering and produce dangerous amounts of heat.

Incandescent Light Bulbs

These are ordinary household light bulbs. You will be lucky to get 1,200 lumens from an incandescent light bulb, but that doesn't mean they are of no use to the indoor cultivator. They can be used to start seedlings and illuminate cuttings during rooting, but only use these if nothing else is available. Fluorescents are much more efficient.

Ultra Violet Light

Cannabis plants have been shown to produce higher levels of THC in response to increased exposure to ultra violet light (UV). Many smaller growers use a facial tanning lamp run on a timer for ten minutes, three times during the 12-hour flowering period.

Light Movers

The most efficient way to use high intensity discharge lamps is to keep them moving within the grow room. Moving the lamps ensures an even distribution of light over the crop, eliminates uneven growth patterns, and produces a more uniform and consistent crop. Because they are moving, the lights can be lowered closer to the plants without burning the leaves, thus promoting faster growth and higher yields. The light also covers a larger area, saving on the cost of additional lamps and electricity. There are two types of light movers available to indoor cultivators.

Linear Movers

These movers carry the light unit back and forth over a six-foot, straight rail. A 30-second delay is applied at either end to ensure maximum coverage. Linear movers increase the effective growing area by approximately 50% and are both easy to install and cheap to run, using only five watts of electricity. Linear movers are ideal for narrow growing areas.

Circular Movers

They are less efficient than linear movers; the 360° movement can result in lower light levels towards the center and edges of the growing area. However, growers have reported using these setups to increase yields in grow rooms where the plants cover the complete floor space. Three-arm movers are the most effective but if possible, try to avoid circular movers and opt for a linear light rail unit.

Reflectors

High-pressure sodium lights are sold as complete units with a ballast and a shade, called a reflector. The type of reflector your lamp has will be determined by the price you pay. There are two basic types: open-ended and closed. The open-ended reflector allows heat to escape and can be mounted closer to the plants, while closed reflectors are more suited to light rails. Aluminum mirror polish is the standard finish for most reflectors and is adequate for indoor cultivation. More efficient systems have a highly reflective anocoil insert. This dimpled surface reflects approximately 10% more light from the bulb than other reflectors at the same mounting height.

Air-cooled reflectors are also available and are ideal for small areas where heat build-up is a problem. These reflectors are sealed units with a toughened glass shield that allows the light to pass through but retains the heat. The excess heat is drawn out through 4" ducting using an extractor fan and dispersed. You can improvise your own air-cooled lamps by placing a sheet of glass between the light and your enclosed plants.

Timers

HID lights use high inductive currents when starting up. Most timers will burn out under this surge, leaving your lights permanently on, so it is important to use a heavy-duty timer when controlling the day length in a grow room. Contactors, which are heavy load relays, can be wired to start either individual or groups of lights. The contactor removes the load from the timer and is easy to install. If you are unsure of the wiring, consult an electrician.

A qualified electrician can wire a contactor to a four-gang extension lead for you without knowing its use. Choose a three-pole, 28-amp inductive, 75-amp

Grow cabinets from BC Northern Lights come completely furnished with easy-to-use electrical systems for lighting and atmospheric controls.

resistive contactor if you intend to use four 600w or two 1,000w lamps. Alternatively, ready-made kits are available from most hydroponic retailers.

How to determine fan size in cubic feet/hour:

Calculate the volume of the grow area you intend to ventilate. This is done by multiplying:
Length x Width x Height = Volume of your room in cubic feet (ft^3)

Air should be replaced every 3 minutes/20 x per hour. Therefore, multiply the volume of your grow room by 20.
For example, a room: 5ft x 5ft x 7ft high = 175 ft^3

175 ft^3 x 20 changes per hour = 3500 ft^3 per hour fan

Install a 3600 ft^3 fan (or a combination of smaller fans equal to 3600 ft^3) to be on the safe side.

Ch9 Jack by Ch9 Female Seeds is an excellent strain known for its vigor, flavor, and high yields.

5. Temperature, Humidity and Carbon Dioxide (CO₂)

Behold, the bush burned with fire.
Exodus III. 2.

It is vital that you monitor humidity, temperature and carbon dioxide levels in your grow room.

Daytime temperature within your grow space, without adding supplemental CO_2, should be 70-80°F. If you are adding CO_2 then it can rise to between 80-90°F. In the last two weeks of flowering the daytime temperature should be kept between 70-80°F and CO_2 reduced to adjust for the plants' lower metabolism. Night temperatures should be kept above 60°F to prevent stress, stimulate hormones and reduce stem elongation. Temperature can be measured using a maximum and minimum thermometer; it will indicate the extremes of temperatures reached. Water and nutrient solutions should be heated in their storage tanks to around 75°F. Use an aquarium heater; they are inexpensive and available at aquarium suppliers.

Due to the heat given off by HPS lighting systems, it is unlikely that you will ever need to heat a grow room during the daylight cycle. During night time cold spells, however, a thermostatically controlled air-blowing heater will maintain the temperature. Fan heaters designed for greenhouse use work well. During the summer months your main problem will be reducing the temperature to manageable levels. The recommended readings are not absolute and while marijuana will survive fluctuations of temperature, excessive heat will cause the plants to grow tall and thin. Portable air-conditioning units can be purchased second-hand to keep grow rooms cool, and venting the room will also assist by removing warm air and maintaining good air circulation.

Use office desk fans to create air circulation. Suspend the fans upside down from the ceiling or place them on prepared ledges. Alternatively, you can buy fans that come with their own stands. Circulation is important within the grow room to distribute carbon dioxide (CO_2) supplies evenly, and also to keep odors and temperatures down. The plants need to sway gently in the fan breeze, a movement that helps to strengthen their stems. Larger setups need horticultural fans that are mounted high in the room.

Humidity

Humidity is the water vapor content of air, and is measured in percentages using a hygrometer that should be positioned on the grow room wall. Humidity during vegetative growth can be kept at an even 50%, but during flowering it should be reduced to between 30% and 40% to ensure that botrytis, or mold, does not attack the buds. Humidity and air temperature are relative: warm air holds more water vapor, thereby lowering humidity levels, while cool air holds less water vapor and therefore raises the level of humidity. It's unlikely that humidity levels will ever be too low in a grow room environment due to plant transpiration and the amounts of water used. High humidity levels are easily controlled by using a dehumidifier.

Carbon Dioxide (CO_2)

Carbon dioxide is essential for plant growth. The atmosphere contains about 350 parts per million (ppm); however, plants can tolerate greater levels of CO_2 than are naturally available. In the early stages of plant evolution the earth's atmosphere had much higher concentrations of CO_2 and plants have not lost

These lamps are air cooled to prevent temperature problems in the garden, and the fans help air circulation.

Use oscillating desk fans to keep the air circulating in your grow room.

Using carbon dioxide to increase your garden's yield is a complicated task, but the rewards can be huge.

the ability to utilize it. By increasing the level of CO_2 in your grow room to around 1,000 ppm you can expect an increase in yield of approximately 25%. This level is the most cost-effective but can be increased by a further 500 ppm with a corresponding increase in yield.

The most common method of supplying CO_2 to grow rooms is with cylinders. You can rent cylinders from welding supply companies or borrow them from bar owners, who use them to pump beer. Hydroponics suppliers stock

The pistils of this plant from Alpine Seeds have moisture on them. Be careful when this happens as the water can cause the light to burn your plant when it evaporates.

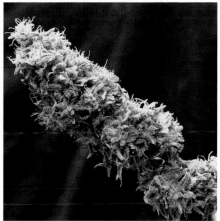

HydroPlex's Spinner system offers a secure environment for your plants where temperature, humidity and carbon dioxide levels are all carefully controlled.

Blue Donkey Dick from Karmaceuticals is a high yielding strain that can provide an increased yield through CO2 treatment.

valves and timers that are screwed into the cylinders and adjusted to inject the atmosphere with gas. There are controllers on the market that you simply program with the size of your grow room and the ppm you require: the valve then opens automatically. Plants do not need CO_2 during the night cycle, so the equipment is off during this time.

To determine the amount of CO_2 your room requires, first calculate the area of your grow room in cubic feet (length x breadth x height). The CO_2 levels will naturally be around 300 ppm so to take levels up to the optimum of 1500 ppm you will need to raise it by 1200 ppm. Multiply your room volume by 0.0012 to give you the amount of carbon dioxide needed in cubic feet.

Smaller plants that have just been started will need a third less CO_2, so set your regulator to inject the required amount every hour. Use a CO_2 testing kit to check that the grow room levels are correct and, if necessary, adjust your delivery. When using carbon dioxide it is better to have a closed system that doesn't vent the room to the outside to ensure you don't waste any of the gas. Temperature is controlled by air conditioners set to re-circulate.

Alternative supplies of CO_2 can be generated with growth gas heaters that burn propane gas to emit atmospheric carbon dioxide. While gas heaters can be useful in winter months, they give off too much heat for most indoor setups. You can supply smaller crops with CO_2 using other methods that don't allow you to accurately control the levels of gas, but that give higher readings. One method is to make a solution of 5 teaspoons of sugar in 4 cups of warm water and then add a brewer's yeast tablet, available at home brew suppliers, to the

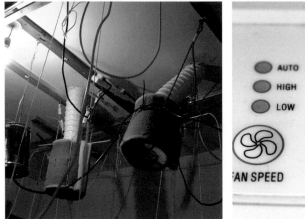

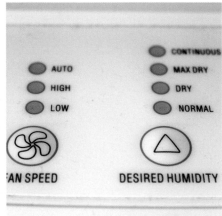

These air filters keep the environment in your garden clean and healthy.

Use a good dehumidifier like this expert grower to keep your garden's humidity at an optimum level.

BC Bud Depot's God Bud is a classic strain that can offer huge yields if grown with a carbon dioxide boost.

solution. Place the open bottle into the grow cabinet and replace weekly. As it ferments the solution will produce half the volume of sugar consumed as gas.

Another method is to add vinegar or lemon juice to sodium bicarbonate (baking soda), which causes it to froth up and release CO_2. Mix a small amount in a container and then place it into your cabinet and close the doors. Small cabinets only need a teaspoon of baking soda, but you need to do this on a regular basis.

CO_2 is comprised of carbon and oxygen. Plants use most of the carbon and exhale the oxygen. The carbon is combined with nutrients and water to produce phosphatides and sugar. Liquid carbon can be added to the nutrient solution instead of using CO_2 gas supplementation, which can be useful, especially during the flowering stage. However, it means changing the nutrient solution every three days, which is not cost effective for larger grow operations. There are also problems associated with pH levels and growers are advised to use hydrogen peroxide (H_2O_2) in the nutrient solution, added on a daily basis, to keep down anaerobic bacteria and fungi. Liquid carbon is not suitable for re-circulating or organic setups and its use is still controversial. Some growers maintain that it is ineffective.

Dry ice gives off CO_2 as it melts. If you have access to a regular supply of dry ice you can use it, although it's an inefficient way of delivering the gas. Dry ice is frozen carbon dioxide that degrades at around 10% per day in a freezer. In the heat of a grow room it melts rapidly, delivering excessive levels of CO_2. While the excessive levels aren't harmful, they are a waste of the gas.

Carbon dioxide supplementation increases yields but is time-consuming and unnecessary for good results. Some growers report that high levels of CO_2 in the flowering room at, or approaching, harvest time can actually lower the potency of your crop. It's better to stop feeding the gas 10 days before you harvest.

There are security implications when moving large tanks into and out of your growing location. An alternative is to ensure the plants have a good supply of fresh air drawn in from outside the grow room, providing the plants with CO_2 at 300 and 350 ppm during daylight hours. Filter the ducts with nylon pantyhose to keep out insects.

Moby Dick is an incredibly powerful sativa-dominant strain from Dinafem Seeds.

6. Choosing Your Plant

The fruits of the spirit.
The Litany.

Quality seeds can be purchased online by mail order from many reputable suppliers, and most companies specialize in feminized seeds that will produce all-female crops. Feminized seeds are produced from a genetic female plant that has been treated with hormones; inducing the female plant to produce male flowers. This pollen is used to pollinate female flowers and produces seeds that do not contain any male chromosomes. This means the plants will all be female; however, it also means that they will carry a hermaphrodite chromosome. Feminized seeds on average should produce a 0-20% hermaphrodite-to-female ratio whereas a standard seeds male-to-female ratio is 50%.

Whilst you have a greater chance of getting hermaphrodite plants using feminized seeds you are also virtually guaranteed genetic females. In practice, feminized seeds can save growers both space and time and only require that you keep a careful eye out for any hermaphrodites. However, most growers want to produce crops without having to repeatedly buy feminized marijuana seeds, which are more expensive than untreated seeds, so most experienced growers prefer to clone their plants by taking a good cutting from a mature plant of known characteristics. You can safely clone from a known female that has been grown from a feminized seed, and therefore you should only need to purchase new seeds when you wish to change the variety you are cultivating. Seed suppliers are listed in the back section of this book.

Most growers choose Cannabis indica varieties for their indoor crops. Cannabis sativas grow too tall and produce lower yields. Outdoor skunk growers also opt for indicas, but there are sativa hybrids available that perform well. Remember that these seeds will be the basis of your future stock and mother plants for several generations, so choose carefully. Most varieties of Cannabis indica are easy to cultivate but novice growers should avoid some of the "Big Bud" varieties, as they are notoriously difficult to clone.

Seeds should be small, brown and speckled. Lighter colored seeds will not be mature enough to germinate. Store your seeds at low temperatures in

Quality seeds can be purchased online by mail order from many reputable suppliers. These seeds are feminized and do not contain any male chromosomes.

Hermaphrodite plant with male and female flowers clearly evident.

This seedling is growing quickly towards the light. It is still encased in the seed shell and the taproot is visible below.

sealed jars to keep them viable for a longer period by slowing down the rate of respiration. Fresh seeds will have a 90% germination rate but this dramatically reduces over time. After three to four years the germination rate will have dropped to about 20%. Dormant seeds need to be made up of an average of 20% water so store them away from heat sources.

Good indoor varieties include:

Kong	*Flowers in 45 to 50 days once induced.*
Northern Lights	*Flowers in 45 to 50 days once induced.*
Crystal	*Flowers in 50 to 60 days once induced.*
Blueberry	*Flowers in 45 to 50 days once induced.*
Big Bud	*Flowers in 45 to 50 days once induced.*
White Rhino	*Flowers in 55 to 70 days once induced.*
Bubblegum	*Flowers in 45 to 50 days once induced.*
White Widow	*Flowers in 50 to 60 days once induced.*

Yields

There will be always be natural variation in your crop and not all of the plants will produce the same weight of buds. Indoor cultivators won't get the same individual plant yields that are possible outdoors with fully-grown cannabis plants but you can still produce high-quality, potent crops in your hydroponic garden that are generally more potent than any outdoor crops, especially those that have been cultivated in cooler climates with less sunlight during the season.

Assuming your grow room light levels are at least 50 watts of High Intensity Discharge (HID) light per $1ft^2$ (12 inches x 12 inches) you can average a minimum of:

- 2 oz (56g) of dried buds per plant from small plants given a two-week vegetative growth cycle and flowered with 6 inches between the plant stems.

And a maximum of:

- Well in excess of 9 oz (250g) average of dried buds per plant from pruned plants given a longer vegetative growth period, increased individual growing space and very high light levels.

A gram per watt per 30 days is a potential yield measurement favored by some growers, but it can be confusing and is far from accurate. It doesn't take into

Kong from Holy Smoke Seeds flowers in 45 to 50 days once induced and is a great indoor variety.

White Rhino flowers in 55 to 70 days once induced and is a highly reliable indoor strain.

account any rooting time for clones or the vegetative growth period. It is not possible to produce a crop from scratch in 30 days, you will need to run your system on a vegetative cycle for a minimum of 14 days beforehand and need to take into account at least another 14 days to allow for seedlings to develop or clones to root. It also doesn't take into account the number of plants or the area. One plant under a 1,000-watt High Pressure Sodium lamp (HPS) will not give you anywhere near 2.2 pounds (1,000 grams) of dried bud.

Yield per unit is one method you can use when working out grow area potential on setups, as we can safely assume everyone uses at least 50 watts of High Intensity Discharge (HID) per 1 square foot of grow area. Regardless of whether your grow is organic or hydroponic, this would be a square base lit by 50 watts/6000 lumens and we can call it 1 unit; aiming for minimum yields of around 2 oz (56g) per unit.

Super Crystal from Homegrown Fantaseeds is a good, reliable indoor strain that grows well both organically and hydroponically.

The formula is:
(1 ft²) + 50 watts HID = 1 unit

And once your clones have rooted:
1 unit + (14 day grow) + (30 day bloom) = 2oz (56g) per unit

If your plants have 1ft (12 inches) between stems then you are placing 1 plant per unit and getting an average:
2oz (56g) per plant

Yield per unit is of course an over-simplification and assumes you have optimum growing conditions with plants as close to the light as possible and even light distribution, but as a guideline to your potential yield it works well and covers all setups. Even large commercial grows can be broken down into multiples of 1 unit and whilst many growers can yield much more than the average, a yield of 1½ oz (42g) of correctly dried, top quality buds per unit is acceptable for many cultivators.

This vegetative female plant is very happy in her organic potting mix and will yield a good harvest of buds.

These crop weights are intended as guidelines only. Plant yields are dependent on several important factors such as variety, light levels, environmental conditions, time of harvest, and cultivation techniques. For example, using intensive rotation – such as the Dutch Sea Of Green (SOG) – it is possible to produce a crop of high quality marijuana buds every two weeks. However, the yield will be lower than with plants given a longer vegetative growth period. Yields from SOG plants grown with 6 inches between individual plant stalks, in rotation, can average between 10 and 14 grams (dried buds per plant).

Alternatively a Cannabis indica variety such as a Shiva Shanti, grown under an HPS lamp and receiving 6,000 lumens, with optimum environmental conditions, and flowered at a height of 16 inches for 55 days, should produce 125 to 150 grams (dried buds per plant).

The Screen of Green (SCROG) technique allows growers to cultivate crops that utilize more of the lumens emitted from their lamps. Micro and mini systems can be built to take advantage of this by using low-wattage lamps. A 100-watt HPS over a single plant, in an enclosed grow unit, will yield 20 grams (dried buds per plant).

The plant density in SCROG is less than with other systems, which is a benefit should the crop be discovered by the authorities. Using a 600-watt HPS over a single plant results in yields that can be more than 70 grams (dried buds per plant).

Outdoor cultivators can expect high yields from mature plants, depending on the growing conditions during the season. Cannabis plants do not require constant direct sunlight. As long as they receive about five hours daily and have 1 square yard of growing space, Cannabis indicas can produce yields of around 500 grams (dried buds per plant).

Cannabis ruderalis varieties can yield up to 300 grams (dried buds per plant). Cannabis sativa varieties, in optimum conditions, can yield well over 2 lbs (dried buds per plant).

In practice you will require monster plants to consistently achieve these outdoor yields, although they are possible. Many outdoor cultivators are more than happy to harvest half the above amounts.

You need to decide if the crop is going to be grown organically or hydroponically before choosing a particular production method. Both methods are suitable for indoor marijuana production.

Melon Gum by Dr. Underground Seeds grows extremely well in a SCROG garden.

Use a pH tester to ensure that the water you use in your garden is at a good level. Organic crops grow best at levels around 6.5.

Techniques For Growing

Hydroponics

This term was coined by Dr. William F. Gericke of the University of California. It comes from two Greek root words: hydro meaning water, and ponics meaning 'put/place.' No soil or compost is used. The nutrients are suspended in water and delivered to the plants by various irrigation methods. The main advantages to gardening hydroponically are speed, control, and flexibility. Hydroponic techniques can increase growth significantly.

Organic Crops

These are grown without any pesticides or chemical fertilizers. Hydroponic crops can still be grown organically using organic feed. Organic nutrients are formulated to slowly decompose in soil so their elements react differently in a hydroponic solution. In a hydroponic nutrient, all elements are suspended in ionic form, whereas in organic systems microbes break down the components of the organic feed to make them available to the plant. Organic nutrients suitable for hydroponic systems can be purchased and 'teas' can be made by hanging a stocking containing your organic fertilizer in a bucket of water.

Organic crops are free from any chemical residue that can remain in the plant tissue after harvest. Nitrates and other agents used in chemical fertilizers are harmful to smoke.

These plants are well into the vegetative stage and are being grown organically to great success.

You can make your own organic tea mixes by steeping organic matter in hot water.

Bioponics

Dr. Luther Thomas coined the term 'bioponics' which refers to a cultivation technique that combines the best of hydroponic and organic systems. Bioponics builds on the strong chemical nutrient base while adding biological activity in the root zone for enhanced growth. A bioponic nutrient must be either liquid or perfectly soluble, be rapidly degradable and have a complete nutrient balance. Most bioponic nutrients contain some organic elements, but are mainly made up of chemical salts. Unfortunately, organic nutrients contain organic matter that won't dissolve completely and can become rancid in hydroponic solutions, which makes the solution smell of rotting eggs and blocks filters and pipes.

It is possible to source completely organic bioponic nutrients that will work in hydroponic systems. Biosevia are organic nutrients that are completely soluble in water and designed to be used with hydroponic systems. Biosevia is a molasses-based fertilizer, similar to bio bizz, but also contains humates and fulvates. It works in a hydroponic system by using a special filter that contains a colony of trichoderma in a sponge, which is inside the bio filter. Temperature of the solution is also an important factor and you have to keep assessing the condition of the plants in order to predict a drop in nutrient strength. pH is adjusted using organic buffers.

Skunk Berry from Peak Seeds is a great indoor/outdoor strain that offers a powerful high.

7. Organic Cultivation

Earth laughs in flowers.
Hamatreya.

Buds grown organically taste great and provide a very natural high.

Organic cultivation in its purest form means using no chemical fertilizer or pesticides on your crop and emphasizes the health of the soil. It is possible to achieve good results organically; however, most cultivators refer to crops grown in soils or potting composts as "organic" despite the fact that chemicals are used. You can achieve more consistent results by using controlled doses of soluble fertilizer, but you must be careful.

Organic-based systems have advantages over hydroponic setups. Inexperienced growers find soil, or compost-based cultivation, more forgiving as the medium provides a natural buffer for pH levels. Smaller scale growers can save on their start-up costs by building organic systems that require far less equipment than hydroponic setups. Many commercial cultivators still grow organically, even in large-scale farms. There are growers who claim that organically produced buds smoke and taste better than hydroponic crops, but there is no real evidence to support this theory. It is virtually impossible to distinguish between the two, especially if the hydroponic crop has been fed fresh, pH-adjusted water prior to harvesting in order to flush out any chemical residue.

Take care when selecting the type of soil to use in potting mixes. Ordinary topsoil, unlike commercially available potting composts, is not sterilized and can contain harmful organisms and insect larvae. Topsoil dries out far too quickly for use in pots or containers and has variable nutrient contents. It's advisable to purchase a good quality potting compost to cultivate your crop. If this is not available, it is possible to make your own.

Compost

Compost is made from organic materials. The best compost is manure, which contains organic material that has been ingested, digested and broken down by animals.

Making Your Own Compost

You can make compost yourself by building a compost heap and allowing vegetable material, grass trimmings, and other organic waste to decompose. Providing air, nitrogen and water will assist the microbes in carrying out the decomposition.

Air

Start your heap with a base of bricks or blocks to vent and raise it. Place thin sticks and branches on top of the bricks or blocks before adding 10" of organic matter. (You can create chimneys that provide air to the heap by inserting posts into the stack and then removing them later.) The side of your compost heap should be vertical, supported by blocks or wooden slats.

Nitrogen

On top of the first 10" layer of organic matter add either manure, horticultural nitrogen fertilizer, or dried blood to provide nitrogen. Alternate with lime every other layer.

Water

Try to keep the heap moist but not saturated. Add water to the heap if the contents dry out. Once the organisms begin to break down the vegetable matter in the compost heap, they generate a lot of heat. The heat kills off all the weed seeds and undesirable organisms so once this process starts, cover the top of the heap to contain it.

After six weeks, turn the compost with a garden fork to ensure that it is well mixed. After a further six weeks the compost will be ready and can be blended with peat and sand to produce a good quality potting compost.

Loam

Some of the best commercially available potting composts are loam-based. Loam can be made by cutting out sections of grass turf and stacking these sections top side down. Build your stack one-yard high and

Fresh clone with a coco coir cup.

Healthy organic female 5 weeks into flower.

place compost between each layer. The loam will take 12 months to form and will require sterilizing. This is best done outside by heating a large drum of water and passing the steam through the loam, which is placed in a perforated container above it. Alternatively, pour a 5% bleach solution through the loam. Small amounts can be sterilized in an oven or microwave where the loam should be heated until steam is given off.

Preparing Your Potting Mix
Ingredients
- 7 parts sterilized loam or organic compost. (Mix the compost with equal amounts of soft sand before use.)
- 3 parts sterilized sphagnum peat moss. (Add four parts if using compost.)
- 2 parts soft sand. (Add even with organic compost that already has sand mixed in.)

To each 50-pound mix add 4 ounces of base fertilizer and 1 ounce of lime.

A good base fertilizer is composed of:
- 2 parts bonemeal
- 2 parts superphosphate of lime
- 1 part sulphate of potash

Once you have mixed your potting compost it is advisable to check the pH level, which is a measure of the soil's acidity. Organic cannabis grows best at levels of around 6.5, with 6 and 7 being acceptable extremes. The pH level can be tested with a probe that is inserted into the soil or with a chemical testing kit. Both are available at garden stores.

To raise pH levels add small amounts of ground lime.
To lower pH levels add acid peat or sulphate of ammonia.

Commercially available potting composts do not need pH adjusting and are already sterilized. Choose a loam-based mixture. If this is not available, a general purpose potting compost will produce good results. Tomatoes have similar nutritional requirements to cannabis so any compost mixes designed specifically for their cultivation are ideal.

To improve the water-holding ability of the potting compost you can add

Creating a great potting mix requires several components, such as peat moss, sand, perlite and an organic soil mix.

Organic bonemeal soil supplements provide great nutrients for your garden's soil mix.

Use a fork to mix the soil once you've added your soil supplements, like perlite, bloodmeal and bonemeal.

perlite, vermiculite, soilless mixes or coconut coir to the blend. These are all naturally occurring, nutrient free soil additives or amendments, available from garden stores.

🌿 Add 1 part perlite to 1 part potting compost (50% mix)

🌿 Cannabis thrives in loose or sandy soil that drains well and supplies the roots with oxygen.

Compost Blends
These basic recipes can be used to blend your compost for a perfect organic mix:

50:50 mixes
50% Compost + 50% Perlite
50% Compost + 50% Soilless mix
50% Compost + 50% Coconut fiber (coir)

30:30 mixes
30% Compost + 30% Perlite + 30% Coir + 10% Worm casts.
30% Compost + 30% Soilless mix + 30% Coir + 10% Worm casts.
30% Compost + 30% Vermiculite + 30% Perlite + 10% Worm casts.

Commercially available potting compost will contain enough nutrients for the first four to six weeks of plant growth, depending on the size of your pot or container, but check young plants regularly for signs of any deficiency, especially if you are using your own compost blends. It is important not to overdo the fertilization, so feed little and often. There is a good selection of organic fertilizers available from horticultural suppliers, but many growers prefer to use natural organic feeds.

Manure
Manure is an excellent resource for organic production. It supplies nutrients and organic matter, stimulating the biological processes in the soil that help build fertility. However, as raw/fresh manure breaks down in the soil, chemical compounds such as skatole, indole, and other phenols can be released and absorbed by the growing plants.

Organic soil associations recommend a 120-day gap between un-composted/fresh or raw manure application and harvest for most edible organic

Moby Dick by Dinafem Seeds is being grown in a SCROG with a good organic soil mix.

crops, where the ripe part may come into contact with the soil; and a 90-day gap for corn and soybeans, which are protected by husks or pods. Cannabis comes somewhere between the two at around 100 days. Some manure from intensively farmed cattle and poultry may also contain contaminants, such as growth hormones, antibiotic residues, pesticide residues and other undesirable organic substances, but these can be eliminated through the high temperatures produced by composting, which reduces the problems associated with fresh/raw manure usage. Fresh manures (including poultry) must be well composted before use.

Composted manure can be safely applied directly to crops. Many commercially available organic fertilizers are based on composted animal manures, supplemented with rock powders, plant by-products like alfalfa meal, and additional animal by-products like blood, bone, and feather meals.

Moby Dick by Dinafem Seeds grows great in growbags under a SCROG with compost and perlite in the soil mix.

The approximate NPK values of animal manures are:

Animal	N	P	K
Dairy cow	0.57	0.23	0.60
Beef steer	0.73	0.48	0.55
Horse	0.70	0.25	0.77
Pig	0.49	0.47	0.34
Sheep/goat	1.44	0.50	1.21

Rabbit droppings are also very high in N and P, whilst still having good K levels. Sheep and goat manures are also highly regarded by organic growers. Pig manure is the least effective and many organic users won't use it, as pigs can carry pathogens that are infectious to humans.

Guano

Guano is the name given to bird and bat droppings. The nutrient content of commercial guano products can vary considerably based on the diet of the birds or bats. Seabirds subsist largely on fish; depending on the species, bats may thrive largely on insects or fruits. Another major factor is the age of the source deposit. Guano products may be fresh, semi-fossilized, or fossilized. Guanos are also rich in 'bioremediation microbes' that assist in cleaning up soil toxins, and guano is safe manure for organic cannabis crops; but it is also an expensive option.

The approximate NPK values of guano are:

Guano	N	P	K
Desert bat	8	4	1
Cave bat	3	10	0.1
Fossilized sea bird	1	10	1
Pelleted sea bird	12	12	2.5

Alternative Organic Fertilizers

There are many other naturally occurring, organic fertilizers that can be used for cannabis crops. These are readily available from horticultural suppliers. However, take precautions when using any blood or bone meal products. Always wear rubber gloves and do not inhale the dust.

Type	N	P	K
Alfalfa Pellets	3	1	2
Bloodmeal	12	0	0
Bonemeal	2	11	0
Corn Gluten	6	0	0
Fish Emulsion	5	2	2
Kelp	1	0.2	2
Insect Manure	4	3	2
Soybeanmeal	6	1.5	2

Organic fertilizers tend to work best when used in combination, as some can be slow to break down in compost potting mixes. To ensure organic crops get a complete balance of nutrients growers can supplement their feeding regime with any of the following:

Organic female plant in a compost perlite mix. This plant will have a nice yield after flowering.

Blood and Bone Meal are great organic nutrients that can be purchased in pellet form for good, slow release feeding.

These plants have a good compost perlite mix and will produce very fresh, great tasting buds.

Fish Emulsion
This is readily available as a supplement and is high in nutrient content.

Kelp
Along with seaweed extract this is an excellent source of soluble and mobile trace minerals.

Seaweed Extract
Contains growth stimulants and is high in nitrogen, phosphorous and potash. Apply directly to the soil.

Sulphate of Potash
This supplies potassium, which is an essential partner to nitrogen and phosphate in maximizing crop yield, as well as strengthening resistance to disease.

Worm Castings
These are excreted by worms and contain humus and other organic material. They are generally high in nitrogen but don't add more than 25% to your compost mix as they can impair root development.

Aquarium Water
This contains fish waste, suspended in the water, which can be used as a nutrient tea for organic crops.

Organic Teas
These are extracts brewed using a nutrient food source. Organic teas can have variable nutrient content depending on the source used and growers should not use fresh manures to make solutions as they can contain harmful pathogens (disease causing organisms), and the brew stinks. Compost, worm castings, seaweed and guano are better nutrients to use.

There are several variations of organic tea and these are:

Compost Tea
Compost teas are distinguished from compost extracts by the method of production and the way they are used. Teas are actively brewed with 'microbial food' and a 'catalyst source,' which are added to the solution. An air pump is also used to bubble and aerate the solution, supplying oxygen for the brewing

process. The aim of the brewing process is to extract beneficial microbes from the compost itself, then grow and enlarge these populations of microbes during the 36-hour brew period.

The compost provides a source of microbes. The microbial food comes from molasses, kelp powder, or fish powder and the catalyst amendments come from humic acid, yucca extract, or rock dust. These additives promote the growth and multiplication of microbes in the tea. When compost teas are sprayed onto leaf surfaces, these beneficial organisms occupy 'spatial niches' on the leaf surface and use up 'leaf exudates' that disease-causing organisms would otherwise feed on.

Young plant being grown organically in a John Inness mix with no perlite.

Compost Extract

Liquid compost extract is made from compost that was traditionally suspended in a burlap sack, in a container of water, for two weeks. Nowadays growers immerse a nylon stocking filled with compost in a bucket or tank, stirring occasionally. The brew time is from 7 to 10 days. Compost extract is a rich source of soluble nutrients that can be used as a liquid fertilizer at every watering; however, monitor your plants' condition for any sign of overdose as compost extract can have variable nutrient content.

Herbal Tea

These are organic extracts made with common plants such as stinging nettle, horsetail, comfrey, and clover that can be grown/collected locally. Fill three-quarters of a container with fresh green plant material, and then fill up with tepid water. The tea is allowed to ferment at room temperature for a week. The finished product is then strained through a nylon stocking stretched over a sieve. The strained extract is diluted:

- 1 part herbal tea extract: 5 parts water and used as a soil drench.
- 1 part herbal tea: 10 parts water and used as a foliar spray.

Trough Production

Large-scale production of compost teas requires a tank, trough and pump. A 12-inch diameter PVC pipe is cut in half, perforated with holes, and lined with burlap. Compost is placed into the trough, which is supported 3 ft above the tank. The tank is then filled with water, and microbial food sources added. A sump pump sucks the solution from the bottom of the tank and distributes it, via a perforated hose, along the top of the compost. The solution runs through the compost and drips back into the open tank below. The pump then re-circulates the liquid. Within 7 days you will have a large population of beneficial organisms in the solution.

Commercial organic tea brewers are available but it is far easier and more cost effective to make the equipment yourself.

Pot and Container Sizes

Deep, six-inch square plastic pots are useful for most indoor cultivation techniques. Square pots allow you to pack the plants tightly together during the early stages of development, in order to make the most use of the available light. If these aren't available, any container larger than 6" is adequate, providing it has drainage holes in its base. Many organic growers use cheap plastic buckets. Plastic tomato cultivation pots are cheap and readily available. They are suitable for hydroponic pot culture which requires 1 to 2.5 gallon capacities, but they are on the large side for rotation cropping. Pots over 12" are too big for serious indoor organic cultivation.

Growbags are plastic sleeves that are pre-packed with potting compost. They can hold between one and three plants. Insert a 3" pot through a hole in the polyethylene to make watering easier. Cutting drainage slits in the base of the bag will prevent waterlogging. Some growers purchase potting compost in plastic bags and simply flatten them, cut slits into the top, and use them as growbags.

You can use plastic bags to grow plants in if nothing else is available. Alternatively, packs of ready-made cultivation bags are available from horticultural suppliers. Outdoor growers can use thick bin liners or polyethylene garbage bags. The first outdoor crop I ever grew was in garbage bags, as I couldn't afford any pots. The bags still yielded around 1 lb per plant.

All pots and containers used indoors should stand in saucers or waterproof trays. You can purchase them in various sizes or make them from builder's polyethylene fixed to a wooden frame. Children's wading pools can be used as trays for some indoor cultivation techniques.

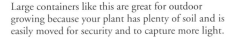

Large containers like this are great for outdoor growing because your plant has plenty of soil and is easily moved for security and to capture more light.

Growbags with an organic soil medium are being used in this successful indoor garden.

Does the moon influence cannabis planting?

The moon has 4 Phases or quarters (lasting about 7 days each). The first 2 quarters are during the waxing (increasing light) between the New and the Full moon. The third and fourth quarters are after the full moon when the light is waning. Planting by the moon is an ancient tradition but scientific research validates it. The Earth is in a large gravitational field, influenced by both the sun and moon. The tides are highest at the time of the New and the Full moon, when sun and moon are lined up with Earth. Just as the moon pulls the tides in the oceans, it pulls the moisture in the earth causing it to rise and encouraging germination and growth.

Soil moisture content is highest at the time of the Full moon and seeds absorb more water at this time, making germination and growth easier.

Auto Blue Kush from Autofem Seeds is a great strain that offers a very cerebral high.

8. Starting Your Crop

Necessity hath no law.
Speech. 1664.

From Seed

When germinated, cannabis seeds are approximately 50% male, 50% female, unless you are using feminized seeds (see Breeding). It is possible to increase the female-to-male ratio by treating the seeds with chemicals before germinating.

Ethylene, a naturally occurring gas given off by ripening bananas, has been found to increase the feminization of seeds. Before germination, place the seeds in a sealed plastic bag containing banana peels for 14 days. Wrap the skins in tissue to absorb any moisture they give off. Keep the bag in a warm place and air the seeds regularly, replacing the skins as they ripen.

Sensa Soak is marketed in the Netherlands as a commercial seed feminizer and is used as a soak before germination.

Increases of between 10 and 25% more females have been achieved using these methods. For best results, germinate untreated seeds in vermiculite soaked in a weak solution of hydroponic feed, which has been diluted by at least 50%. Place the vermiculite in a shallow tray or container (aluminum foil is suitable) and pour in nutrient solution until it is saturated. Plant the seeds just below the surface, ensuring that they are lightly covered. It is not necessary to place them in a darkened area. Instead, leave the tray exposed to at least 18 hours of uninterrupted daylight and keep the vermiculite moist. The temperature should not exceed 80°F. This method of germination can be used for organic plants but for true organic gardening you should start them in a 'seed' potting compost, or a proprietary soil-less compost. They will only require fresh water instead of a dilute feed.

Within one to seven days the seeds will begin germination. The first stage is the absorption of water, followed closely by the emergence of the radicle or root. As the radicle forces its way downwards the hypocotyl or stem extends toward the light, still covered by the seed case. As the cotyledon, or first leaves, enlarge they shed the seed husk, allowing the first true leaves to emerge. Don't be tempted to pull off the seed casing as you can damage the hypocotyl.

Dinafem Seeds have a highly reliable germination rate. Note the taproot emerging quickly from the base of the seed.

As soon as the seedlings are between ¾" and 1" tall, remove them carefully from the vermiculite and plant them into pots, cubes or polystyrene cups, ensuring that they are well watered. They are now ready to be placed into the nursery or vegetative growing area.

Damping Off

Damping off is a fungal infection that kills seedlings. The base of the stem rots and the plant falls over and dies. Some growers spray seedlings with a diluted, preventative systemic fungicide as a precaution. It's not essential to spray, just ensure that you give the seedlings the best possible start by cleaning all your equipment thoroughly before use, and by using fresh water (or a weak nutrient solution) to feed them. Low light levels; low temperatures, high humidity and waterlogged medium all contribute to damping off.

Cloning

Cloning is simply taking cuttings from a mature plant. It ensures that you have a 100% female crop. Plants that are in flower are difficult to clone so females are identified through the flowering of test cuttings. Cuttings are taken from the plants while they are in the vegetative state, and then carefully labeled. These cuttings are then rooted and flowered. It is possible to induce cannabis to flower and then, as soon as the females are identified, place them back under 24 hours of continuous light, forcing them to revert to the vegetative cycle. However, this process can be time consuming and most growers prefer to use cuttings. Female marijuana plants can be cloned as soon as they have developed healthy side shoots. The older the plant, the more shoots you will have.

Once you have a healthy mature female plant that shows signs of vigorous growth you can make genetically identical copies of her that will exhibit exactly the same traits. Start by cutting young growth tips, about 3 to 4" long, from the mother plant. Use a sharp, sterilized pair of scissors. Most horticultural guides will tell you that scissors pinch and damage the stem tissue but that doesn't affect the strike rate of young cuttings and scissors are easier to use than

Seeds from Dinafem are carefully checked by quality control before being made commercially available.

This branch from the clone mother is ideal for taking a cutting.

This branch from the clone mother is ideal for taking a cutting.

Prepare the branch for cloning by choosing the ideal place to cut.

This beautiful Green Crack clone from the pros at SinsemillaWorks has taken root and is doing well.

Doby from breeder and grower Sativa Tim is a great all-around strain that clones extremely well. Note the vigorous root growth.

Cuttings take root in styrofoam cups before being transplanted into larger containers.

Scissors or a sharp knife are perfect for taking cuttings. Be sure to cut on an angle to cause the least amount of damage to the mother plant.

Clone gel is used on the cutting to promote the formation of roots.

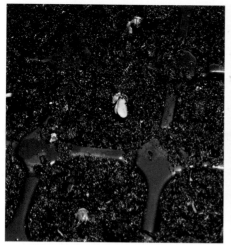

Seedlings emerge with the seed husk still attached. Note the center plant with its cotyledons already appearing.

This healthy beauty from OGA Seeds needs to be transplanted into a bigger home. Remember to tease the roots out before you re-plant.

razors. Cut the stem at a slight angle to expose a larger area, and then dip the stalk into a rooting gel. Gels are available from all good gardening retailers and are better than rooting powders. Place the rooting gel you are working with in a separate container to avoid cross contamination of any possible infections. Remove any large leaves and place the cutting stem ¾" to 1" into the potting medium you've chosen.

If you are gardening organically you can use peat pellets that have been soaked overnight in water. A lot of growers don't like them, though, and an alternative is 3" pots filled with a good quality 'seed' potting compost. Simply firm the seed compost around the stem.

Hydroponic gardeners can use rockwool starter cubes, floral foam or, alternatively, small pots can be filled with perlite or vermiculite. These hydroponic media can later be potted into soil for organic cultivation.

Whatever your potting medium, ensure that it is saturated before inserting the cuttings, but don't allow the cuttings to stand in water. You need to drain off excess liquid, as cuttings root more successfully in a well-drained medium and won't develop fungal infections.

Place the clones in a high-sided propagator with a clear plastic lid and put it under a fluorescent or MH lamp on 18 to 24 hours of daylight. Depending on the season, a greenhouse can be perfect for starting young clones and won't require any lamps. It is important to maintain humidity for the early stages of the clone's life, as they have no roots. Mist them three to four times daily for the first few days, then daily with a 50% diluted feed. Ensure that the temperature remains near 75°F. You can remove the propagator cover after a few days, but continue misting the young clones and making sure that the rooting medium doesn't become waterlogged. Cuttings are repotted as soon as they start to develop roots: usually 10 to 14 days after they have been taken. Once a cutting has developed roots it can be treated as a young plant.

There is an even less complex method of cloning using only water, light, and the cutting. The cutting is taken as with the other cloning methods; however, the clone is placed into a glass of water that has had foil wrapped around the outside to prevent too much light striking the root area. The clones are then placed under your chosen propagating lamp. They will even strike under a 100-watt incandescent light bulb in around 10 days.

Air Layering

This interesting technique for propagating cuttings from plants produces strong clones from the mother. However, it's time consuming and can slow your harvesting down if you are cultivating on a large scale; for example, if you're using a Sea Of Green setup. When you take a conventional cutting from a female, two fresh growing tips will appear from the node below the damaged area, effectively doubling your clone production. When applying the air layering technique, you don't physically separate the newly formed clone from its mother until it has started developing roots. This delays the healing and regeneration process, but this is a small price to pay if you only require a small number of quality clones. Some plants will produce new growth tips beneath the site while the clone is still attached. The intent of air layering is to produce a rooted clone that is still attached to the mother plant, giving it an umbilical cord that allows water and nutrients to pass into the clone area. Any food produced from its own leaves above the root site is retained and utilized by the new offspring.

Select a vigorous growing tip from the mother plant and with a scalpel cut two horizontal lines just below the node, circling the stem roughly ⅓" apart. Join these two rings with a vertical cut and peel the bark away. Cut through into the phloem, which is the layer beneath the bark that conducts food away from the leaves and into the plant. The phloem is tougher than the outer bark so it's not difficult to feel the depth with a little practice, just handle the scalpel gently. Scrape the phloem away with the scalpel blade, using a gentle scraping action. Try not to do damage to the xylem, the layer beneath the phloem. The xylem is responsible for conducting nutrients from the plant to the leaves. It

Seedlings are grown in starter containers until they are ready to be transplanted into the ground.

must be left intact to ensure that the clone is fed during its rooting time.

Next, apply a coating of rooting gel to the node site above the cut. Cover the whole area, including the cut, with damp sphagnum moss. Use plastic cling wrap to hold the moss in place by wrapping it around the stem. Ensure that you leave the top and bottom of the moss exposed to aid watering and drainage. Within 10 to 14 days you'll see strong new roots developing. At this point, you can separate the clone from its mother. Remove the plastic cling wrap and treat the clone as a young plant.

Repotting Your Seedlings

Repot cannabis seedlings into their final growing containers when they are between 4 and 6" tall and show signs of vigorous growth. This helps them to form a healthy root ball in their new pots. Prepare your growing pots by filling them with fresh potting compost to within 1½" of the rim, leaving a hole in the center for the plants. Place young plants in the containers, level with the compost mix, and firm more compost around the base of the stem.

Seedlings that were started in small pots must be carefully removed from their original containers. Place your hand over the top of the pot so that your hand is covering the soil and the plant is resting between your fingers. Then turn the pot upside down. Gently tap the base of the pot and the root ball will slide out and can be repotted into the new growing containers.

Feeding Young Plants

Potting composts contain sufficient fertilizer to sustain the young plants for the first four to six weeks of growth, depending on the size of pots you're using. After this time you have to feed the crop. For consistent and accurate feeding, use a soluble plant fertilizer that is either poured onto the compost as a drench, or sprayed directly onto the plant leaves as a foliar feed. Feed cannabis plants small amounts frequently, as overfeeding can be as harmful as underfeeding. Organic growers can find a range of feeds commercially available that are suitable for cannabis and are more precise than alternative methods of truly organic fertilizing, such as adding manures or nutrient teas, produced by placing organic fertilizers in pantyhose, and steeping in warm water.

Fertilizers are classified by the nutrient content, or NPK ratio, enabling growers to select the most suitable type for their crop. Cannabis has varying nutrient requirements at different stages of its life.

The three main components, or macronutrients, of plant fertilizers are:
- Nitrogen (N)
- Phosphorous (P)
- Potassium (K)

Vegetative Growth

Cannabis in its vegetative state requires high amounts of nitrogen in its feed. Nitrogen promotes vigorous growth and stem development; it also increases protein synthesis in the plant. Drying of the leaves and reddening of the stems, as well as stunted growth, are signs of N deficiencies. Fertilizer with an NPK of 30-15-15 is ideal for vegetative growth. This ratio indicates the percentage of macronutrients, with nitrogen the highest at 30%.

Flowering Stage

Cannabis that has entered the flowering stage requires higher amounts of phosphorous and lower levels of nitrogen. Phosphorous promotes blooming and flower production in cannabis. Dark blue/green leaves and small bud formations indicate P deficiencies. Fertilizers with an NPK of 15-30-30 are ideal for flowering.

Well-organized outdoor garden filled with vegetative plants with stake system in place. These girls will benefit from a fertilizer with an NPK of 30-15-15.

While organic fertilizers are unsuitable for hydroponic gardening, hydroponic feeds are ideal for organic crops. To avoid overfeeding the plants, always dilute the nutrients by 50%.

Growth Promoters for Organic Gardens

Earth Food or Earth Juice is a mixture of activated carbon, amino acids, organic trace elements and lignite suspended in a catalyst of altered water. Available from hydroponic suppliers, it is highly recommended for increasing yields.

Humboldt County's Own Bushmaster. Proprietary kelp extract which speeds up the transition to bloom while decreasing inter node spacing resulting in tighter flower clusters and bushier compact plants.

Hydrogen Peroxide (H_2O_2) is normally associated with hydroponic cultivation; however, it is useful in organic gardening to keep down bacteria and fungi. You can add hydrogen peroxide solution to your water at each feed in the form of Oxy-plus 17.5%. Alternatively, use a 35% solution of H_2O_2 diluted at a ratio of 10 drops per four cups of water.

Gorgeous flowering plant from 420Clones.com. Use fertilizer at an NPK of 15-30-30 during the flowering stage.

This grow room is full to the brim with Auto Bud by Autofem Seeds in Spain. Note the reflective material on the walls, the good ventilation, and the healthy plants. Nice!

O.G.P. is the brand name for an 'organic growth promoter' manufactured in New Zealand and available in the U.S. It contains extracts of beeswax and alfalfa with high levels of gibberellins that can promote strong cell growth during the vegetative period.

Panchagavya is a Sanskrit word and means a blend of five products obtained from cows, which are considered sacred to Hindus. The three direct constituents are manure, urine, and milk; the two derived products are curd and ghee. It acts as a growth promoter and immunity booster, increases the weight and quality of yields and also promotes dense root growth.

Recipe for Panchagavya:

Cow manure mixed with water - 11 lbs
Cow's urine - 3 quarts
Cow's milk - 2 quarts
Curd - 2 quarts
Ghee - 2.2 lbs
Ripe banana - 12 bananas
Coconut water - 3 quarts
Sugarcane juice - 3 quarts

The measured amount of cow dung and ghee are added to the container first and kept for three days to ferment. On the fourth day the remaining ingredients are added to the container and kept for seven more days. After ten days of incubation, *1 quart Panchagavya solution is mixed with 2.5 gallons of water, and then applied as a solution to the compost. The Panchagavya can also be used as a foliar spray.*

Somasundaram et al., (2004) reported that Panchagavya contains growth regulatory substances such as Indole Acetic Acid, Gibberellic Acid and Cytokinin along with essential plant nutrients. It also contains beneficial, effective microorganisms, predominately lactic acid bacteria, yeast, actinomycetes, photosynthetic bacteria and certain fungi besides beneficial and proven biofertilizers such as Azotobacter, Azospirillum and Phosphobacterium. Jayasree and George (2006) observed a significant high yield and quality in chili plants, Capsicum annuum treated with Panchagavya. Ravikiran (2005) stated that Panchagavya is not only an effective pesticide, but also a natural fertilizer, growth promoter and boosts immunity in the plant system, helping repel pests and control disease (Prabu, 2006).[8.1]

The taproot extends into the soil and the head bursts forth. Soon the tiny cotyledons will emerge.

Soak your seeds overnight in a jar to promote germination, but don't leave them in there too long.

African Free by Eva Seeds should be staked for extra support due to its bountiful harvests.

Seaweed extract is available from most horticultural suppliers and contains growth stimulants. It is particularly suitable for organic production where it is used as both a root drench and a foliar spray.

Snow Storm Ultra. Enhanced flower aroma and flavor. 1 tsp. per gallon of water and applied every one or two waterings.

Sulphate of potash supplies potassium, which is an essential partner to nitrogen and phosphate in maximizing crop yield, as well as strengthening resistance to disease. It is applied as a surface dressing to compost or soil.

Triacontanol is a root stimulant which, when used in small quantities, can increase yields. Alfalfa contains nitrogen and trace elements; however, the real benefit comes from a fatty acid alcohol called triacontanol which occurs naturally in the waxy surface of the plant's leaves. To make alfalfa tea, add 12 cups of alfalfa pellets to a 32 gallon garbage can, add water, stir and steep for 24 - 48 hours. You can add five cups of Epsom salts and eight ounces of fish fertilizer if you wish to experiment with the solution. It is better to test your tea on an individual plant first. If you experience no problems you are good to go.

Watering Systems for Organic Crops

Most organic growers store their water supply in garden water barrels or large plastic tanks in order to age it. Aging lowers the levels of chlorine in the water, allows it to be heated with aquarium heaters and, if necessary, lets you adjust the pH levels. Black plastic water tanks, available from household plumbing retailers, are generally the favored storage tanks to use and come with their own lightproof lids. Larger tanks for commercial setups can be built from building blocks and waterproofed with a pond liner. It is not advisable to use water straight from the water mains, especially in winter when the temperature drops even lower in the underground supply pipes. Organic crops can easily be watered by hand using containers or hoses. Cultivators wanting to automate the process can use most hydroponic setups to water organic crops, with the exception of flood and drain or Nutrient Film Technique (NFT) systems as they tend to saturate the potting compost.

Leaching the Soil

It is important to leach your potting composts at least once every two weeks with aged water, in order to flush out any build-up of salts. The salts come from the fertilizer solution and are deposited by evaporation in the warm grow areas. Pour aged water into each pot until it floods over the level of the soil, and then allow it to drain through. Discard the water that collects in the trays.

Supporting the Plants

Plants grown intensively in rotation will only produce a main cola with very few side shoots. However, plants grown for longer vegetative periods usually need supporting during their flowering phase, hopefully due to the weight of the buds! Short canes can be used to provide support for individual plants and are cost effective; however, some growers like to use cord supports, secured to the ceiling and attached to individual branches. Groups of plants can be supported by stretching six-inch nylon mesh horizontally above the crop. The plants grow up through the mesh and you raise it as they develop. This is a good way of supporting a large crop, although it can also be used very effectively on small flood and drain tables to support plants.

Outdoor crops usually develop thick stems and many growers collect these after harvest to use as canes and walking sticks. It is advisable to give outdoor plants some form of support to protect them in high winds, especially if you have planted a late crop or have pruned the plants to produce two or more main colas. Growers use bamboo canes, cord or fencing wire stretched between posts, or they drive tree support stakes into the ground next to each young plant and secure them as they develop.

Alternatively, some growers cut flexible lengths of thin branches and push both ends into the soil to form an arch under each plant. These arches allow you to support individual branches more effectively, especially on cropped plants, and are better than individual canes or stakes. Check outdoor plants regularly, particularly after any heavy weather, to ensure that none have been uprooted or damaged. Damaged stems can be saved by splinting, taping and supporting the injury.

Footnotes:
8.1 http://www.eco-web.com/edi/index.htm

This Sensi Star is well-staked for extra support during the flowering stage.

9. Hydroponic Cultivation

An oppressive government is more to be feared than a tiger.
Confucius.

Hydroponic cultivation is growing without soil, using water that contains all of the nutrients and minerals required by a plant. In a hydroponic garden, the cultivator can control and adjust the feeding requirements to optimum levels; however, systems need careful monitoring as mistakes with the nutrient solution can ruin a crop

Measuring pH Levels in the Nutrient Solution
The pH level is a measurement of acidity or alkalinity. On a scale measuring 1 to 14, neutral would be 7 and the lower the reading, the more acidic the solution is.

🌿 1 to 7 is called an 'acid' and 7 to 14 is called an 'alkaline' solution

The ideal pH range for cannabis cultivation is 6.5 in soil and about 5.5 in most hydroponic solutions. Be aware that extremes of pH will cause serious injury to cannabis plants. The pH is measured in the solution using either a digital meter or pH test papers. You dip the test papers into the solution and compare the color changes to the chart that is supplied. Meters are more accurate and convenient to use. Serious growers should invest in a professional pH meter unit with a detachable probe.

Adding phosphoric acid, sulfuric acid or white vinegar lowers pH in nutrient solutions. Add small amounts and check until the meter shows the required reading. Sodium hydroxide, potassium hydroxide or baking soda will raise pH levels. These pH adjusters are toxic and aggressive chemicals so always store them safely and protect your skin and eyes when using them.

Measuring the Nutrient Strength
The standard measurement of nutrient concentration in hydroponic solutions is known as Total Dissolved Solids (TDS) and is expressed in parts per million

(PPM). To gauge the TDS in a solution you require a meter that measures Electrical Conductivity (EC) or Conductivity Factor (CF), which is the ability of a solution to conduct an electric current. Pure, distilled water contains no minerals and so cannot conduct electricity. As nutrients are added the conductivity will increase. Measuring this gives the cultivator an accurate method of determining nutrient strength. TDS is confusing and many U.S. growers are now converting to EC (CF) units of measure.

The standard used for the measurement of EC is milliSiemens per centimeter (mS/cm^2). In order for your meter to show a reading in TDS it has to convert the EC reading using a mathematical equation; however, different meter manufacturers use different factors (0.50 to 0.72) to calculate the PPM they display, although the EC/CF reading will be the same for all meters. To convert EC to CF multiply by 10. Standard hydroponic nutrient solutions are EC 2.0 milliSiemens (or $2.0mS/cm^2$) or 20 CF units. Hydroponic solutions should be within the parameters 1.5mS - 2.0mS.

Nutrient Requirements of Cannabis Plants

Essential nutrients in hydroponic fertilizers are classified as either macronutri-

These plants are 2 weeks into the vegetative state and are looking particularly healthy in their hydro set up.

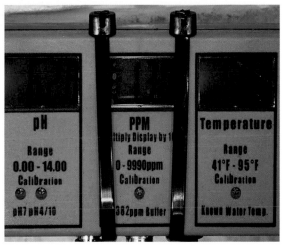

Hydroponic systems needn't be huge; this small cupboard from Dinafem will be incredibly effective.

The guys at OGA keep a close eye on all their systems' readings, which is essential when growing in a hydro system.

ents that are required in large amounts or micronutrients that are required in smaller quantities. Along with essential nutrients, plants require carbon, oxygen and hydrogen, which are supplied by water and the atmosphere.

Water (H_2O)

Most hydroponic feeds come in either grow or bloom formulations, as plants have different requirements at different stages. Hydroponic feeds are also formulated for hard or soft water. Hard water has high levels of bicarbonates in the form of magnesium and calcium salts that cause a build-up of salt deposits, locking up trace minerals. It is easy to identify hard water areas by the build-up of lime scale in kettles. The main problem for the hydroponic gardener is that the bicarbonates require large amounts of acid to neutralize them before the pH can be adjusted. Growers in hard water areas need to use hard water formulations. If you only have a small number of plants, try using mineral water. Mineral water contains trace elements and carbonated waters contain CO_2, as does rainwater. Tap water is treated with chlorine and in some areas fluoride, so most growers allow the water to stand or age before using it. Excessive amounts of chlorine will cause a hardening of the crop. Run tap water before filling your reservoirs to disperse any sediment present. Hot water has high sodium and calcium deposits and should be used very sparingly, and only to warm solutions.

When fed properly and given the right amount of light, this guy will be a fantastic producer.

Both light and space are utilized brilliantly in this hydro set up.

Hydroponic Feeds

Nutrient solutions that are designed for soil cultivation are of no use to the hydroponic grower. The feed solution must contain all of the macro and micronutrients the plant requires, and they must be in the correct balance. There are a wide variety of hydroponic solutions available that will suit indoor cannabis growers.

Hydroponic nutrient packs usually come supplied in two separate containers labeled "A" and "B" for convenience. The reason behind this is that the components are incompatible with each other and cause precipitation when mixed. Once diluted into the solution there is no problem. Liquid nutrient packs are easier to use than powder formulations as the powdered feed must be dissolved before it's added to the plant reservoir. Nutrient packs recommended for hydroponic cannabis cultivation include the following:

Botanicare
CNS17 Hydroponic Grow (3-2-4)
CNS17 Hydroponic Bloom (2-2-5)

Canna
Aqua Vega A & B (6-2-8).
Aqua Flores A & B (5-3-10)

Dutch Masters
One Grow (One part no mix nutrient solution. Just add to tank)
One Flower (One part no mix nutrient solution. Just add to tank)

Dyna-Gro
Dyna-Gro Liquid Grow (7-9-5)
Dyna-Gro Bloom (3-12-6)
Earth Juice
Earth Juice Grow (2-1-1)
Earth Juice Bloom (0-3-1)

Fox Farm
Grow Big Hydroponic (3-2-6)
Tiger Bloom (2-8-4)

General Hydroponics
Flora, 3-part nutrient solution:
FloraGro (2-1-7)
FloraBloom (0-5-4)
FloraMicro (4-0-1)

Pure Blend
Metabolic Bloom Organic Compost Formula For Hydroponics & Soil:
Grow Formula (1-0.5-1)
Bloom Formula (0.5-0.5-1)

These packs all come with detailed instructions concerning dilution rates and are easy to use. It is important that cultivators choose a nutrient solution that is right for them and suits their hydroponic setup. Growers using rockwool may choose a solution formulated for this medium; fertilizers that are more acidic compensate for the higher pH levels caused by rockwool. However, with careful pH adjustment, all of the above nutrients can be used in rockwool setups. To optimize the uptake of the nutrient formulation you have chosen, gently heat the solution with an aquarium heater to around 75°F. The solution temperature can be monitored with a submersible thermometer purchased from an aquarium retailer.

Growth Promoters and Additives for Hydro Systems

Hydrogen Peroxide (H_2O_2)

Can be added to the solution to increase its oxygen content, thereby increasing nutrient uptake and improving photosynthesis. The addition of H_2O_2 produces thicker plants with shorter internodal lengths and also keeps down bacteria in the solution. H_2O_2 is sold commercially as Oxy-Plus in a 17.5% stabilized solution. Alternatively, it can be purchased from hairdressing wholesalers, who sell it as hair bleach. Add one teaspoon of 35% H_2O_2 per 5 ¼ gallons of nutrient solution, twice a week. Dip test strips, purchased from your hydroponic supplier, into the reservoir to give a reading. The optimum level is 30 to 50 ppm.

Nitrozyme

A growth enhancer that can be added to the nutrient solution or used as a foliar feed. It contains cytokinins, which are hormones derived from a North Atlantic sea plant. They aid in cell division and enlargement. Use Nitrozyme during early plant development but not during flowering.

Seaweed Extract

Contains natural growth stimulators and is available commercially in North America and Europe. It is excellent for both organic and hydroponic cultivation, and can be used as a foliar spray or root drench. The extract will mix readily with any foliar feeds you choose to use.

Adding a non-ionic wetting agent to the spray will increase uptake of foliar feeds. Wetting agents work by increasing the surface tension of water, allowing the nutrients to penetrate deep into the leaf tissue. Alternatively, add a few drops of liquid dish detergent, rinsing the plant leaves regularly with fresh water to avoid blocking the stomata. Recommended growth enhancers for hydroponic cannabis crops are:

B'Cuzz Bloom

Completely water soluble, activates biological life in the substrate, and contains micro-nutria in chelate form which offers enzymatic action on several fronts. Available for Soil, Hydro or Coco.

Hydro system in the Kannabia Seeds grow facility. The Grodan cubes hold the plants inside the clay pebbles on the table. Note the overflow tray at the front.

B'Cuzz PK13/14 (0-13-14)
Flowering booster; ensures firm, dense flowers.

Emerald Triangle Bushmaster (0-.1-0)
Bushmaster slows down and halts the vertical growth, creating more compact plants. At the same time the vertical growth ceases, the plant starts to become very bushy, producing lateral branching and eventually producing much more surface area for flowers to form, thus greatly increasing the yield. Works well in soil or hydro.

Emerald Triangle Gravity (0-.1-0)
Uniquely prepared kelp extract and phosphorous-based additive will harden your flowers from the top to the bottom. A little goes a long way. Use once or twice about 3 weeks before the end of a plant's cycle. Adds size and weight to flowering plants.

Look out for any signs of nutrient imbalance in your plants. This grower should act quickly to save his crop.

Emerald Triangle Purple Maxx (0-0-3)

Humboldt County's Own Purple Maxx is completely organic. Purple Maxx used to be called Stacker and has been shown to improve essential oil production. Purple Maxx is a combination of organic compounds that encourages plants to "stack" their flowering sites closer together, producing more flowers.

Emerald Triangle Snow Storm ULTRA (0-0-3)

Humboldt County's Own Snow Storm Ultra is a potassium supplement which assists with essential oil production. Snow Storm has been separated from the original Purple Maxx product.

Sensa-Spray

Hormonal stimulant applied as a foliar spray in the mid-life of the plant. Increases bud development.

Superthrive - vitamin and hormone supplement
Add to your nutrient solution at the rate of 1 drop per gallon.

Flushing

Hydroponic cultivators can produce smoother tasting marijuana flowers by flushing the plants prior to harvesting. Flushing removes any chemical residue that may have built up in the crop, and is recommended because nitrate salts (a form of nitrogen in NPK) are not healthy to smoke. The hydroponic feed is replaced with pure pH-adjusted water for the last three days of flowering. There are commercial hydroponic flushes available that are added to the water; however, some growers prefer to reduce the strength of the nutrient solution, as opposed to flushing it through with water. A gradual reduction over the last two weeks before harvest tends to work best. Aim to have the solution at 25% strength by the last day.

Troubleshooting Hydroponic Systems

If problems occur with your crop, first check that all plants are suffering from the same symptoms. The plants themselves are the best indicator of problems within your setup, so check your crop daily. New growth problems are almost always associated with the nutrient solution - usually a deficiency of nutrients, or a build-up of toxicity. Either way, the remedy is to replace the solution in the reservoir after flushing the system through with fresh water.

- Leaf Droop: Over or underfeeding of the plant. An over-dry medium. Sudden extreme temperature fluctuations. Insect attack.
- Yellow Leaf: Underfeeding of the plant. Saturated medium due to poor drainage. Low light levels.
- Black Leaf: Excessive heat from lights or cold temperature fluctuations occurring during the night cycle. Parasitic insects.
- Copper Leaf: Overfeeding of the plant. Saturated medium. Imbalance in nutrient system.
- Drooping Leaf: Over or underfeeding of the plant. Dry medium. Fungus gnat larvae attacking plant roots.
- Irregular Leaf: Overfeeding of the plant. Incorrect balance of the nutrient solution. Parasitic insects.
- Stunted Growth: Over or underfeeding of the plant. Low light levels. Parasitic insects.

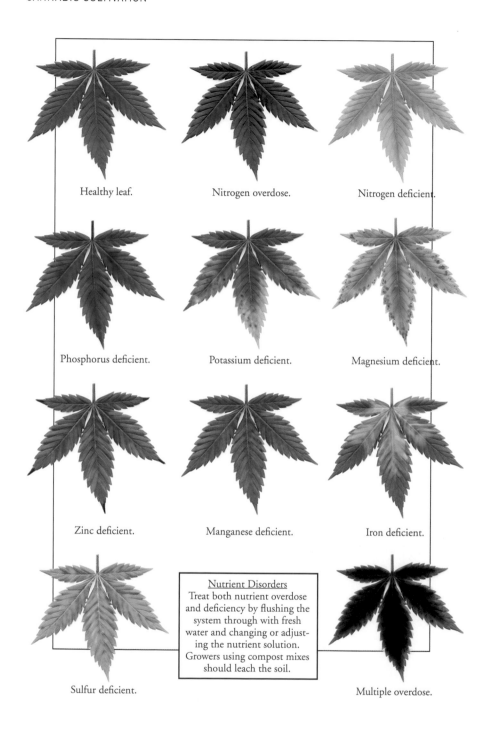

Healthy leaf.

Nitrogen overdose.

Nitrogen deficient.

Phosphorus deficient.

Potassium deficient.

Magnesium deficient.

Zinc deficient.

Manganese deficient.

Iron deficient.

Sulfur deficient.

Nutrient Disorders
Treat both nutrient overdose
and deficiency by flushing the
system through with fresh
water and changing or adjusting the nutrient solution.
Growers using compost mixes
should leach the soil.

Multiple overdose.

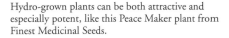

Hydro-grown plants can be both attractive and especially potent, like this Peace Maker plant from Finest Medicinal Seeds.

While it's unusual for hydro systems to be outside, it's not impossible, as this aeroponics system shows.

Hydroponic crops recover quickly once the nutrient solution has been changed and adjusted. As a precautionary measure, flush the system with fresh water every eight weeks. Most problems with your hydroponic crop will be environment-based and caused by parasites or disease, incorrect temperatures, and/or humidity and light levels, rather than with the nutrient solution itself.

- Low light levels will produce weak, thin plants with pale leaves: a condition known as chlorosis.
- Temperature problems will cause wilting and black or brown leaves, irregular growth and weak plants.
- Humidity problems will cause fungal attacks and stunted growth.

Daily Check List
1. Assess the condition of the plants. Are there any signs of insect attack? Check the condition of the new growth, and the color and vigor of the plants.
2. Assess the condition of the growing medium: Do algae formations exist? Is the medium waterlogged? Are the visible roots white and healthy? Does the medium smell fresh?
3. Assess the environmental conditions. Are the temperature, humidity and light at the correct levels?

4. Assess whether the system is functioning correctly. Check solution for pH and EC/CF. Test pumps, fans, vents and CO_2 equipment.

5. Assess to ensure that light is not escaping or entering the grow room.

Hydroponic Media

The most productive way to grow cannabis hydroponically involves using an inert, sterile medium to support the plant roots. The medium does not contain any nutrients or minerals of its own; they are supplied to the plant during the irrigation process, either by hand or using an automated system. Gravel, sand, foam and even beads have all been used for hydroponic cultivation. The best media are described below.

Rockwool

Rockwool is a lightweight, sterile growing medium available in slabs, cubes or granules. Rockwool can be used in all hydroponic setups, although its pH value is quite high at around 7.5. The nutrient solution must be adjusted to compensate for this high pH value. There are specially formulated feeds designed for rockwool setups but, as long as the nutrient solution is kept more acidic, any hydroponic packs can be used. Rockwool will easily hold up to 10 times more water than soil, but like all hydroponic media it is less forgiving and provides no buffer against fluctuating pH levels. Rockwool provides an ideal environment for algae growth on its exposed surfaces and, although this growth is not harmful to the plants and doesn't compete for food, it can encourage fungus gnats and caspid flies, so cover all exposed surfaces with aluminum foil or lightproof polyethylene. Dry rockwool is an irritant so wear gloves when handling it.

Greenmix and Golden Wool

Greenmix and Golden Wool are tufts of rockwool granulate that have a mixture of water absorbent and repellent properties that makes them particularly good for hydroponic cultivation.

Perlite

Perlite is an inert granular growing medium that is produced at very high temperatures and used in containers to provide a lightweight, sterile, absorbent material in which to cultivate. Saturated perlite will hold just as much air as rockwool and can be reused but needs careful cleaning to remove any dead roots and must be sterilized. It is advisable to cover the tops of the pots with foil to prevent algae from forming.

This little plant is growing in clay pebbles and looks healthy and happy.

Coconut Fiber

Coconut fiber holds more water and oxygen than rockwool, which is an advantage in passive hydroponic systems. Unlike most hydroponic media, coconut fiber is completely natural: it contains organic compounds and is environmentally friendly. Dutch cultivators have been using 50% coconut fiber mixed with 50% expanded clay pebbles with excellent results. Choose a coarse coconut fiber prepared for hydroponic cultivation. Coconut fibers intended for adding to potting composts can be too finely graded and high in sodium.

Clay Pebbles

Clay pebbles are porous, lightweight and pH-neutral and can be used in active hydroponic setups, but are not good at lifting nutrients from reservoirs in passive systems. Used alone in ebb and flow systems, clay pebbles are too light and can result in the plants falling over during the flood cycle. As clay pebbles can be reused indefinitely, they are cost effective and make a useful medium to mix with coconut fiber. Clay pebbles are usually imported and sold in metric sizes. The most popular sizes are 8 to 16mm (about 5⁄16" to 5⁄8" in diameter). Choose a brand that looks irregular in shape with no smooth round pebbles, as the small crevices and pockets help feeder roots form.

Vermiculite

Vermiculite is a very absorbent, lightweight growing medium that holds water well. Because it is excellent at drawing nutrients in passive hydroponic systems such as wick units, vermiculite is used as the bottom layer under perlite. Vermiculite can become waterlogged when used on its own, but is ideal for germinating seeds.

Hydroponic Systems

Hydroponic setups are classified as either active or passive. Active systems use pumps to distribute the nutrients to the plants and passives do not. Those suitable for organic watering systems are marked: ●

Aeroponics

Aeroponics is a hydroponic method of propagating and growing plants in air. Plants are grown with their roots suspended in a lightproof, sterile and enclosed air chamber where a nutrient vapor is pulse-sprayed onto the developing roots - in some systems more than 200 times every 12 hours. Aeroponic propagation is not new, and was first used in 1944, but advances in modern technology have allowed us to build more efficient aeroponic systems. Most growers prefer to buy ready-made aeroponic setups, but it is possible to build a unit yourself providing you understand the principles.

An aeroponics chamber can be constructed from a black plastic domestic plumbing tank. The clone is put in a net pot or perforated container holding an inert growing medium, such as rockwool or clay pebbles. The container sits in a small opening cut into the removable lid and is supported to allow the roots to hang in the lightproof chamber. A drain placed at the bottom of the tank allows you to collect the nutrient mix in a reservoir and re-use it by placing a pump in the reservoir to force water up a pipe to feed a misting nozzle that is fixed into the growth chamber. It is best to connect the pump to a digital timer programmed to spray at 15-minute intervals. You can build a unit like this using a powerful submersible pump, connected by a hose to misting nozzles taken from hand-held garden sprayers, and it will work well. Use a commercially available hydroponic feed at the manufacturer's recommended dilutions (pH 5.5) and add either seaweed extract or one of the many growth-promoting supplements that are commercially available.

Aeroponics is not the best system for novices but with a little experience it can produce very high-yielding crops. Research has shown that aeroponic

Aeroponic Chamber

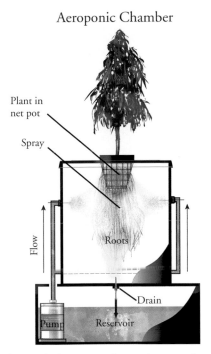

Plant in
net pot

Spray

Flow

Roots

Drain

Pump

Reservoir

Aeroponics is not meant for a novice grower but with a little effort it can produce very high yields.

Aeroponic cloning can be a great way to preserve the genetics of your favorite plant.

Aero Cloner

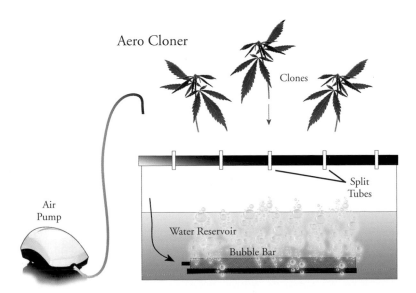

Clones

Split
Tubes

Air
Pump

Water Reservoir

Bubble Bar

In an aero cloner, the clones sit in the split tubes and if the system is working correctly, splashes of water should spray the clone stems but not submerge them. The aero cloner box should be black to keep out light.

Deep Water Culture (DWC)

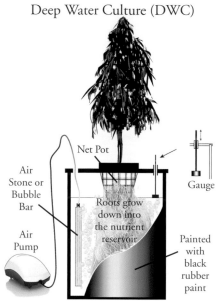

Net Pot

Air Stone or Bubble Bar

Gauge

Roots grow down into the nutrient reservoir

Air Pump

Painted with black rubber paint

The lid of your aeroponic clone box should fit tightly, whether you are growing inside or out.

This aero bubbler/DWC system shoots the nutrients straight onto the roots. The nutrient solution must be kept at one-third strength at all times.

cultivation produces better yields than any of the other hydroponic techniques. Clones placed in aeroponic rooting chambers have an almost 100% strike rate. Even without the use of hormone rooting agents, cuttings are produced faster and have incredible root development when removed from the chamber. Once rooted, your clones can be moved either to a larger grow chamber or placed into another medium, either hydroponic or organic.

Aeroponic Cloning

An aerocloner is simple to make using a lightproof, plastic container with a tight-fitting lid. The size of your container is governed by the number of clones you want to produce. If you only require a small number then kitchen storage containers are ideal. Lightproof your containers by painting the outside with black rubber paint.

Next, the container base is fitted with an aquarium bubble bar that can be bought inexpensively at an aquarium supplier. The bar requires an air pump, available at the same supplier, and is connected using flexible tubing. Choose one that produces a fine stream of bubbles and secure it to the base of your container using silicon glue. The bubble bar should cover most of the container length so larger setups will require additional bars.

The container is now partly filled with pure pH-adjusted water and the air pump is switched on. The bubble bar creates tiny splashes at the water's surface that spray the clone stems. You will need to adjust the water depth to ensure the spray hits the stems but does not submerge them. The clones are supported in a series of ⅜" holes drilled into the container lid that enables the plant stems to hang just above the water. The clones are first placed in 1" lengths of ⅜" plastic tubing. Split the tubing down one side so you can easily remove the rooted clones. These tube supports should fit neatly into the holes in the lid.

Here we can see a pot with a wick hanging from the bottom. The water travels up this wick to the plant.

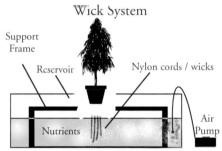

Wick system have their limitations but can be useful in some set ups. Organic growers can use wicks to draw nutrient free water to the crop but as with hydroponic wick systems, ensure that your reservoir is light proofed and covered.

You can test the aerocloner by closing the lid and running the air pump. If it is running correctly you should see splashes of water coming up through the empty holes in the lid. Once you have your cuttings in position and the air pump running continuously, they should root in about 7 to 10 days. There is no requirement to feed the clones.

Deep Water Culture (DWC)

The basic requirements for healthy root growth are water, nutrients and oxygen. Providing that cannabis roots receive a plentiful supply of oxygen, they can be kept permanently submerged in a light (⅓" strength) nutrient solution. This allows growers to set up a very simple, hydroponic bubbler system that can produce surprisingly heavy yields. Ensure that your container holds a minimum of four gallons, with the optimum size being about five gallons. A plastic bucket with a tight-fitting lid is ideal but should be lightproofed to prevent unwanted algae growth within the chamber. Oxygen is supplied to the nutrient solution by an aquarium bubble bar or airstone that is connected to an air pump with flexible

Capillary Floor System (CFS)

In a CFS plants are placed into an X cut in light-proof polythene covering the capillary matting.

Capillary Watering Setup

Capillary watering setup. The capillary matting is laid onto polythene and then the plants are fed from the reservoir in a similar fashion to a wick system.

tubing. The bubble bar is placed in the container through a small hole in the lid. If you are using an airstone, ensure that it is weighted down so that it sits on the bottom of the bucket.

The container only holds one plant that is placed in a 6" net pot containing your chosen medium and fits tightly into a hole cut into the plastic lid. Ensure that the nutrient solution is kept between ⅓" to 1" above the bottom of the net pot. This is best measured using a gauge made by pushing a thin plastic drinking straw into a small square of polystyrene. Next, cut a 1½" section from a larger diameter straw and glue this into position in a small hole cut into the container lid.

The polystyrene floats on the nutrient surface and the nutrient level is shown by the thin straw that slides up and down the larger section glued to the lid. You can easily calibrate the high and low measure by marking the sliding straw.

Leave the airstone running continually and keep the solution's pH constant at around 5.5. Ensure that your nutrient solution remains at ⅓ strength throughout the plant's growth cycle. This can be easily calculated using the manufacturer's recommendations.

Pot Culture

Pot culture is the simplest form of hydroponic cultivation and involves growing each plant in its own container, filled with any of the popular hydroponic media. Most growers prefer perlite, coconut fiber or rockwool granulate. Despite its simplicity, excellent results can be achieved using this system. It is, however, difficult to automate. Choose a pot with a 2.5 - 4 gallon capacity and place it into a deep saucer or tray to act as a reservoir.

Always water from the top, allowing the reservoir to fill up. Small plants will require watering every two to three days but mature plants will require daily feeding. Allow the reservoir to almost empty before feeding again as this draws air down into the medium. Leach the medium every two to three weeks to prevent a build-up of salts.

Gravity Fed System

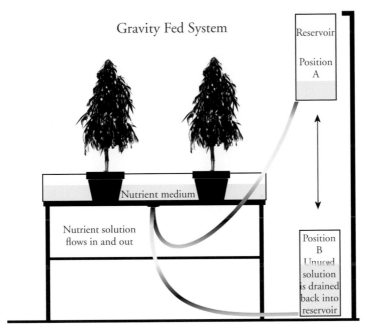

In a gravity system the nutrient reservoir moves up and down according to a feeding schedule.

Flood and Drain or Ebb & Flow System

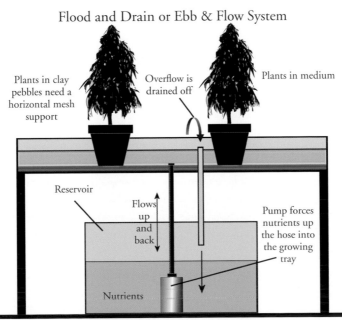

This flood and drain system uses a pump to bring the nutrient solution up to the tray table. The roots develop under a cover.

This ebb & flow system from Hydrofarm is spotless, just as these systems should be. Remember to clean your equipment thoroughly between crops.

Wick Systems

Wick systems are a simple but effective method of growing hydroponic crops. Nylon cord is threaded through the drainage holes in the bottom of the pot so that it passes up one hole, across, and down out of the opposite hole. This is repeated so that you have two lengths of cord threaded through, leaving four ends hanging down. Trim the lengths so that they are about six inches long. Next, add a layer of vermiculite to a depth of one inch and fill the remaining space with perlite or coconut fiber. Then suspend the pot over the nutrient reservoir and water it from the top to saturate the medium. As the plant feeds, it will draw nutrients up the wick by capillary action.

The reservoir can be a small container of nutrients for just one plant, or a larger system can be built using a child's wading pool with a mesh framework supporting the plants above it. Organic crops can be watered with this setup: the nutrients are replaced with fresh water and drawn up into the potting compost.

Capillary Floor System (CFS)

I have used this hydroponic method to passively cultivate large numbers of marijuana plants and cut down on costs. Thick polyethylene sheeting is laid onto a level grow room floor, under HPS lighting, in long narrow strips between one and two yards across (depending on your lamps' wattage). Run your lamps on lightrails to ensure even distribution. A framework of 2" x 2" timber is laid around the polyethylene edge, that is then stapled to it, producing a large waterproof tray.

Capillary matting (the thickest available) is then laid over the polyethylene right up to the 2" lip. Ensure that any joins are overlapped by at least 1". The capillary matting is now saturated with nutrient solution and then covered with thick, lightproof, reflective plastic sheeting. Where the plastic cover meets the tray edge, it is sealed with duct tape to prevent evaporation.

Mendo Purp from PureBred Growers is a solid plant that does well in hydro and soil systems. Be aware that its root mass stays very compact, so container size is an issue.

Individual plants are prepared by placing them into 6" pots of perlite, co-conut fiber or wrapped 4" rockwool cubes. A cross is cut into the polyethylene cover, taking care not to cut into the matting or base plastic, and the edges lifted so that the pot or cube sits on the mat. The plant roots will grow out into the matting, but the plants will need supporting, as they cannot form a verti-cal root system. The root growth is not affected by this: the roots just spread horizontally across the mat. Place uprights around the matting and stretch a horizontal section of wide mesh nylon netting between the posts. The plants grow up through the netting, which can be raised as they develop. Water the matting by hand or from hoses connected to a reservoir.

The system is easily automated using a sump pump and timer but ensure that your feed hose runs up one yard vertically before branching off: this pre-vents siphoning once the pump has stopped. You need to calculate how long the feeding takes and set your timer accordingly. The matting needs to be saturated but not swamped. These setups need feeding with nutrient-free water, once ev-ery 7th feed. Collect a sample of this from the matted area and test its pH and EC. Your next feed can then be adjusted to compensate for any fluctuations.

Gravity Fed Systems

Nutrient solution can be placed into a lightproof reservoir that is then sus-pended and lowered manually, to water the plants. The reservoir needs a small breather hole in the top to allow the solution to flow properly. A section of hose is connected to the base of the table to allow the solution to run in and out of the flood area, where it acts in the same way as a flood and drain table.

By lowering the reservoir beneath the flood area after each watering, the unused solution can be drawn back into the reservoir through the delivery tube. Grow tables require flooding twice a day, which can cause problems for some cultivators, but an alternative drip system can be built and left for several days with proper management.

It is possible to incorporate a drip system that works by gravity feed, but it requires a large reservoir to ensure you have sufficient water pressure to deliver the nutrients evenly to each plant. The reservoir for a gravity drip system is permanently positioned above the height of the grow table. The solution run-off is collected in a container positioned under a drain hole at the base of the grow table and manually poured back into the reservoir.

These systems are easy to design and build yourself. They allow the grower a degree of automation and do not require any power to work pumps. They are particularly well suited for greenhouses and outdoor hydroponics in

Drip System Using Flood Table

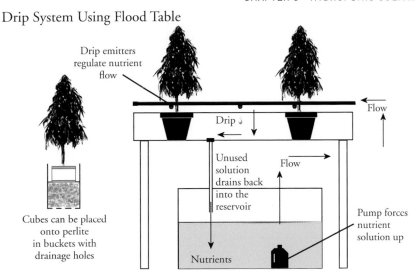

Drip emitters regulate nutrient flow

Flow

Drip

Unused solution drains back into the reservoir

Flow

Flow

Cubes can be placed onto perlite in buckets with drainage holes

Pump forces nutrient solution up

Nutrients

This drip system uses a flood table with drip emitters coming from the main supply to feed the plants in the setup.

remote areas.

Gravity setups can be used to water organic crops but you must take care not to saturate the growing medium. It is not advisable to use automated flood and drain tables for organic cultivation but the gravity setup at least ensures that you only flood when the plants require it.

For this reason gravity systems are marked: ◖

Flood and Drain

Also known as "Ebb and Flow" these setups are very effective and consistently produce high-yielding crops. Plants are grown on a waterproof tray table with 6" sides. The table stands over a reservoir filled with nutrients and is connected by a ½" hose that is attached to a submersible fountain or sump pump. The plants stand on the table in pots filled with perlite, Golden Wool, clay pebbles, coconut fiber or you can use wrapped 4" rockwool cubes. Some growers fill the table itself with clay pebbles and plant directly into it.

At least twice during the day cycle the submersible pump is switched on by a programmable timer. The pump forces nutrients up the hose and into the growing tray. The plants are watered from the base up with the liquid forcing stale air out of the pots as it rises. When the pump stops, the nutrients drain back down the hose under the force of gravity and into the reservoir. This action draws fresh air into the pots as the solution drains out of the

Bottle Systems

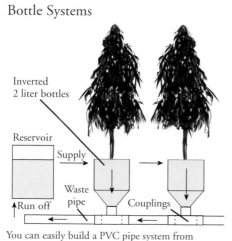

Inverted
2 liter bottles

Reservoir

Supply

Waste
pipe

Couplings

Run off

You can easily build a PVC pipe system from inverted plastic drinks bottles.

medium and ensures that the plant roots are well aerated. An overflow is fitted to ensure that the tray doesn't overfill. It is important for the table to be level so that all the plants receive the same amount of nutrients. The nutrients should be checked regularly and adjusted. An aquarium heater will keep the solution at 75°F and although some growers like to add a fish tank air pump to keep the feed fresh and aerated, this is not necessary as the solution is regularly moving.

These systems are easy for the grower to build using plywood, waterproofed with glass fiber or polyethylene. The reservoir is made from plastic water storage tanks available at plumbing supply outlets. Alternatively, these flood and drain systems can be purchased ready-made from hydroponic suppliers.

It is advisable to cover the tops of the trays with reflective, lightproof polyethylene, secured along the edges. Cut into the cover to place your plants on the tray. This prevents evaporation, inhibits the formation of algae, and the reflective surface bounces light back to the underside of the plants.

Nutrient Film Technique (NFT)

This method of hydroponic cultivation involves continuously recirculating nutrients around the plant roots. The plants are grown on a gently sloping tray that runs into the reservoir. A pump in the reservoir forces nutrients up to the top of the tray, where they run back down under the force of gravity. Capillary matting ensures that the nutrients are evenly distributed to the plants.

The plants can be in 4" wrapped rockwool cubes or 6" pots of perlite, Golden Wool or coconut fiber. Cover the capillary matting with lightproof polyethylene and cut out sections for the plant pots or cubes to sit in.

The reservoir has a removable lid that allows you to test and adjust the solution as required. An aquarium heater keeps the solution at 75°F and the nutrients are well aerated by the constant movement so you don't need an air pump. You can easilybuild this system or one can be bought ready-made from your hydroponics supplier.

Plastic Channel Table

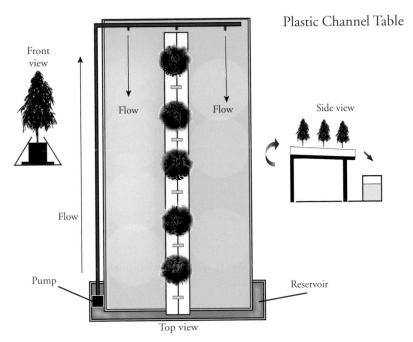

A plastic channel setup utilizes a gently sloping surface to deliver water back to the reservoir.

Tube System

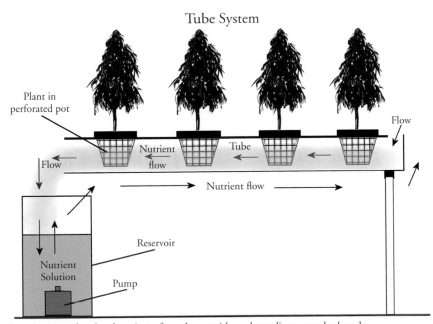

This tube system has the plants in perforated pots with a tube to direct water back to the solution container.

Rockwool Culture Slabs

Rockwool culture slabs are widely used in European commercial horticulture and are a convenient way of growing cannabis plants. The 6" and 8" slabs are best suited to cannabis cultivation. Grodan produces plastic trays that the slabs fit into and they make an excellent passive system that can be watered by hand in smaller setups. The plants are brought on in 4" wrapped rockwool cubes that are placed into cuts made in the plastic cover on the slab to allow the roots to grow down through it.

Placing the slabs into open-ended sloping channels makes an excellent recirculating, active system. Position the channel above a reservoir so that the nutrients can be collected and reused. Generally, crops are cultivated in rows of these channels that are positioned on a raised timber support. The nutrient run-off is collected in a section of plastic roof gutter or eaves troughing that is placed across the bottom of the channels and directs the solution back into the reservoir where it can be recirculated. The nutrient solution is delivered to the base of each individual plant with a constant drip system.

Drip Irrigation

These setups use small bore spaghetti tubing that branch off a larger feed hose to deliver a constant flow of nutrients to the base of each individual plant in the system. The flow is regulated by the use of special drip emitters that fit on the end of the tubing and are available from horticultural suppliers, along with the spaghetti tubing. The tubing is supported on a small plastic stake that is placed into the medium to ensure the dripping solution is directed to the base of the plant. As an alternative to fitting expensive drip control valves, you can simply bend the last 1" of pipe back against itself and hold it securely in place using garden wire. This can then be adjusted to regulate the flow. Drip systems can be either closed, where the nutrient is collected from the run-off trough and recirculated, or open where the feed is allowed to run to waste. Open systems are not recommended for cultivators, as they are a waste of resources. Providing your nutrient solution is regularly monitored and adjusted, it can be recirculated for weeks.

Perlite, Golden Wool, coconut fiber or rockwool cubes are all good growing media to use in drip systems. The setup can also be used to water organic crops, and is especially useful in greenhouse cultivation where you may have large numbers of plants to irrigate. The drippers can be set to deliver the plants' exact water requirements. Any feeding you need to carry out is simply added to the reservoir ensuring that each plant receives the correct amount of nutrients. The fertilizers are delivered slowly over a longer period than conventional watering, which is a more efficient way of delivering nutrient solutions to the plants.

These systems can be built using corrugated plastic roofing sheets and standing each plant container or cube on them. The sheets are held in position with a simple timber frame and angled downwards to allow the solution to drain off. A section of roof gutter or eaves troughing is attached across the bottom of the run to collect the used nutrients and can either lead to the reservoir or to a drain. Submersible pumps are used to move the nutrients through the system and, due to its constant flowing action, the solution does not need aerating.

The Plastic Channel Technique

This setup is built onto a gently sloping surface made from plywood. The system needs to stand roughly 3 feet off the floor at the high end and less at the low end so that a child's wading pool can fit underneath and act as the reservoir. Alternatively, you can build the system higher and use a water tank. The reservoir needs to be wider in order to catch the run-off. Or, fix a section of

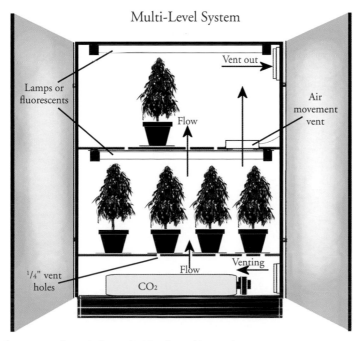

Multi-Level System

Multi-level systems are fantastic for maximizing the usable space in your grow area.

This BC Northern Lights grow cupboard can easily house a micro system without anyone knowing you are growing inside.

guttering or eaves troughing across and underneath, to direct the flow back into the reservoir. A 16" strip of thick, lightproof polyethylene is laid from the top of the plywood run to the bottom, dead center, and allowed to overhang slightly.

The very top of the strip is tacked in place before a 4" strip of capillary matting is run centrally down the whole length. Cannabis plants in 4" rockwool cubes are placed down the strip, leaving 12" between the stems. Once you have filled the strip, the two edges are folded up over the cube in a triangular shape and secured with staples, bulldog clips or clothes pegs.

All that you should see are the plants growing from the spaces left in the triangular channel. This procedure is repeated, leaving one foot between centers, until the board is full. A hose is run up from the tank and branched so that each run is fed. A submersible pump is fitted to the hose and then nutrients are pumped up to the top of each channel and allowed to run down under the force of gravity. Ensure that you have left enough of an overhang at the base of the channel to direct the nutrients back into the reservoir. Cover the remainder of the reservoir with polyethylene to act as a lid. Heat the solution to 75°F and leave it feeding continuously.

The plastic channel technique is used in larger setups and is a cost-effective way of building a system that can be used indoors and out. The system helps to keep humidity levels manageable in grow rooms, as the nutrient is not easily evaporated by the heat of the lamps.

Tube Systems

Plastic drainage pipes can be used to build effective active hydroponic systems. Six-inch tubes are cut to the desired length, usually two yards, and placed on a wooden frame constructed to support them. The frame slopes gently and has semicircular cuts to accommodate the base of the tubing. It is usual to have four pipes sitting next to each other in the frame, but larger setups can be built. The ends of the four pipes are sealed with rubber caps that are available from the building supplier where you purchase the plastic tubing.

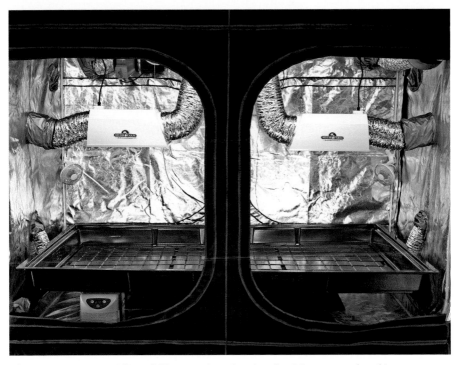

There are many commercially-available pre-made cupboards to fit mini systems, such as this one from Hydrohuts.

Staking can give your plants support in flowering, if they are struggling to hold their huge buds.

No matter what size your grow space is, you could create a very effective hydro system.

The pipes need a series of circular holes, 8" to 12" apart, cut in a straight line along the top. Use an electric drill fitted with a special cutting bit and make the holes large enough for a 3" net pot to sit in them, supported by its top lip. A reservoir is fitted underneath the frame and each pipe is connected to a ½" feeder hose that is placed in a purpose-made hole at the top of the pipe's highest end. The feeder hose is branched off a submersible fountain pump and a drain is connected to the bottom of the pipe that flows back to the reservoir. The pots are filled with clay pebbles and the plants inserted. The top of the pot is covered with foil to light-seal it and the system is started. The plant roots are fed continuously with a rapidly moving oxygenated nutrient solution and will grow down into the tubing. Excellent results are possible with this system.

As an alternative, you can build a PVC pipe system from inverted plastic drink bottles, painted white with the bases cut off so they can be fixed into couplers on 2" plastic, plumbing waste pipes. A ball rolled from durable netting material is placed in each base to act as a particle filter and the plants are then placed into the inverted bottles in rockwool cubes or an inert medium. A drip system is used to feed each plant and the run-off is collected via the connected pipes and held in a reservoir for recirculation. This system is particularly good at keeping down humidity in your grow room, and the waste pipe and couplings can be purchased cheaply from do-it-yourself stores.

Multi-Level Systems
You can maximize space within your grow area by growing the crop on shelves

Notice how reflective materials have been utilized in this hydro set up. The more light, the better!

420Clones.com grows great plants in clean, efficient hydroponic systems.

Hydroponic systems can be very easy to maintain and require little effort.

set at different levels. This system works particularly well for closet setups using fluorescents, but these lights have a high heat-to-light ratio and cabinet systems need careful monitoring to ensure that overheating problems don't occur. Plants are kept short and bushy by regular pruning, and CO_2 is supplied either by vents, fermentation or from gas bottles.

Perforate the shelves in cabinet setups with a series of holes made with a ⅜" drill bit. If the system is open and not using CO_2 position the exit vent in the closet roof and the intake vent in the base. This ensures that fresh air is drawn up through the setup. A small desk fan can be added to facilitate the air movement. Closed systems do not require venting, and this is one of the most effective ways of using bottled CO_2. The surfaces of the closet are lined with a reflective material to ensure good light distribution, especially when using fluorescents. An alternative to using a closet or enclosed space is to build a freestanding set of shelves and then enclose them in light reflective sheeting. To create access at the front, have a flap that can be rolled up and secure it with Velcro. Shelf systems can be built onto a wall, where space is at a premium.

The common method is to make a three-shelf arrangement that allows you to cultivate in a mini Sea Of Green (SOG) setup. One shelf is used for clones and mini-mothers, the next shelf is used for the two-week vegetative stage and the third is used for flowering. The shelves should be lightproof and enclosed so you basically end up with a closet arrangement, but you can use

OGA grow rooms utilize a whole range of available nutrients and feeding solutions on their plants.

Well-organized clay pebbles and drip hydro set up by the experts at Kannabia Seeds in Spain.

lightproof polyethylene instead of wood. Velcro the edges down and ensure a tight seal that can easily be opened and resealed.

Micro Systems

Micro systems are run with lamps that are 100 watts or lower. These systems are ideal for the hobby grower and if you maintain your light levels at 100 watts per square foot you can expect yields of more than 1 ounce (per square ft). Small HPS lamps are ideally suited for use in micro and mini systems as they provide the highest output per watt of electricity consumed. Fluorescents and MH are not as efficient and heat build-up can be a problem when using them.

To optimize yields in these small setups you need to have your plants cropped (see Pruning) and well inside the productive range of your lamp (this is a sphere of around 20" for a 250-watt HPS, dropping to around 10" for a 100-watt HPS). It is light intensity that we are interested in, and strangely, two lights with the same total wattage as a single lamp will actually supply less intensity. This is worth noting if you intend stripping down HPS security lights for use in your system.

Micro systems are generally used to grow small numbers of pruned clones in an enclosed space. A micro system designed to house a single female can be built by constructing a plywood cabinet with a 12 inch square grow area that is lined with Mylar or aluminum foil. The actual height of the grow area needs to include the depth of your pot or rockwool cube, depending on your chosen cultivation method. In addition, include the depth of your lamp in what will become the light housing area. This area is custom built to fit your lamp.

(Box height = 12" + height of pot/cube + light housing)

The unit is lit by a small 70-watt HPS that is adapted from a garden security light. In order to prevent heat build-up in the cabinet grow area, the light is fitted above a sheet of glass that rests on battens secured inside the box. The area above the glass is enclosed and fitted with an extractor fan that is light-proofed by attaching a section of ducting that is bent twice through 90°. This prevents light contamination. Fans can be adapted from bathroom extractors or even old car parts that can be run on transformers. Some micro growers link the lamp heat extractor to a vent in the grow area itself, but if you are using CO_2 supplementation this has to be carefully controlled or you lose the gas.

Micro systems are better left as closed systems that can be given additional CO_2 through either fermentation in the grow area or gas cylinders that feed the area through a small pipe. The cylinder will last for several months since you only need to release small amounts of CO_2 gas into the growing chamber.

If you are growing hydroponically then you should install a passive wick system that is fed by a small reservoir underneath the grow cabinet. Small holes are drilled into the floor of the cabinet to allow the wicks to pass down into the nutrient solution. It is possible to build an active system into a micro grow cabinet, but you are better off using a drip setup as flood systems will raise the grow area humidity to unacceptable levels. The plants are usually only given a two week vegetative cycle before flowering to ensure there is little side shoot development. If you want to give the plant a longer vegetative period then you will need to prune it in order to keep it short and bushy.

Mini Systems

Systems are referred to as mini when they utilize lamps between 100 and 270 watts. A mini system can be constructed in exactly the same fashion as a micro grow cabinet. The same principles apply, only you install a stronger lamp. The grow area is made larger to take advantage of the extra lumens available. A 2 ft square growing area can hold two female clones using a 250-watt HPS housed above a glass screen. Plant mini setups at a density of one plant per square foot.

The alternative to the grow cabinet setup is to use the Screen of Green (SCROG) method. Larger SCROG setups are covered later in the book and the same principles apply to mini SCROGs. A screen of chicken wire is stretched between the lamp and the flower tops, which are grown up to it, and then bent through 90° and trained horizontally underneath it. You plant at the same density but you can expect to yield around 2 ounces plus per plant as the buds are grown in optimum light conditions under the wire.

Cindy 99 from Dr. Greenthumb Seeds is a highly potent strain that produces copious resin and THC.

10. Compact Cultivation

It is so small a thing,
To have enjoyed the sun!
Matthew Arnold. (1822 – 1888).

Stakes and chicken wire are used to protect this outdoor crop.

Becoming self-sufficient in cannabis with a compact grow requires little space and will not make any noticeable demands on your household electricity bill, unlike larger gardens, which will require more light and electrical equipment. A hobby grower can produce a regular supply from any small closet or purpose-made grow space with little effort. It just requires knowledge of a few basic principles needed for a successful compact crop.

Once you have assessed your needs you can determine the size of the crop you wish to grow; for example, smokers who are using around a quarter of

This compact garden can easily produce enough ganja to keep you supplied for months.

an ounce of cannabis buds per week will want to crop around one ounce a month. This would require at least 1 plant, returning 1 ounce of buds, to be harvested every month in rotation. Cannabis plants take 8 weeks to mature, so by staggering the harvest areas and cropping one female every 4 weeks you will guarantee a continuous, monthly supply of buds. Dividing the flowering area in half and harvesting one area every 4 weeks will easily achieve this.

The flowering area is fed by a smaller grow area that contains your bonsai mothers, young plants, and clones. These areas will require at least 50 watts per square foot of lighting and this is best supplied using converted security lamps or low-wattage HID grow lamps purchased from your hydroponics supplier. Secondhand "Lowbay" industrial lights can be purchased online using Ebay or other auction sites for a fraction of the cost of horticultural lamps and are easily adapted to your space.

Most growers remote the ballast outside of the grow space and vent the area with a powerful, silent fan. Squirrel or centrifugal fans are equally as effective. Fluorescent lamps can also be used in compact grows but bear in mind that they can produce more heat than high-intensity discharge lamps. Air-cooled lamps and "cool tube" lamps are really effective in compact grows. Cool tube lamps have an HID bulb contained within a glass cylinder that is connected to ducting.

Air-cooled lamps use an enclosed reflector. Air is drawn through the ducting using an in-line fan and removes the heat directly from the source, leaving the glass almost cool to the touch. This is useful in cabinet type grows as it enables the plants to be much closer to the bulb, allowing you to grow larger plants in less space.

You can make a cool tube yourself using a cylindrical glass Pyrex tube. These used to be manufactured in the United States for making bread and are sometimes available online at auction sites. You can also improvise a glass tube by removing the base from a cylindrical glass flow-

Closet gardens are highly effective due to their compact and discreet nature.

er vase; this must be done carefully using a diamond-bladed tile cutter. These are readily available in tile shops and have a water-cooled spinning disc that will cut the glass. Be sure that you wear eye protection and gloves if you do try this as the glass can break. I have seen these homemade tubes in operation and they are very efficient and appear to handle the heat without any problems.

Stealth Cabinets

The choice of space will depend on your situation. A closet or under-stairs storage space can easily be adapted to suit a compact grow. Cultivators can also build purpose-made cabinets that are designed to handle their requirements. Stealth cabinets can be constructed to look like innocent pieces of furniture.

It is fairly straightforward to convert an old chest of drawers or bedside cabinet into a stealthy grow space providing you follow the guidelines for maintaining an optimum growing environment. When designing and building stealth cabinets compact cultivators are limited only by their imagination. An old fridge in the garage or basement can make an excellent stealth cabinet, accommodating a small vegetative area in the old freezer compartment

A DIY aeroponic bubbler system like this can produce large amounts of bud in a small place.

while the flowering area takes up the larger space. You can cut venting into the back of the fridge unit and hide the venting. One of the most effective stealth cabinets I have seen was made from a converted fridge freezer that was set up very discreetly in the corner of a grower's garage.

Maintaining an optimum environment in a stealth cabinet is not difficult; the main concern for the cultivator is ensuring that the area doesn't overheat. This is best achieved by using good quality extractor fans, and many compact growers will tell you that these are more important than the lamps. Lamp failure in a compact grow situation results in reduced yields, but extractor fan failure can be a serious fire hazard.

The aim of all compact growers is to keep plants cropped and small. This will obviously result in a reduced yield, however an ounce per plant is easily achievable from your bonsai harvest and, providing an optimum growing environment is maintained, many growers can yield much more than this.

Bonsai Plants

Bonsai is the art of growing and maintaining miniature trees; this may also include hardwood perennials; however, cannabis is a soft-wooded annual. Cannabis plants are not true bonsai in the Japanese sense of the word as they only live for one season, but this doesn't mean that it is not possible to bonsai cannabis plants. Mother plants are ideal candidates for bonsai treatment as they are constantly kept in the vegetative state and this technique allows growers to keep a selection of different varieties in an undersized space. A small cabinet can quite easily accommodate four to six different strains so hobby growers can rotate each one in turn and enjoy a different variety each month if desired. Mother plants kept in a constant vegetative state will develop thick, branch-like trunks and, with regular pruning and trimming of the foliage, will remain short and bushy. A bonsai mother can produce 10 to 20 cuttings every 14 days under an HID lamp or every 20 days under a fluorescent light, and you can keep a mother plant in this bonsai state for years, only replacing her if she shows loss of vigor.

These lights can be raised as the plants grow, meaning the garden's size is easily controlled.

BC Northern Lights produce some of the best stealth grow cabinets available. Close the door and no one's the wiser.

These carefully pruned OGA Seeds strains can produce a lot of pot in a small space.

Once you have chosen a healthy and strong mother plant from your cuttings you need to allow it to grow on and develop branches before you trim it back to 4 side shoots. As these side shoots then grow and extend they have to form an open cup type of shape; any new shoots that grow into the central cup shape are then removed. When the main shoots reach around 6" they can then be used as your first set of cuttings. Ensure that when you cut them back you trim just above the first leaf node of new growth to allow the mother plant to produce more shoots. You need to be taking cuttings from your bonsai mother plants every 2 weeks, regardless of whether you require the cuttings. This keeps the plants short and manageable.

Another important part of the bonsai technique involves root trimming. Twice a year the bonsai mother is removed from her pot and the rootball and 1" of potting compost and root is cut from the 4 sides and base. The best way to do this is by using an old serrated bread knife. The plant is then placed back into the pot and fresh compost is added to fill the trimmed edges. This new compost is then firmed in using your fingers; square pots are easier to work with as you have a defined edge and round pots are harder to trim when you root prune. There is no requirement to trim the rootball of your flowering plants; the leaves and branches are only trimmed and pruned during vegetative growth to keep a small compact shape that won't smother the flowering area. If necessary they can be further trimmed out after 2 weeks in the flowering cabinet but this is not always required and can reduce yields. Any large fan leaves are removed to encourage sideways growth.

The flowering section of your cabinet or stealth box grow is ideally suited to some of the other techniques described in this book, and while it is far better to grow bonsai mothers organically, you can still use hydroponic techniques providing you can still trim back the rootball. This is tricky using rockwool but other mediums such as perlite are ideal.

The flowering area can easily incorporate a hydroponics setup, and many cabinet growers use the Screen of Green technique, as this allows optimum use of the light canopy. You can construct small bubbler systems to fit into the grow space; many growers make use of plastic food containers and these work well in stealth cabinets.

Additional carbon dioxide supplementation can be engineered via cylinders or you can use any of the alternative techniques described earlier in this book.

Lowryder is an excellent auto-flowering plant from High Bred Seeds by The Joint Doctor. This plant is easy to grow and produces tons of bud in a very small space. Great for compact cultivation.

11. Cultivation Techniques

It is quite a three-pipe problem.
Sherlock Holmes.

SOG setups can provide you with rooms full of fast flowering buds like this one.

◗ Dutch Sea Of Green

Sea of Green (SOG) is one of the most effective techniques for producing regular cannabis crops. Using this method, it is possible to harvest a crop of sinsemilla marijuana every two weeks. There is a reduction in yield from each individual plant, but the numbers grown more than compensate.

This technique involves rotating your crop, staggering each new cloning session by two weeks. The flowering section is divided into four grow areas and is fed in two-week rotations with fresh clones. This allows you to crop every two weeks indefinitely. The SOG method is used by a lot of commercial growers, but is equally well suited to smaller setups. Shelf systems using SOG are very effective in supplying the hobby grower with a regular yield of flowers. Separate shelves are used for each stage of the rotation with either four flowering shelves, using their own lamps set on 12-hour cycles, or one shelf divided into four areas.

When gardening with the SOG method, be aware that the setup requires you to have large numbers of plants in the rotation. This can cause you problems if the crop is discovered by the authorities. They will base any fines or prison sentences on the potential value of your crop and you will be astonished at the monetary value the police will give your setup, ensuring that you receive the maximum sentence possible. In my last case, the authorities didn't even find any plants in the warehouse, only 38 x 1,000-watt HPS lamps and evidence that cultivation had taken place. Based on their forensic scientist's report they gave the setup a value of more than $2 million. The 'live' factory they 'discovered' was in fact a property I had bought to renovate and consisted of one tray of cuttings under a 125-watt MH. They confiscated the house.

SOG plants are flowered after two weeks of vegetative growth, in pots or cubes spaced at 6" between stems. It follows that the optimum sized container is a 6" square pot. The plants are either in potting compost for organic growers or in perlite, Golden Wool, coconut fiber or Rockwool cubes for hydroponic feeding.

The first step for SOG production is to set out your growing spaces. For this technique you will require two separate grow rooms.

A. This grow room will be on a minimum of 18 hours of daylight and house the mother plants, the cuttings and the plants in vegetative growth. It will require two HPS lamps and a fluorescent setup for the cuttings.
B. This grow room will be on a strict 12-hour day/night cycle and will be the flowering room. It will house four crops at all times, but these will be in rotation. The crops take up the four corners of the room and need four separate HPS lamps.

A total of six HPS lamps will be required, plus fluorescents for the cloning table.

For illustration, we will assume that the grower wants to harvest around nine ounces of cannabis every two weeks. Using this method, the average yield per plant is between ⅓ and ½ ounce of correctly cured buds, so this would require that approximately 20 plants be harvested every two weeks.

Dutch Sea of Green

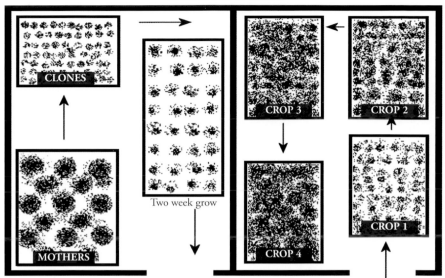

Room A: 18 hours on, 6 hours off   Room B: 12 hours on, 12 hours off

The Sea of Green method, popularized in Holland, uses limited space very effectively.

This is a stacked garden by the experts at Sinsemilla Nursery. They maximize their SOG setup by using vertical space as well as floor space. Contact them to arrange a consultation and learn their methods.

The selections room at Alpine Seeds is where the best plants are chosen for breeding.

BC Bud Depot's The Black strain grows well in SOG setups. Here we see the flowering room.

ASG Seeds utilize a Dutch SOG setup to grow some great cannabis. Here we see the vegetative room.

Room A

Set this room up first. In the example, we have chosen to use 600w HPS lamps with a small fluorescent table for our cuttings, but the lighting you choose will be dependent upon the size of your crop.

Four mature females are required as mothers, to provide us with 20 cuttings every two weeks. These females are the first to be installed in pots containing your chosen medium and placed under the first sodium light. After two weeks, the first set of cuttings is taken. We take 25 to allow for any that fail to strike. The cuttings are placed under the fluorescent lights and will take two weeks to develop roots.

Two weeks later, we take 25 more cuttings to replace the original 25 that we have rooted under the fluorescents. Twenty of the newly rooted cuttings that were under the fluorescents are potted into 6" square pots containing your medium and moved under the second sodium lamp that has been set up in the pre-flowering area. The pots stand next to each other at 6" between stems. Two weeks later we take a further 25 cuttings, and they replace the 25 that have rooted. Twenty of the newly rooted cuttings are potted into 6" pots and placed into the pre-flowering area. The twenty from the pre-flowering area are moved into Room B for flowering.

Room B

This room is set up with the remaining four sodium lamps, placed over four separate flowering areas. The first twenty plants are now in area one under the first lamp.

Meanwhile, back in Room A, we are taking 25 cuttings at a time on a 2-week cycle to replace those that have rooted and potting 20 of them into 6" pots and placing them in the pre-flowering area. After two weeks, another twenty from the pre-flowering area are moved into Room B for flowering under the second lamp.

Again, after another two weeks, twenty more from the pre-flowering area are moved into Room B for flowering under the third lamp. And then, finally, after yet another two weeks, another twenty from the pre-flowering area are moved into Room B for flowering under the fourth lamp.

Cannabis takes eight weeks to mature once it has been placed into flowering, so two weeks later we can harvest the plants from the first flowering crop, under lamp one, and that space can be filled with the next generation.

This setup can continue indefinitely, giving you a crop every two weeks. The mothers will need replacing, so it is always a good idea to have a few extras

OGA Seeds have an extremely well-organized SOG system in place. Here we see some fresh clones.

This is a cuttings and clone mother room at Sinsemilla Nursery. These plants are under 18 hours of light for vegetative growth.

in Room A. This technique works both organically and hydroponically and it is possible to build any of the active systems into the rotation. For most people a floor and tray based setup is adequate, with the watering being carried out by hand. There is no limit to the size of this operation as extra lights can be added. Those who are growing smaller amounts can simply scale down and use smaller lamps or fluorescents.

Screen of Green (SCROG)

We touched on the Screen of Green (SCROG) technique in the mini/micro cultivation section. It is covered in more depth here but the principles are basically the same. Screen of Green is not an intensive farming method like the SOG method, but it produces excellent yields and requires less plants in your grow room. This is certainly a factor to consider when planning any cultivation, as it will directly affect your punishment, should the plants be discovered.

The vegetative growth period is two weeks longer when using SCROG but you can expect yields of up to 3 ounces per plant at a density of 1 plant per sq. foot.

A screen of chicken wire is suspended 12" above your chosen planting medium and supported with either suspended chains from the ceiling or posts around the grow table. Posts are most cultivators' first choice when building these systems, as chains have to be secured to the floor to stop any movement. A 600w HPS lamp will cover 12 square feet and produce fast growth. It follows that the optimum width of your screen will be slightly over 3 feet with these lamps. Using SCROG allows you to cultivate nine clones per square yard.

Sour Grapes by Apothecary Genetics grows well indoors, and likes some extra netting for support.

These clones will be placed directly into a SCROG with a foot between each plant.

This area will yield over a pound and a half of dried buds, which more than compensates for any extra time spent in the vegetative stage.

To use SCROG commercially using 1,000w HPS, which will ideally cover 20 square feet, you first prepare a long grow slightly over 4 feet wide and suspend your lamps centrally on lightrails. The lightrails should be spaced, from the end of one to the start of the next, slightly over 4 feet apart. The number you suspend is determined by the length of your SCROG run.

Once you have installed your lighting fixtures you can then set up the SCROG screen, which must be securely mounted. The best method of mounting depends on your grow location. Most growers build a flood and drain table with posts around the edge and the chicken wire is suspended horizontally between the posts. The frame should be 12" above the top of your pots or cubes. It is possible to build a SCROG run that is floor-based using CFS as described in the hydroponics chapter. The plants are secured to the underside of the wire as they develop, and are well supported by the screen, but it can be awkward stooping to tend the plants. Both hydroponic and organic cultivation methods can be incorporated into the SCROG run.

Place your clones into the SCROG run leaving approximately 12" between stalks and working your way down the table. Then leave the plants to grow as normal with the same environmental conditions as recommended for any of the other systems.

Between three and four weeks after being placed into the SCROG run, the plant tips will begin breaking through the wire mesh screen. Allow them to grow through by about 1" and then pull them back through the screen and arrange them underneath, holding them in position with loose wire ties.

The flowering stage can now be started. Give the plants 12 hours of uninterrupted darkness each night cycle. Train the flower tops to fill the whole screen as they grow, and hold them loosely with ties. This doesn't affect growth, which can be over 1" a day if you have optimum environmental conditions, so attend to the plants regularly at this stage. Any leaf growth that obscures the buds or comes through the screen is clipped back hard, along with all foliage and shoot growth between the growing medium and the buds wired underneath the screen. This area receives little light and the foliage will die back causing possible fungal infections. All that you should see under the screen are stems rising to a canopy of thick buds that are in optimum light conditions. If you have problems training the plant stems, crimp them slightly by bending them. The plant will recover quickly from crimping and continue growing with no ill effects.

You may need to tie down the middle of your screen as the plants push up against it and bend it towards the lights. Use nylon cord that can either be secured to the table or, if you are using an alternative cultivation technique such as CFS, you can tie weights to the end of the cord.

Once growth slows, you have little maintenance to carry out on the screen. As long as the environmental factors are running at optimum levels you will be ready to harvest about eight weeks after inducing the flowering period.

This grower is making a branch hook for their harvested bud from TH Seeds.

Most growers try and utilize every lumen they can from their lamps, which makes economic sense. By creating vertical chicken wire screens around the sides of the growing table, in addition to the horizontal one, plants can be trained up and around the edge. This creates a box of foliage around your lights that is remarkable to see, but is more suited to the hobby grower. You can grow a box of green using a 70w HPS security light fitting; however, the sides tend to be sparse and thin. A mini system using a 250w HPS lamp is more effective, due to the extra output of lumens. Micro system growers are better off using a horizontal SCROG run with a reflective screen replacing the vertical wire. If you are growing commercially it can be time-consuming to construct boxes of green around your tables, but you may want to try it. Alternatively, replace the vertical wire with a reflective screen. There is plenty of light available from the 1,000w HPS, and it is uniformly distributed by the lightrails. Even on smaller setups utilizing 400w and 600w lamps there are still lumens being wasted.

The alternative to flat screen SCROG is to train plants vertically up the outside of the wire screens. Remove the lamp from its reflector and suspend it vertically, like a light bulb from a ceiling rose and arrange the screens in a box shape around it. Keep the bulb central and 8" from the edge with larger lamps, and about 4" in mini and micro systems. You will require an access point at the front for maintenance. Place the plants into your chosen growing medium, around the outside edge of each screen and train them up the sides. Place two plants per screen using 600w HPS lamps.

Large buds like this one can be achieved through careful management of your grow. Be sure to stake a plant like this.

An alternative to the box arrangement is the tube of green. Plants are grown on the outside of a tube of wire with the lamp hung vertically in the center. This works well in micro systems.

All of the SCROG methods of cultivation can be incorporated into a rotation system similar to the SOG. The SCROG screens are in the flowering section and the area is divided to stagger the harvest. These screens are filled in rotation from a mother room nearby. The vegetative stage takes longer, so you are unable to crop every two weeks as you can with the SOG method; however, this is not a concern with most growers as the yield per plant ratio more than compensates for it. SCROG is an excellent technique for indoor cultivation as it ensures you supply optimum light levels to the flower tops at all times. This is a great advantage in smaller mini or micro setups, and for commercial farming it ensures a uniform and predictable crop.

Heavy Yielding Plants

Heavy yielding techniques require that you grow plants individually or in small numbers. The best yielding plants tend to be grown hydroponically and many growers use NFT, but it is possible to get good results using potting composts enhanced with growth promoters. You can also use estrogen to boost plant growth if you want but it is not necessary for good results. Plants intended for heavy yield production are grown in very high light levels with one to four plants under a 1,000w sodium in an air-cooled reflector, enabling the plants to be very close to the lamp. A reflective tent is built from bamboo canes wired together and covered with reflective sheeting, or alternatively a laundry drying rack can be used. The reflective tent completely surrounds the plants and lamp, ensuring that no light is wasted.

The plants are allowed to establish themselves and develop a strong stem before they are defoliated. All of the leaves are stripped back, leaving just the branches. The plants are then regularly trimmed of large leaves right up until flowering: the leaves will start to grow back misshapen but this is normal. Once the plants reach a height of around 16" the light cycle is changed to 12 hours and the plant is induced to flower. The flowering phase will take approximately 50 days.

Continual and severe defoliation produces what are known as polyploid plants: basically mutations. Polyploidy is well known in the plant world and mutations can take many forms. What is of interest to the cannabis producer is that these mutations can produce abnormally high yields, although there is no increase in potency or THC content.

Grubbycup's Stash is a great strain from Grubbycup Seeds which is known for high yields due to polyploidy.

OGA Seeds use pruning shears to trim their buds. The gunk on these will have to be cleaned off using rubbing alcohol or rolled into a fat piece of finger hash!

Polyploidy can be chemically induced in marijuana plants with colchicine, which is found in crocus plants and can be extracted from the bulbs by crushing them. Dilute the juice with an equal amount of warm water and add a few drops of non-ionic wetting agent. Paint this solution onto the growing tips four times a day for three days; the plant will start to produce abnormal leaves that are misshapen and irregular. Although the colchicine has been extracted from a plant, it is poisonous and should be handled carefully wearing gloves.

Secondary Budding

Cannabis plants grown under artificial light will flower when the daylight length is reduced from 18 plus hours to 12 hours. Buds start to appear along the females' growing tips, as flowers begin to form.

After five weeks, while the buds are still immature but formed, secondary budding is induced by changing the day length to 24 hours of permanent daylight. This forces the plants back into the vegetative growth phase and fresh growing tips sprout from the newly formed buds. The flowers that were already forming will continue to grow, which has the effect of lengthening the area that is producing the bud.

The plant is grown on for a further four weeks before changing the light cycle back to 12 hours of uninterrupted darkness to induce flowering once more. The extra time required to flower your secondary bud crop is compensated for by a 25% increase in yield.

Pruning

Cannabis plants, when left alone, will reach heights in excess of 15 feet. This is obviously not practical for indoor cultivation so plants are kept short and bushy by pruning. Growing tips are pinched out of the young plants after they have developed their fourth set of leaves. The more you trim, the slower the plant grows, but this keeps the internodal length short and causes the plant to produce two new growing tips on either side of the injury.

This is desirable for the cultivator as it means the plant will produce extra branches or 'leads'. Side shoots are similarly pinched out, along with any large fan leaves that may obscure light from the developing buds. It is possible to produce five or more shoots from the pruned node by a little careful surgery on the growing tip. Instead of removing the complete tip in the conventional way where the whole node is cleanly removed, cut through the tip itself just below the centerline, aiming to leave around 10 to 15% intact. The vegetation that is left contains rapidly dividing cells that will continue to form into shoots.

OGA Seeds monitor their light cycles carefully to ensure big, solid nugs like this one.

Once flowering has started these shoots will also develop buds, increasing the density of top flowers. It is not necessary to pinch out plants that are being cultivated in the SOG method as they will only produce one main cola, with little side shoot development. However plants grown with more distance between centers should be trimmed, but can handle up to 10 leads, providing you maintain good light levels.

Ultra Violet Light

Cannabis plants produce more THC in response to receiving higher levels of ultra violet (UV) light. THC is thought to protect the plant from the harmful effects of sunlight. It is possible to reproduce this effect in the grow room environment by exposing the plants to 30 minutes of UV light during the day cycle. This exposure is usually divided into three 10-minute sessions. The UV light is delivered to the plants using sun bed tanning equipment. An area of two square yards will require 8 x 6 foot long tubes. Facial tanners can be utilized for smaller setups. Four x 1-foot long tubes are used in conjunction with 400-watt lamps.

Regeneration

It is possible to harvest two or even three crops from your cannabis plants by a process known as regeneration. This is done by carefully harvesting only the top third section of your females. The lower section is removed from the flowering area and placed into a vegetative growth cycle. It is better to leave the females under a continuous light source for the first 10 days to speed up the reversion process, but they will revert under 18 hours of daylight.

Remove the buds from the ends of your plants' branches but leave all the fan leaves intact. It is important to leave as many of the smaller flowers on as possible, as these are the regeneration sites for new vegetative growth. The more flowers that are left on, the greater the potential for re-growth. The plant needs to be fed a high nitrogen growth formula feed. If you are cultivating hydroponically, this is easily done by switching from the bloom formulation to the required grow formula feed. If you are growing organic crops you should give the plant a weekly drench with seaweed extract and apply a 30-15-15 NPK fertilizer as a foliar spray. Some growers adjust the feeding of flowering females they want to regenerate well before harvest to ensure that the plants don't suffer from nitrogen deficiencies. It is important to have as many fan leaves on the plant as possible, so avoid any leaf pruning during vegetative growth.

Within 10 days of starting regeneration you should see signs of re-growth on the plant. The first vegetative growth may be misshapen but this is nothing to worry about, and future growth will appear normal. Once your plant has started growing back in the vegetative cycle, you will need to trim off any minor shoots and growth to allow the main stem to develop properly. Remove most of the lower vegetable material to ensure the plant's energy is directed into the main stems. The plant can now be treated as normal and once it has established itself, placed back into the flowering room. A second harvest is possible in six to eight weeks after regeneration since the plant already has a strong stem and good root development. To regenerate the plant again, you follow the same procedure. It is not recommended that you try a fourth regeneration, but I know of growers who do. Alternatively, you can use the female as a mother plant.

The Black from BC Bud Depot is an incredible indica that offers a soothing and instantaneous high.

12. Harvesting and Drying Your Crop

I can resist everything except temptation.
Oscar Wilde. 1854–1900.

Indoor crops are harvested within 45 to 75 days, depending on the variety and cultivation method. Most indoor marijuana is Sinsemilla, or seedless, since fertilized buds are less potent and their weight is composed mostly of seeds. The earlier you harvest your buds, the more THC they will contain. As the bud matures, it degrades THC into CBD and CBN, which gives marijuana less of a high and has a more lethargic affect on the user.

❦ When ⅓ of the pistils have changed color = more of a high
When ¾ of the pistils have changed color = heavier smoke

Before you harvest female buds they should be pungent and glistening with a thick coat of translucent crystals. The false seedpods should appear to be bursting with resin and the tiny white pistil hairs protruding from the false seedpods should be brown or reddish and withering. The plant should be sticky and resinous to the touch. Check the buds under a magnifying glass and observe the individual glands: they should be covered with balls of resin. Finally, harvest a few selected buds and flash-dry them to correctly assess the quality of the crop.

Choosing when to harvest is a matter of personal preference so experiment with your plants. Cut each plant at the base of the stem and remove it to your cool, dark drying room to prevent fungal attacks. Hang the plants upside down on a line and leave them to dry out slowly; the slower you dry out the flower heads the smoother the end product will be, as chlorophyll, which gives marijuana its 'green taste', is removed through this slow curing process. Drying takes up to two weeks if the buds are to be properly cured, but applying a gentle heat to the drying area can speed up the process. Be sure not to over-dry the buds; they should give slightly when pressure is applied, and the stalk of

Be careful when handling particularly resinous buds as you can receive a powerful contact high.

each bud should crack when bent. However, over-dry buds will crumble and powder, so try to get the balance right.

Correctly dried and cured cannabis contains around 15% moisture.
- Below 10% and the buds will be too brittle.
- Over 15% and the marijuana is in danger from fungal spores.

Hanging the plants has several advantages over drying them flat. Firstly, the small leaves that surround the flowers will dry around the buds, which help to protect the delicate stalked capitate trichomes. These tiny translucent structures are the glands that give the buds their frosted appearance and they contain the cannabinoid oils. These oils are chemicals unique to the cannabis plant and are collectively referred to by the name of the main psychoactive ingredient, THC. The larger leaves can be trimmed away later in a process known as manicuring.

Secondly, you are less likely to have fungal attacks since you can ensure that your drying room has good air circulation around the drying crop. Some growers place a small desk fan in the room to keep the air moving.

The beautiful orange pistils on this plant indicate that she's ripe for harvest.

Hanging buds to dry helps to preserve the delicate THC glands.

The third reason is aesthetic. Buds that have been dried hanging upside down appear more presentable. Most growers prefer to leave the buds in the shape they have dried, and this is by far the best way to ensure that none of the delicate glands that hold THC are knocked off or damaged. However, this is not practical if you are dealing with a large crop of buds, and if you need to transport any quantity you will have to compress the harvest to a certain size. Compressing is not ideal but is the best way to package buds for wholesale.

You don't need to make Dutch bricks that are shaped with a press; it is sufficient to just compact them by hand into resealable plastic bags. If you are using vacuum packers or heat-sealers to package your crop it can be compressed and shaped in the bags before sealing.

Smaller flowers can be made to look more presentable by compressing them by hand, or, if you have a large quantity, you can use a mold. Some growers make tubular molds. The material is placed into a pipe that is held on a firm surface. A rod of a slightly smaller diameter is knocked into the open end with a hammer, compressing the buds. The tube is then turned over and the rod is struck onto a hard surface, pushing the compressed flower-tops out.

Others construct flat molds from wooden frames that can be compressed in a vice, or in a small press constructed from three steel plates with holes drilled in each corner and four steel bars bolted to the top and bottom plates. The third plate slides in between them and a car bottle jack is used to drive it

This custom-built structure is perfect for ensuring the buds are dried evenly.

Harvesting may be hard work but it's every grower's favorite time of year.

against the top plate. You can purchase presses that are designed for compacting old newspapers into bricks for the fire and they are ideal if you need to compress any quantity into a uniform size.

Commercial Skunk is nearly always compressed into bales to facilitate smuggling and it is usually packed slightly moist. Once it has been vacuum-sealed into polyethylene bags, the bales are wrapped tightly with parcel tape. This keeps the buds fresh and prevents fungal spores from forming. This technique doesn't give the end user the best deal: once opened the buds lose weight as they dry. The producers are trying to optimize their profits, but at least you know the buds haven't been tumbled to remove some of the THC. Many buyers lick their buds before a purchase; if they taste sweet it can indicate that they have been sprayed with a sugar solution in order to increase their weight. If they are gritty then they may have been treated with more serious contaminants.

Grit Weed

This is deliberately contaminated herbal cannabis that has been treated with a variety of grit-like substances which have been added to the plant prior to harvest in order to increase the weight.

The results of an excellent trim!

Currently these include:
- Large Glass Particle Contamination
- Industrial Etchant Spray Contamination
- Sugar or Sand Contamination
- Micro Contaminants

Test buds by licking them. If you feel a gritty sand-like residue when you clench your teeth together then it may be contaminated with silica or spray. If you don't feel any grit-like substance between your teeth but the weed tastes very sweet (sugary) then chances are it has been dusted with fine sugar to add weight. Micro contaminants are difficult to detect.

What is astonishing is how the authorities have seen this as another example of why cannabis is dangerous. They claim it is now extremely harmful to use because of what unscrupulous dealers are adding. This practice would not occur if marijuana was made legal.

This plastic bin is filled with a great harvest of carefully trimmed buds. Remember that the leaves and excess trim can be used to make hash, cannabutter and oil, so be sure to save as much as possible!

13. Outdoor Cultivation

Give me a spark of nature's fire, that's all the learning I desire.
Robert Burns. 1759–1796.

It is possible to grow cannabis outdoors where yields of around a pound per plant can easily be achieved from Cannabis indica plants and up to 2lb from some Cannabis sativas. In his book, Marijuana: A Growers Lot, the Australian author, Kog, describes harvests of up to 5lbs a plant from a Cannabis sativa variety called "Old Mother Sativa." Crops are planted out after the last of the frosts, and are generally ready for harvesting in the last weeks of fall. Unlike indoor cultivation, the grower has little control over the environmental factors that affect plant growth and depends on a good summer to harvest a high-yielding crop. However, cannabis is a hardy plant and, provided there are no frosts early in the season, and fungi, animals or parasites do not attack it, it will give good yields.

Cannabis sativa is perfect for drier climates that don't become too damp. If you're growing in this type of environment, such as California, use one of the hybrids available like Skunk #1 from Dutch Passion (25% Afghani, 25% Mexican Acapulco Gold and 50% Columbian Gold). However, Cannabis sativa varieties are unsuitable for outdoor cultivation in cool climates as they tend to grow tall and thin, yielding less than Cannabis indicas from the tougher Hindu-Kush strain, which is less sensitive to cool weather. Try a good outdoor variety like the purpose-bred Holland's Hope, which is very mold resistant, Early Skunk, Early Girl or Iranian Autoflower. If these are not available, most Cannabis indicas will yield well outdoors even during a poor summer, but watch for mold during flowering.

Choosing Your Location

Finding a secure place to grow your outdoor crop of marijuana is the main problem you face as a cultivator. The distinctive shape and size of cannabis is easily recognizable, so you have to take steps to ensure the plants are not discovered. Drug crops do not need constant direct sunlight, five to six hours a day is sufficient, so try to screen the plants.

Holland's Hope from Dutch Passion.   Early Girl from Sensi Seeds.

This dense foliage is less recognizable than large individual plants.

When scouting for your location, look for areas where people do not go. Good outdoor locations include the following:

- Greenhouses and polytunnels
- Back yards (providing they are not visible to neighbors)
- Balconies (as above)
- Rooftops (as above)
- Scrubland and derelict areas
- Parks (private areas can be found)
- Farmland
- Railway embankments
- Expressway or highway embankments
- Woodland clearings
- Tree tops (plants can be suspended in containers)

Skunk #11 from Dutch Passion.

- Military areas (crops have been cultivated behind no-go areas)
- River banks (once the tap root has grown down they don't require watering)

These are just a few examples of where crops have been successfully grown and I'm not going to reveal any more, for fear of compromising any outlaw farmers. When selecting your own location, remember it is better to grow large crops in an area that won't be linked back to you, should they be discovered. Most cultivators spread their crop over several different locations, to ensure that at least some are harvested, and this is a good policy to adopt.

🌿 Try to find an area that has a water supply nearby. Carrying water in to the growing location can compromise the site and is hard work.

Preparing Your Location

Once you have found a suitable area in which to grow your plants you can start preparing it. Locate the crop in the most inaccessible part of the site; if there are brambles and thick undergrowth, cut an access path in and clear the center. Ensure that the crop will receive as much light as possible by removing

This small plot was prepared and filled roughly a foot and a half deep with compost.

A generator pumps water up from the lake and the plants receive a consistent supply of fresh water from the irrigation tubes.

This is a fantastic outdoor strain from Australia called Rainbow Dreaming. It is a Jack Flash x Carrot (Australian Sativa) that outdoor growers are raving about.

With good soil and regular access to water you can produce like the best growers.

overhead foliage and branches. Always use the same track in and out of the growing area in order to avoid leaving obvious trails. Set warning traps on the approaches that will tell you if anyone has used your path. Try to use all the available cover to your advantage. Be aware that if the authorities discover your crop they may mount an operation to catch you on your next visit.

Those growing in more remote locations need to construct some form of fencing to deter animals from destroying the crop. The best fencing is plastic mesh netting that is cheap to purchase and light to carry. It can be secured around the edge of the intended growing space and acts as a barrier. When the crop is planted, additional protection is given to each plant by placing it into a 12" long by 6" diameter chicken wire sleeve that is supported on a short cane woven through the mesh. Once this is completed, work can begin on improving the soil.

Soil Types
Soil was formed millions of years ago from rock that was powdered by the actions of wind, rain and frosts eroding its surface. Some types of soil are formed directly from the rocks underneath their surface; others were deposited by the wind. Freshly formed soil has all the elements that were in the original eroded rock, but it requires a vital addition in the form of decayed living matter, known as humus, in order for it to support plant life. Soil comes in many varieties due to the differences in the rocks that are broken down in its formation, so it's not always possible to get the correct soil type for your crop. Soil is categorized as being either light or heavy.

Light
Light soil is composed of large particles. Sand is the lightest soil, and you can see the individual particles.

Heavy
Heavy soil is composed of the smallest particles. Clay is the heaviest soil. The definition of heavy or light doesn't refer to the weight of the soil but to the ease with which it can be worked.

Beneath the surface topsoil is another layer known as the subsoil. This tends to be humus-free but rich in minerals providing a balanced nutrient supply for those plants, such as cannabis, that can root deeply enough to reach it.

Good soil increases your germination success rate as well as your end product.

Soil is further categorized by type.

Peat Soils
Peat soils are formed under water from compressed, decomposed plant material. They are only found in specific areas; however, if they can be located they are ideal for cultivation.

Sandy Soils
Sandy soils require large amounts of organic material and manure to make them suitable for cannabis growth. They tend not to hold water, so they need monitoring to ensure they don't dry out.

Loam Soils
Loam is a mixture of clay and sand. Well-fertilized loam soils are ideal for cannabis cultivation.

Clay Soils
Well-drained clay soils are suitable for marijuana crops; however, care must be taken to ensure they don't become waterlogged. Most can be improved with manure and soil treatments.

The soil in this area is substandard, so the grower chooses to use grow bags instead.

Identifying Your Soil Type

The best test for soil type is to dig out a section of earth and compress it in your hand. Heavy soils will form into a mass, whereas lighter soils will crumble. Pull the sample apart between your fingers and observe the color and texture and look to see if it is sandy, clay, or dark and peat-like. Soil analysis is based on the quantities of nutrients contained in any given sample, and it is possible to get an accurate indication of the quality of your soil by using a test kit. Some growers send their samples to be analyzed by a laboratory analysis service, which provides an extremely accurate picture of the soil's macro- and micro-nutrient content.

The pH level is also important, and you can use either a dip test or a probe that is pushed into the ground and gives an instant reading of the pH.

Examine the soil for pests and weeds. Leather jackets, the maggots of the European Crane fly, and wireworms are obvious to spot in your sample digs. It is not feasible to examine the soil for disease by using pathological plating and incubation tests so growers need to check the surrounding foliage for signs of any disorders. If the plants show signs of damage or wilting you could have a problem.

Once the soil has been analyzed you can remedy any shortfalls by adding fertilizer or manure to the area. There is no requirement to dig the soil over. It is a common misconception that soils need to be turned. For light soils, a no-dig approach is actually better, as digging speeds up the breakdown of organic matter in the soil, which is to be avoided.

Add fertilizers by spreading them over the surface, and allow them to be absorbed by the soil. Many growers use concentrated bone meal fertilizer on outdoor gardens as it has the added effect of deterring deer and rabbits. However, since the outbreak of vCJD (mad cow disease) in Europe there have been concerns about its use. Bone meal is made from the spinal cords of carcasses, the high-risk area for the infectious agent that causes the disease. Infected carcasses could find their way into processing plants and you could put yourself at risk when inhaling and handling the fertilizer. Instead, use chicken manure pellets or fresh manure if it's available to you. Alternatively, if the soil is particularly poor, use a slow release, granular chemical fertilizer and follow the manufacturer's recommendations for surface dressing. We are looking for a balanced NPK reading but unlike growing indoors this isn't an exact science. As long as the soil is well drained and healthy we can supply the remaining nutrients on a regular basis with foliar feeding to the plant leaves. The same fertilizers that are recommended for organic indoor cultivation are suitable for outdoor growing.

Some cultivators choose not to grow their plants directly in the soil and use growbags, pots or plastic bags filled with potting compost. These work well, especially for smaller setups in back yards and on balconies, but containers require watering regularly, whereas mature plants in the ground with a well-established root system and deep tap root can survive on their own for longer periods. Only plant one or, at most, two plants into a growbag outdoors.

It is possible to grow outdoor crops hydroponically. Many growers also use these systems in greenhouse setups, and they produce consistently high yields. It is easy to set up a small hydroponic unit outside if you want, and any one of the active or passive setups described in the hydroponics section will work well.

Preparing Your Crop

Cannabis grown from seed that has not been feminized will produce a crop that is composed of approximately 50% each of both males and females. This is undesirable for marijuana cultivators, especially outdoors where large crops are easily compromised. A crop of known females can be half the size of an indeterminate crop and still yield the same amount of bud.

Cultivation in the cooler areas of Europe and North America is mostly carried out using clones that have been prepared indoors at the beginning of March. The clones are given two weeks to root and are then transferred to peat pots filled with fine potting compost and put in a greenhouse or on a window ledge to harden off. The greenhouse can be a simple construction made from polyethylene sheeting. During the first weeks of April the clones are placed outdoors during good weather and brought back inside every evening. By mid April, when the young plants have reached a height of 6 to 8", they are packed into cardboard boxes and transferred to the growing area. This is best done at night, but it depends on your location. Tape a larger plant pot over the top of each clone to protect it during transit.

The alternative to using cuttings is to germinate your seedlings earlier and place them in a greenhouse or on a window ledge to harden. The same procedure is carried out as is used for the cuttings; however, as soon as the plants are just over 2" and 3" tall they are forced into the flowering stage by giving them 12 hours of uninterrupted darkness every night cycle. To do this, place them in a specially prepared darkened area or, in the case of a few plants, into a box. Within two weeks they will begin to exhibit signs of gender. After two weeks, remove the young plants from the flowering cycle, even if they are indeterminate (not showing gender). The plants will continue to flower as they revert back to the vegetative state, and can easily be identified. If you want to keep a male, select the strongest plant and cut it back hard. Remove the forming male flowers, and only leave a few lower shoots. Male plants die soon after flowering so it is important to encourage fresh vegetative growth.

Within a few weeks of removing your females from the flowering cycle, they will be growing back in the vegetative state without any ill effects. If you are prepared well in advance of the growing season, bring your plants on indoors under artificial light. You don't need any specialized horticultural lamps, as seedlings respond perfectly well to a 100-watt incandescent household light bulb. Position an adjustable desk lamp over the plants, keeping it as close as possible without burning the leaves. You will be surprised at the results.

The third method of gender identification involves growing your seedlings on until a cutting can be taken from each of them. The cutting and plant are each labeled to identify the mother and clone, and the cuttings are rooted and flowered. It's possible to root the cuttings under 12 hours of daylight, which will save you two weeks. The mother plants are grown on either in the greenhouse or taken to the grow area, but they are kept in containers until their sex is determined. Once they have flowered, you can trace the parent plant and, if it is male, remove it.

Unpruned cannabis sativa.

You can also identify the sex of your plants by selectively flowering a lower branch. Cover a branch for 12 hours every 24 hours with a sleeve made from black construction paper, which blocks out light but still allows the plant to breathe. (Covers made from plastic will create the perfect environment for fungal attacks, so avoid using them.) Within two weeks the plant will begin to show signs of gender.

Planting Out

Cannabis, when grown outdoors, can reach heights of 15 feet. Depending on your situation, it is best to prune your plants to keep them short. However, you will want to encourage thick, bushy side growth, so spacing of the individual plants is important. Plants that are crowded and competing for light will grow tall and thin with little side shoot development.

Plant out your female crop with a one-yard distance between stems. Pacing a large step between plants will help you measure out that distance. Dig a hole with a trowel and, if you only have a small number of plants, add a handful of water-absorbing crystals of the type normally used in hanging baskets. This practice will assist the young plant by giving it a small reservoir of water, but it can work out to be expensive in large operations. The plants are then watered in and, if it is a wildlife area, a sleeve of chicken wire is placed over each clone, and a cane threaded through it. The young plants will need watering regularly until they have developed a strong root system.

You can water your crop by hand with containers or gas cans that you bring from your water source. If there is a river nearby and the situation allows, crops can be watered using a small gas-driven pump. The types used in the construction industry for pumping out ditches are excellent and can be rented or bought. If you don't have a nearby water supply, dig a hole and line it with a polyethylene tarpaulin. Cover the top with more polyethylene pegged out and weighted with a stone in the middle. Bury the polyethylene edges or you could trap small mammals, which are beneficial slug and insect predators. Pierce the center of your rain trap with a few small holes and leave the well to fill up naturally. Foliar feeding is best carried out with a horticultural backpack sprayer. The same sprayer can be cleaned and used for treatment sprays. Take care not to overfeed your plants. It is better to use a diluted application of foliar feed and watch how the plants respond. Remember that younger crops require less feed than mature or budding plants.

Foliar feeds should be combined with a surface dressing of either manure or granulated fertilizer that is sprinkled around each plant at the recommended

Amending the soil can be a solution if it is not of great quality.

This crop is difficult to identify from a short distance away.

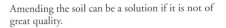

rate (which depends on the feed you've chosen). Lightly fork the fertilizer into the soil around each plant, ensuring that the area under the branches is evenly covered, and water it well in. Two weeks before flowering, give the area a light surface dressing of sulphate of potash. This encourages better flower formation and resistance to disease. Three weeks after planting out you need to weed the plot to remove any wild plants that may be competing. Only clear an area around the plant itself, as you need vegetation to give you cover and weeds help the soil to retain moisture. You will need to repeat this again as more weeds develop.

Disguising Your Plants

Cannabis is easily identifiable so hide and disguise your plants to avoid them being spotted, especially when growing plants in your back yard or on balconies. Pruning your crop will develop short and bushy plants, and this should be your first step. Pinch out the growing tips when the plants are short and keep them small during the vegetative growth phase. Try starting your plants later in the season so they will be smaller and remove or trim some of the larger, more distinctive fan leaves. Some growers bend the top of the plant over and tie it down to allow the side shoots to grow upwards, which gives the appearance of a row of mini plants rising from the main stem. Plastic flowers and fruit can also be attached to the plant to disguise it further: wire them on with gardening wire.

Greenhouse and polytunnels offer a protective environment in which the grow can be controlled, like this expert garden of Mastadon Kush from Emerald Triangle Seeds.

Using containers makes it easier to move the plants if necessary.

This huge greenhouse of Paradise Seeds plants shows what successful growers can achieve outdoors.

A ton of skunk from Shantibaba at Mr. Nice Seeds.

These beauties from Mr. Nice Seeds are a true sea of green.

Some growers train their plants along a trellis that is fixed to a south-facing wall in much the same way as vines are grown. Alternatively, pinch out the growing tip when the plant reaches 12" and grow the two new side shoots out horizontally, in either direction of the trellis. Cut back any unwanted growth. The side shoots will grow out quite a distance and artificial flowers or fruit can also be attached as a further disguise. These plants are strange to look at but actually produce quality buds as the flowers receive good levels of unshaded sunlight.

Plants can also be trained to grow along the ground. Just pinch out the growing tip at the third internode and then train the new tips to grow sideways by wiring them down to either side of the cannabis plant. Trim and wire new growth as it develops. You are not limited to two side shoots; many growers have them going in four directions. These plants need protection from pests and insects such as snails and slugs, and tend to produce small yields. However, they can be effectively grown along the fronts of balconies with the plant rooted in a growbag and the branches held down with weighted cord.

Treetop Cultivation

The more agile farmer may be interested in cultivating a crop high in the treetops. Plants grown this way receive optimum sunshine but are left exposed to any unexpected bad weather, so a good crop is dependent on a fine summer. The plants are grown in large 8 to 10-gallon plastic containers that are spray painted green and brown, and covered with ripped sacking or camouflage netting to resemble foliage. This disguises the plants from the ground. The containers are then filled with equal quantities of potting compost and perlite mixed 50-50 with coconut fiber or rockwool granules. Or, if you can obtain a sufficient quantity, use water-absorbing crystals. Plant a single female in each container, water it well, and tape a polyethylene lid around the top to prevent evaporation. Then hoist the containers up into the branches and lash them into position. Some growers like to build platforms in the canopy to create a cannabis treehouse, holding several plants.

Safety is a factor when watering your treetop plants and it is advisable to invest in a pair of rubber soled climbing boots, a harness and some quality climbing rope. Secure rings into the trunk that you can attach yourself to. Hoist water up in containers when the plants need it, which can be weekly when they are mature, and also during hot weather. Towards the end of the growing season you will lose a lot of cover as the trees shed their leaves, so you will need to position your plants fairly high up in the canopy and ensure that they are difficult to see from the ground.

Greenhouse Cultivation

Greenhouses and polytunnels offer the outdoor cultivator a protected growing environment that can be controlled to a certain extent by the use of fans, heaters and even horticultural lighting. Lamps can be installed to supplement natural light and will make up for any shortfalls in the season. Greenhouse cultivation can be either hydroponic or utilize compost in containers, although for larger polytunnel setups planting directly into the soil is preferable. Cannabis plants will strip any ground they are planted into and heavy fertilization is required to bring the soil back for the next season's crop. Plants grown in greenhouses can be forced into early flower production quite easily by reducing their exposure to daylight. Use covers to block out the light.

Greenhouse Grow Rooms

An alternative to greenhouses and polytunnels is to convert a shed or outbuilding into a grow area by removing the roof and replacing it with glass or plastic panels. Disguise the panels with white greenhouse shading paints if the area is visible from other buildings. The walls of the grow room are lined with reflective material. Warm white fluorescent tubes are installed along the walls to add a low-cost supplement to the natural sunlight and ensure good growth on the bottom branches of the plants. Only run the lights during daylight hours to

For great plants, nothing can beat natural light.

avoid compromising the setup. Use fans to recirculate and cool the air, and in southern climates use air conditioners to prevent heat buildup. In colder climates heat is generated from fuel-burning greenhouse heaters that also release CO_2.

The plants can be grown both organically and hydroponically. In some buildings it's possible to remove the floor and plant directly into the underlying earth, but it is better to dig out the original soil and replace it with potting compost each season using specially constructed holes for each individual plant. It is easier to use a hydroponic floor-based setup such as CFS rather than digging out your planting areas. A floor-based setup will produce crops as good as if not better than the earth grown system, but it depends on your situation and location. Some medical cannabis users are physically unable to do the digging and lifting required and an automated hydroponic system is the ideal solution.

Daylight Reduction

Just as you force the young plants to flower earlier in the season to determine their gender, you can also force outdoor crops to flower for an early harvest by giving them 12 hours of uninterrupted darkness. Most growers will do this in the late summer when the plants have already benefited from the best of the sunshine and are strong and healthy.

Forcing the flowering can be labor intensive as plants need moving or covering on a daily basis. However, it is worth the effort as your plants can be flowering early and producing their buds in good levels of sunshine. Plants grown in containers are easier to force as they can simply be moved into a light-proof area for the 12-hour period. Plants that are in the ground need covering, which sometimes causes heat buildup problems, so shading is usually started in the evenings. You need to build a frame around the plant so that the cover can be easily placed without

You'd have to climb a mountain to get to this plant. Its remote location keeps it away from prying eyes.

touching the plant leaves. This is especially true if you are using polyethylene covers as they can cause the foliage to become damaged and wet, leading to fungal infections.

Use either thick black polyethylene or black/white polyethylene as your cover and ensure the edges are light-proofed by securing all joins with masking tape. Alternatively, large, cardboard boxes can be waterproofed and used.

A Ton of Skunk

Two thousand female Cannabis indica skunk plants, if successfully cultivated and harvested, even in cooler climates, will yield approximately 2,200 pounds or 1 ton of dried buds. The area required to cultivate 2,000 plants with 3 feet between each one is 20,000 square feet, which is an area roughly 50 paces long by 40 paces wide. Have the soil tested professionally and adjust it if necessary. The easiest way is with chemical fertilizer spread by hand or machine. You don't have to plough the field, but the weeds need to be cut back and left as mulch on the surface. You will have to repeat this at regular intervals to ensure that nothing competes with the crop. Don't use weed killers, as you need some cover to retain moisture in the soil, and cannabis, once established, will outgrow

For faster outdoor harvesting it's worth investing in professional trimming machines.

These large colas are almost ready for harvest.

Your yield might need a little protection.

any local wild plants. The area will need some form of fencing with mesh or wire in order to deter wildlife.

First you'll need to prepare your seed stock — double the amount to account for the males, unless you have access to a large quantity of feminized seeds or enough mothers to supply you with 2,000 cuttings. Many growers prefer to use seed, preferably F1 hybrids, and this is done either indoors, with a crop that is flowered and fertilized, or by preparing well in advance and growing an outdoor seed crop the previous season. When farming on this scale using indeterminate seeds, try the feminizing treatments to increase the female to male ratio by about 20%. You will need to germinate over 4,000 seedlings in the first week of March, which is very labor intensive. However, with proper organization, it is manageable. Weigh 100 seeds using digital jewelers' scales; you can then calculate your number of seeds by weight.

Germinate your seedlings in trays of vermiculite and, as they appear over the next week to ten days, transfer them to 4" plastic pots filled with seed-grade potting compost. Place these pots into a greenhouse or polytunnel and allow the seedlings to grow on. When they reach a height of 3" to 4", force them to flower by giving them 12 hours of uninterrupted darkness. This is best done by growing the young plants on carts or trolleys that can be wheeled into and out of your flowering shed. To use a polytunnel for the forcing, cover it with black, light-proof plastic as they do at mushroom farms. It is better to have two polytunnels facing each other, end to end, one for flowering and one for growth. The plants can then be wheeled between the two. You'll need a generator to run fans but propane burners, which will also give off CO_2, can supply heat if needed.

Within two weeks the gender of the plants can be identified and the females placed permanently into vegetative growth and the males discarded. When the females are 8 to 12" in height, transfer them to the grow area. Start in the far corner and pace out the spacing; work in a grid leaving 3 feet between plants, and dig a small hole for each one. Then transport the plants, 50 at a time, in a wheelbarrow. Remove them from their pots and plant them. Provide water from your source using pumps or hoses and support the plants with fencing wire or thick cord stretched horizontally between 3 feet high posts along each row.

Treatments and feeding can be carried out with a horticultural backpack sprayer combined with regular, dried fertilizer applications to the area under each plant. Harvest the crop in late fall and dry it in the forcing shed before manicuring and compressing it into one-pound bales for vacuum packing.

OG Genetics regularly prune and trim their outdoor plants which makes for an easier harvest.

Where the authorities allow the cultivation of cannabis plants, cultivators prefer to grow mother plants in greenhouses with additional horticultural lighting to ensure that they stay in the vegetative stage. Cuttings are taken and rooted, then later planted out or placed into greenhouses, where they are grown both hydroponically and organically with reduced spacing between individual plants. By reducing the plant's daylight and using HID lighting it is possible to produce several crops in rotation. This is a good, intensive way to farm marijuana but requires a large nursery setup, whereas the Ton of Skunk method is low-tech, requiring only a forcing shed and, if possible, a polytunnel.

Harvesting Your Outdoor Crop

The same principles apply to outdoor and indoor crops when it comes to assessing the readiness of your harvest. If you are unsure, harvest a few select buds and sample them. If you intend to sell the crop, wait until they are at their heaviest, which can mean that some of the THC has been degraded into CBD and CBN's. With practice, you will be able to judge when the plants have a good balance of THC and material weight. Harvesting in remote locations is better carried out at night, but it depends on your situation. Trim down the plants using pruning shears or a sharp machete. Cut off each individual branch and then the main stem and lay them on a plastic sheet. When you have collected the crop, the sheet can be rolled and tied neatly; the harvest is then removed to a safe area for drying.

If you only have a small amount of buds then dry the branches by hanging them from a line in a darkened, cool area. If you have a larger crop it is better to clip the buds from the branches and trim the leaves off while they are still wet. The buds can then be hung on a line or dried flat on newspaper, but ensure you turn them regularly. Allow the buds to dry out slowly, which will remove most of the chlorophyll and give a smoother, better tasting harvest. Ensure that you don't over-dry the buds. The small stalks should be brittle to the touch but the bud needs to have a slight elasticity. Buds that are too dry will crumble and disintegrate when packed.

Store your dried buds in a cool dark place. Seal them into plastic bags and then cover the bags with parcel tape. Light can encourage both decomposition and the growth of fungal spores.

If you are dealing with any quantity of marijuana buds it is a good idea to invest in a small heat-sealer and some lay-flat plastic tubing. You make the bags up from the tubing by heat-sealing each end and cutting it from the roll. Place a small piece of newspaper in with the buds to absorb any moisture and don't try to pack them too wet, as they will deteriorate rapidly.

Heat-sealers can be bought for a reasonable price. Check your phone book for packaging wholesalers or local kitchen equipment retailers as there are units designed to assist you in home freezing that work well. You can use heat-sealing equipment to give you a form of vacuum packing that helps preserve your harvest by first sealing the buds into a tightly fitting bag. Apply pressure to the bag once it has been sealed and force any trapped air into one corner. Then pierce that corner with a pin and force the air out of the bag. While you still have pressure on the bag, get an assistant to place a small piece of clear, waterproof adhesive tape over the pinhole. The buds are now sealed in a vacuum. You can purchase the tape from garden centers where it is sold to repair greenhouses and polytunnels.

In the unlikely event that you need to store any buds they can be placed in the refrigerator without any risk of deterioration. Don't freeze your harvest as the freezing process damages the delicate stalked capitate trichomes. They become brittle and break off, affecting the potency of your buds. Store your personal supply in a light-proof box. Single buds can be carried in waterproof plastic money tubes, like those worn around your neck on the beach. Alternatively, compress the buds in a plastic bag and then wrap them in parcel tape.

Breeding great cannabis plants is a passion for Cabin Fever Seed Breeders. This beautiful Blue Geez plant is a Blue Cheese clone x Empress Kush (ChemD x Loompas Headband/Loompas OG).

14. Breeding Cannabis Plants

In nature there are neither rewards nor
punishments, only consequences.
Ingersol. 1833 - 1899.

LowRyder by The Joint Doctor was the first commercial strain to be bred to exhibit autoflowering characteristics.

At some point you may decide to breed from your favorite plants. Cuttings will only produce genetic replicas of the mother and, although this is fine for the purpose of cultivation, it prevents any natural development of your stock. By selecting a female with outstanding traits, you can pollinate her using a strong, well formed male either from the same variety or, better still, from one of the many others that have traits you want to incorporate into your stock.

It is important to define what breeding actually means. Many growers cross varieties and then clone the best examples for their gardens. Although this is a good way to develop certain traits in your harvest, it does not provide you with a true breeding strain of plant. To develop a new strain you need to stabilize the hybrids by inbreeding the stock, which allows you to produce consistent chromosomes and establish common characteristics.

It is better to keep your males and females apart when breeding but if that is not possible, remove males from the grow room as soon as they have been identified. Males do not need much light once they have started to flower but you must keep them in the 12-hour light cycle. Place the plant on a sheet of clean paper in an area that has no air circulation. The pollen will fall on the paper, and can be collected by folding the paper in half and pouring the contents neatly into a test tube or vial. Alternatively, you can cut off a healthy branch and place the stalks in a glass of weak sugar and water solution. Then stand the glass on a sheet of clean white paper and collect the pollen. You can further harvest the pollen by holding a sheet of paper under the flowers and tapping them gently with a pencil. If the flowers themselves fall onto your collection paper, pick them out and discard them.

The pollen is then diluted in what is called a "carrier"; usually flour that has been microwaved for at least five minutes. Once the flour has cooled, it can be added to the pollen you have collected. Only one pollen cell is needed to fertilize a single female ovule, so using a carrier reduces waste.

Add half a teaspoon of pollen to 4 teaspoons of sterilized flour and store the mixture in an airtight vial. Test tubes are most breeders' choice for storing pollen, and a hobby chemistry set will provide you with ample supplies. Try to get tubes with plastic stopper lids rather than corks. Label the tubes with details of the male plant and date them. If you intend to store your pollen for any length of time, keep it refrigerated and it should last for a few months.

It is possible to keep a male cannabis plant alive indefinitely by cutting it back hard, once it has flowered. If you need to delay the onset of flowering in your male plant you can shock it by crimping its top over.

When you have selected the female you want to breed from, simply take

This amazing photo, from weed.co.za, shows a Winlaw Train male plant growing wild in South Africa.

This Alpine Seeds plant is just shooting out pollen!

Here we see a true hermaphrodite with male and female pre-flowers.

Shaking your male plants in an envelope is a great way to collect their pollen.

one of your test tubes into the flowering area. Use a small artist's brush and dip the tip into your tube, then, gently stroke the brush over the fine white pistils on selected flowers. The flowers will be most receptive to pollination two weeks after the flower clusters have formed. The seeds will take between four and six weeks to fully develop and they are not harvested until they have a dark, speckled appearance and seem to be bursting from the pods. The branches are cut and allowed to dry for about ten days. The seeds can then be picked out by hand and stored in labeled airtight containers. They are best kept in a refrigerator for long-term storage.

When choosing your parent plant for breeding purposes, you need to carefully examine the traits of the individual plants, since they are the gene pool of your future generations. Growers can have different requirements from their stock based on environmental growing conditions and the cultivation techniques they choose. The general rule when selecting stock plants is to choose those that grow and mature the fastest. Once you have identified these plants you can then further categorize them by potency and yield. If you are growing outdoor crops in cooler climates you may want to introduce a certain amount of frost resistance to your stock. By carefully selecting your varieties you can

The male is pollinating this grow room full of females. What a lucky guy.

develop this and many other desirable traits. When you cross two different varieties of cannabis plants, the resultant offspring are known as hybrids. These hybrid plants will all be very different from each other. Seeds from the same plant will all exhibit different traits, so it is important to grow a wide selection to maturity in order to examine them for vigor and potency. The best examples are then kept for further breeding. It is better to breed from two plant varieties that show contrastingly different traits. In this way you create what is referred to as "hybrid vigor" and the resultant offspring will exhibit a good selection of the genes of both parents. The first generation of two genetically different, but true breeding and stabilized plants, are called F1 hybrids, and they grow 25% faster and bigger than any other crosses. The offspring of F1 hybrids are called F2, their offspring are F3, and so on, however, these generations after F1 will not exhibit hybrid vigor.

If the plants you have selected to breed from both contain dominant genes for certain characteristics or traits, then the resultant offspring will display either one or the other of these traits. This makes it difficult to combine characteristics from the two parents, as the offspring will only exhibit the dominant trait of one plant. You can overcome this difficulty by inbreeding the seeds from the first cross.

Keeping your plants tagged is essential for good breeding. This OGA grow room is a perfect example.

Nexus from Eva Female Seeds exhibits foxtailing, a trait common to many Asian sativa strains.

StarBud is a famous indica strain from HortiLab Seeds that grows super tight buds covered with resin.

Dinafem's fantastic Blue Fruit holds DJ Short's famous Blueberry in its genetic lineage.

These OGA plants are categorized and clearly labelled so the breeders know exactly what is happening in their grow room.

This means growing the seeds to maturity and pollinating a female with a male from the same batch. In this way, recessive genes become magnified and available, and the new seeds will exhibit a better balance of the traits you are looking for. Inbreeding is a necessary, but not desirable, practice for producing new stock since it means continually drawing from the same gene pool. Some recessive traits may become prevalent that can reduce potency and vigor. However, to produce true breeding plants you need to backcross your females with males from the same strain. It is important to keep records of your plants and their progress. I know of several breeders who photograph and catalog their stock, but there are security implications if the police discover these records, and it will be used against you in any subsequent court appearances to demonstrate your professionalism and intent. Keep your records in a waterproof container and bury them. If you must take photographs, use a digital camera that requires no film processing. Film laboratories are primarily concerned about pornography and check their work before sending it out; however, they may contact the police if they suspect you are growing cannabis.

Feminized Seeds

It is possible to produce seeds that have no male chromosomes in their genetic makeup and therefore, when germinated, produce all female plants. This is desirable to the cannabis cultivator for several reasons; the main one being that it is difficult to select males to breed from. Although it is possible to assess the male's vigor and speed of growth, it is not possible to assess its potency since they do not produce any buds. It becomes a process of trial and error which, when considering the penalties imposed for possessing cannabis plants, is undesirable. Cultivators should seek consistent results from as few plants as possible to minimize their risk. Feminized seeds solve this problem by allowing you to select two females with known characteristics and use them as your gene pool.

This Dinafem team member is pollinating female plants with great precision.

Gibberellic Acid

When applied to female cannabis plants, gibberellic acid causes them to develop male flowers in the treated area. This technique allows us to collect viable pollen from a female plant. The acid is readily available from horticultural wholesalers, and is used by nurseries for plant breeding and hybridization. Spray a few of the upper branches of your chosen female every day for 14 days with a 100-ppm solution. Add a few drops of non-ionic wetting agent to your gibberellic acid solution to improve uptake in the plant. Once your female has flowered you can collect the pollen or simply remove the branches for later collection, as described earlier. The second female, which will carry the seeds, can then be pollinated. Since there are no male chromosomes present in the pollen used for the fertilization, the resulting seeds will all be female. Some varieties are better suited than others for this technique so you will need to experiment with your plants.

It is possible to pollinate the female treated with the gibberellic acid with its own male flowers, in effect crossing it with itself. This process can be used to preserve desirable plants but there is a danger of loss of vigor due to inbreeding. There are some mail order seed suppliers who stock feminized seeds. Check out their websites for more details.

A fine collection of hash made from specialty genetics bred by the geniuses at Alpine Seeds.

15. Troubleshooting Pests and Fungi

There's a sucker born every minute.
Barnum. P. 1845.

Both indoor and outdoor cannabis crops are attacked by the same insect pests and suffer from the same fungal infections. However, these problems become magnified in an indoor environment. Humidity can rise to unacceptable levels, encouraging fungal infections, and parasitic insect attacks are worse since the conditions are perfect for breeding pests.

Spider mites are by far the most damaging of insect pests and although they can be controlled with both insecticides and predator mites, the mantra for all indoor and greenhouse gardeners should be that "prevention is better than cure." Keep areas clean at all times, remove any plant trimmings, and in larger setups, invest in an industrial-grade vacuum cleaner that can suck up water spills. Vacuum the area regularly, paying attention to edges and corners. Wash surfaces and sterilize your equipment with a dilute solution of hydrogen peroxide (H_2O_2). A 17.5% solution is diluted at the rate of $2/3$ of an ounce per gallon of water or you can use a 5% dilute bleach solution. Indoor and outdoor growers should spray crops with a preventative systemic fungicide every two weeks during flowering and humid conditions, using a treatment that contains carbendazime, a chemical that is recommended for fruit and vegetable treatment. Use the recommended application for tomatoes and stop spraying at least ten days before harvest. Ensure that all vents are filtered through ladies' stockings or pantyhose, since the fine mesh will trap flying insects. Never enter your grow areas after working in outdoor gardens or walking through locations with other plants and foliage. Some growers remove their outer clothes and wear paper coveralls in their growing areas to avoid cross contamination.

Troubleshooting Pests and Fungi:
Organic and greenhouse gardeners must never take unsterilized soil or compost into their grow area. In addition, potting compost from previous crops must

Problem	Indication	Treatment
Algae	Green slimy growth. Causes odors. Mainly a grow room problem.	Clean affected area with H_2O_2. Cover surfaces with light-proof material.
Blackfly	Aphid colonies/causes yellowing and weakens plants.	Systemic/Organic spray. Predators may develop resistance to some systemics. Spray/repeat after 10 days.
Botrytis	Gray fibrous mold on buds and stems. Spotted leaves.	Reduce humidity. Remove affected leaves or buds and treat with systemic fungicide.
Caspid Bug	Brown or red spots, holes in leaves. Buds attacked.	Systemic/Organic spray. Drench; repeat 14 days later.
Caterpillars	Irregular holes in leaves. Black droppings. Heavy damage to leaves. Outdoors mainly.	Remove by hand. Organic wax spray. Systemic insecticides.
Damping Off	Seedlings/cuttings stems rot at base.	Reduce humidity. Improve drainage. Check temperature. Sterilize equipment.
Fungi	Powdery white/dark mold on leaves or stems (see Botrytis).	Reduce humidity. Improve drainage. Fungicidal sprays.
Greenfly	Aphid colonies. Twisted growth. Sticky deposits.	Systemic/organic spray. Predators.
Mealy Bug	Colonies of white furry insects on leaves.	Spray insecticide at first sign. Predators.
Sciarid Fly	Black flies. Young are tiny white maggots that attack roots.	Cover pots with foil. Prevent algae from forming. Spray/drench. Predators.
Spider Mites	Tiny clear or red spiders. Webs on bent leaves. Very harmful. Infestations will ruin a crop.	Pepper wax/Pyrethrum spray. Phytosiulus Persimilus (predator mites) is a predator.
Thrips	Tiny black or yellow flies, grubs are visible. Plant has silver streaks on leaves.	Insecticide sprays. Amblyseis is a predator, comes in colonies of 100.
Whitefly	Tiny flies or scales on undersides of leaves.	(Can be vacuumed off in the early evenings using a battery powered car cleaner.) Systemic/organic spray. Encarsia Formosa wasp is a tiny predator.

Cleaning your pots and equipment thoroughly before every grow is essential to keep pests and fungi at bay.

This C99 plant from Mosca Seeds is healthy and pest-free!

be removed and disposed of in case it contains organisms that are developing immunity to your sprays, especially fungi that will mutate very quickly.

Most problems can be dealt with effectively by using readily available sprays or drenches. A drench is simply poured into the plant container, filling it to the rim and then allowed to drain away naturally. Organic gardeners who don't want to use chemicals can find a range of safer insecticides that contain natural fatty acids and are particularly good at controlling spider mites. An example is hot pepper wax, which contains a mixture of cayenne peppers and paraffin wax. Pyrethrum is an organic insecticide made from plants and is the grower's main choice for combatting infestations. Homemade remedies can also be effective, such as a mild soap solution made with liquid dish detergent that can be sprayed onto the leaves, paying particular attention to the undersides of the plant. Rinse the leaves regularly to ensure the stomata don't become blocked.

Some organic growers plant garlic in with the crop. It takes up very little space and repels most pests. If you want to try this companion planting, buy a variety of garlic that has been bred for cultivation, as it will be disease and virus free. Don't use garlic bulbs from the supermarket.

Flycatchers are sticky strips of brightly colored plastic card that can be hung around the plants and are very effective at controlling aphids and whiteflies. They are attracted to the card and stick to the surface. Replace the cards once the surface is covered with dead pests.

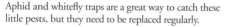

Aphid and whitefly traps are a great way to catch these little pests, but they need to be replaced regularly.

Ladybugs will control both aphids and spider mites and love the conditions of a typical grow room.

Smoke bomb treatments are not recommended for grow rooms as they can compromise a setup, but they can be effective in the greenhouse. I met an inmate in prison who was convicted of running what police at that time described as the most sophisticated grow room ever discovered. It had a computer system installed that controlled the growing environment, automatically adjusting CO_2 and measuring and adjusting nutrient levels. The inmate had written the program himself and was a well-educated and intelligent man, with absolutely no common sense. Even his sophisticated system couldn't keep out the humble spider mite, so to rid himself of the problem he ignited two smoke bombs in the middle of his grow room. Anxious neighbors alerted by smoke pouring from the house called the fire department, which, on getting no response, broke in to fight the fire. If it were an offence to be an idiot in a public place he'd have been charged with it!

Slugs and snails can cause serious damage to young cannabis plants outdoors, but can be prevented from attacking by smearing petroleum jelly around plant pot rims. If you have planted into the soil, slug pellets are effective at controlling slugs and snails, but they are toxic and harmful to the

Ladybugs are easy to introduce to your crop and are very reliable predators.

slug's natural predators such as birds and small mammals. There are non-toxic pellets available and they are worth the extra cost as you are only magnifying the problem if you poison your slug-killing allies. Slug pubs are an excellent and environmentally friendly way of killing slugs and snails. Sink a large plant saucer level with the ground and fill it with beer. Slugs simply can't resist beer and by morning you will find the saucer full of drowned pests.

American breeder and expert grower Sativa Tim always says that sometimes your predators can be distracted from their task, so keep an eye on them.

Predators

Predators are insects that prey on pest species. They are harmless to your crop, and their numbers, once released into the growing area, will be determined by the size of the pest problem. Once the predators have destroyed the pest species, they will die out. In practice, they tend to control the number of pests rather than eradicate them completely. They are, however, effective in continuous yield systems where the grower can't shut the area down. Once you have added your predators, avoid spraying your crop with insecticides. Horticultural suppliers will be able to advise you on the availability of predators. Predators are generally supplied by mail order from specialist breeders.

Some growers add ladybugs to their growing environments whenever they can catch them outside as they are natural aphid and spider mite controllers and thrive in grow room conditions. A ladybug will consume over 5,000 aphids in its lifetime and is an aggressive predator. There is a tiny wasp called Aphidius matricariae, who will also hunt aphids and inject an egg into the host's back. The aphid is slowly eaten alive by the wasp larvae. These wasps are also aggressive predators and will hunt out small pockets of aphids before they become an infestation. Another good aphid killer is Aphidoletes aphidimyza, also known as the Aphid midge. This tiny killer is a native of Europe. It mates a few days after hatching and then lays up to 100 eggs near the aphid colony. Within two days the eggs hatch into tiny orange larvae that begin devouring the aphids for up to two weeks before crawling down into the plant medium to develop into a cocoon. The cycle will repeat until there are no more prey insects for them to eat. The larvae of the European Hoverfly also consume large numbers of aphids. Hoverflies look like wasps but hover around flowers like tiny humming birds. The serial killer of the predator world is Chrysopa carnea, also known as the lacewing. They lay tiny green eggs that hatch in about four days. Lacewing larvae are so aggressive that they will eat each other if they can't find any prey. They viciously attack all soft-bodied pests, including spider mites, and are particularly effective against aphids. They kill even when they don't need to feed, leaving punctured victims to die of their wounds, and they will consume up to 50 aphids per day for three weeks before emerging as adults to repeat the cycle.

If you need a whitefly killer then the Encarsia formosa wasp is ideal. It will hunt for the whitefly, which it can detect at up to 3 feet away, and lay its eggs in the host larvae, killing them. Two weeks later new E. formosa will appear and the cycle is repeated; they are harmless to humans.

If your plants are suffering from the early stages of a spider mite infestation, you can release a tiny predator mite called Phytoseiulus persimilis. They are particularly effective but must be released early to avoid an infestation.

Insect Pests

Spider mites pose by far the greatest threat to cannabis crops and plants exposed to this insect should be treated immediately. If left unchecked, spider mite populations will explode, causing serious damage to the crop and actually killing some plants. The mites appear as either tiny clear or red arachnids (spiders). Unlike other mites, they reproduce quickly and several life cycles will be repeated during a growing season. The cycle of egg, nymph, two nymph molts and adult life can take place in under a month. Spider mites don't migrate quickly and move out from the center of infestation as their population increases. Because they are difficult to spot in the early stages, growers can inadvertently spread the population by taking infested cuttings. Symptoms of attack are the tiny mites themselves moving slowly around the plant, bronzing of the leaves and stems and fine webs on the leaves where mites are active. It will take several treatments to eradicate any infestation; sprays will not kill the eggs. Generally, a once-weekly treatment is spread over 5 weeks. Like most arachnids, the spider mite is difficult to treat with regular Diazinon or Dursban treatments, but Pyrethrum is very effective and therefore recommended. Spray the undersides of the leaves to ensure that you kill as many of the mites as possible.

Aphids and other insect pests are less damaging to cannabis, but weaken plants and can transmit viruses, so they should be treated immediately. If you are releasing predators, there are many to choose from, but even truly organic growers should consider using Pyrethrum as a first line of defense. Watch out for earwigs (Dermaptera), also known as pincer bugs. They feed on aphid eggs, but they also chew cannabis leaves with a passion. Symptoms are irregular holes in the soft parts of the plant's leaves. While not fatal, they can badly damage younger plants. Treat the area with a barrier insecticide powder that you sprinkle around the edge. Greenhouse growers can sometimes mistake baby slug attacks with earwig damage so it is advisable to slug pellet your area as well. Both pests attack at night so by morning you will know the culprit. They should be lying dead on the grow area floor.

Outdoor cultivators can experience problems with roundworms, also known as eelworms. Roundworms are nematodes and there are six species that will attack cannabis plants. They are difficult to diagnose due to their size and because they attack the root system underground. Symptoms to look out for are pockets of plants within the crop showing signs of stunted growth, and problems with wilting during the hotter part of the day, followed by a recovery in the cooler evening. The infestation destroys the root system, starving the plant of water and nutrients. You need to dig down to check the plant's roots. Nematodes that attack cannabis roots cause the formation of root knots or gauls that can easily be seen. They appear as lumps or growths on the roots. Treat the plant with a systemic insecticide and regular root drenches.

The stem nematode, Ditylenchus dipsaci, lives above ground and attacks stems, branches and leaf petioles. Symptoms of this infestation are stunted growth with twisted and shortened internodes. Treat with a systemic insecticide.

Parasitic Plants

Parasitic plants are almost exclusively an outdoor problem and can seriously damage cannabis crops. There are two genera of parasitic plants that will attack crops. Broomrape (Orobanche ramosa) is by far the most serious and attacks from under the ground, sinking specialized feeder roots, called haustoria, into the host's own root system to draw away nutrients and fluid. The sites of these haustoria attacks can develop fungal root infections. Broomrapes live entirely under ground and so are impossible to spot. However, they do briefly send up shoots that flower and seed quickly, before dying back. Broomrapes are responsible for huge amounts of damage to hemp fiber crops and will also attack tomato and tobacco plants.

Dodder, by contrast, sinks haustoria into plant tissue above ground and can easily be seen. Dodder appears as tangles of filaments called Devils Ringlets that twine tightly around stems and branches. Left alone, they will eventually pull the host plant over. The European strain of this parasite is known as Cuscuta europa and, like broomrape, causes serious damage to crops.

Sativa Tim's cat in the garden, keeping an eye on those lady beetles. Remember to be careful of your pet's fur as it can transport pests from one garden to the next.

Some growers have slightly more exotic grow room security.

Be creative in your predator choices; some insects are better at the job than others.

Fungal Attacks

There are at least 80 species of fungi that will attack cannabis and by far the most serious is Botrytis cinerea or Gray mold. Gray mold will attack young seedlings and cause damping off, a symptom of which is brown soft rotting of the vegetable matter at the soil line. The young seedlings quickly topple over and die. The same symptom can occur on cuttings that have been kept in high humidity for too long. Several fungi will cause damping off, including the following:

- Rhizoctonia solani
- Botrytis cinerea (can be effectively controlled with carbendazim)
- Macrophomina phaseolina
- Fusarium solani
- Fusarium oxysporum (used by the U.S. government to destroy drug crops)
- Fusarium sulphureum
- Fusarium avenaceum
- Fusarium graminearum

Powdery mildew is a very common fungus on marijuana plants. Treat it with a fungicide that contains sulfur.

Prevalent organisms that are not strictly fungi but belong to the Pythium species also cause damping off, including the following:

- Pythium aphanidermatum
- Pythium ultimum

Gray mold also attacks the stems of cannabis plants and can be seen as a furry growth around infected areas. The growth becomes covered with fungal spores and the tissue in the infected region becomes soft and rotten. Eventually all growth above the site of attack will die. The other manifestation of gray mold occurs during flowering and attacks the larger resinous buds since, in damp conditions, these buds trap moisture, creating ideal conditions for fungal growth.

The treatment for all fungal infections starts with good prevention. Spray your crop every two weeks with a preventative systemic fungicidal spray, especially during flowering, as it is far easier to prevent attacks than treat them once symptoms appear. Carefully control humidity levels in the growing environment

Leaves often display the first symptoms of both pest and fungi problems. Inspect your leaves every time you enter your grow room.

during flowering. Don't allow seedlings and cuttings to get waterlogged and raise all their media out of any standing water, to allow them to drain naturally. Take cuttings out of a humid environment after two days by removing the propagator lid and, although they don't require high light levels, ensure that you have a light source positioned directly above. In greenhouses, try to ensure that the clones receive filtered, indirect sunlight. If your cuttings do suffer from damping off, they can sometimes be rescued by cutting them $^1/_3$" above the rot line and dipping the stem into a dilute solution of copper sulphate and ammonium carbonate (Cheshunt compound) before applying fresh rooting gel and placing them into a fresh, well-drained medium.

Stem disease is harder to treat and will kill a lot of plants. They must be removed from the grow area immediately. If you have caught the infection in time you can wipe the affected area very gently with a soft cloth dipped in diluted copper oxychloride and then treat the whole plant with a systemic spray. Repeat this every 10 days until there are no more signs of infection. Keep the plants in a dry environment and drench the medium with a dilute fungal treatment before covering it with foil to prevent evaporation from raising humidity in the treated area.

Bud infections are even harder to deal with and the treatment has to be fairly drastic. All infected buds are removed and destroyed. The plant itself must be isolated and placed in a dry environment, in a drenched and covered medium. Treat the plant with a fungicidal spray; however, if it is badly infected it is better to destroy the plant. Prevention of these attacks starts with the early use of systemic fungicidal sprays before any fungi can establish themselves, and by controlling the humidity in your grow area. Clean all surfaces regularly with a 5% dilute bleach solution and remove any dead plant material from the grow area immediately. Outdoor growers should use preventative systemic fungicides as soon as flowering commences, even if there are no symptoms.

Fungal infections can also occur in the leaves of cannabis plants and some can spread into the plant stem; these infections are called leaf spot. Infections are classified by their appearance so identifying the symptoms is made easier.

Yellow and brown leaf spot will not kill cannabis plants but will badly affect the yield. Remove infected plants for spraying with a fungicidal treatment.

Pink leaf spot is a more serious infection caused by Trichothecium roseum. This fungal attack will quickly spread and kill your crop if left untreated. Badly infected crops should be destroyed and the grow area disinfected. It is possible to treat pink leaf spot if it is caught early enough; some growers report that copper oxychloride can be effective. Use it as a spray treatment and repeat weekly until the infection has been eradicated.

Viruses

These are spread by parasitic insects, mainly whiteflies, thrips and aphids. There have been reports of Hemp mozaic virus and Hemp streak virus being transmitted to European crops by feeding insects and although these are rarely fatal, they will reduce yields. Symptoms of viral infections are chlorosis of the leaves that turn into yellow streaks, or chevron stripes across the surface. Occasionally you will see brown flecks on the leaves. Viruses are impossible to eradicate and the whole of the plant is infected, including seeds and pollen that will carry and spread the infection.

Chemical Treatment Compounds

All of these are effective at controlling problems with marijuana plants and are readily available at horticultural retailers. It is important to remember that your crop is intended for consumption and that any chemicals that you apply can linger in the plant tissue. Be aware of what you are using and adhere to any applicable withholding periods.

Bordeaux Mixture
A mixture of copper sulphate and hydrated lime used to control fungal infections.

Cheshunt Compound
A mixture of copper sulphate and ammonium carbonate used to control damping off.

Copper Oxychloride
Controls most fungal infections in cannabis plants.

Sulfur
Used as a treatment for powdery fungal infections.

Organic Pesticides

Derris
Made from the powdered and dried root of a wild plant but still highly toxic. Its active ingredient is rotenone.

If you're growing outdoors, utilise netting and fencing to keep away larger pests such as deer and rabbits.

Pyrethrum
Made from the South African Pyrethrum plant. Very safe for the user and kills all pests that attack Cannabis sativa.

Insecticidal Soap
Derived from fatty acids of plant origin. Very safe to handle but only kills those insects it is sprayed directly onto.

Soft Soap
A traditional mixture of plant origin used to control aphids and as a wetting agent.

Neem Oil
Controls aphids and is used as a wetting agent.

Smoking home made hash from a clean pipe or bong is one of the most pleasurable ways to get high.

16. Extracting THC From Plants

Penser, c'est voir. To think is to see.
Balzac. 1799-1850.

After curing and drying your cannabis crop you will have a collection of mani-
cured and packaged buds ready for consumption. Along with these you will
have a large collection of dried leaves, bud trimmings and possibly male plants.
The leaf material contains a low percentage of THC; however, through extraction it can be concentrated into rich, spicy oil that can be smoked or eaten.

There are many different ways to remove the oil from dried marijuana
plants. However, in most countries it is difficult to obtain the chemicals that
are necessary to complete the extraction. Fortunately, acetone can be purchased
easily if you know where to look, and it is one of the best chemicals available
for hash oil production. Acetone is a solvent that is used in fiberglass molding

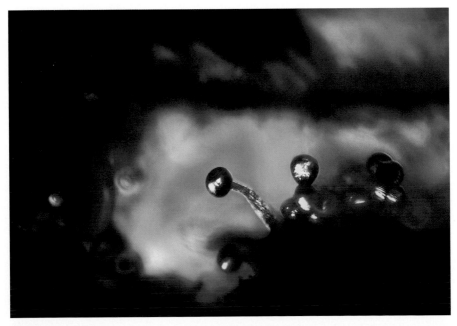

The trichomes are the part of marijuana plants that hold the THC.

and for cleaning brushes and equipment. Boat builders and auto mechanics all use the chemical, and individuals can purchase it from wholesalers without any questions being asked. Check boating and trade magazines for suppliers. You can also find it in hairdressing and beauty salons where it is used to remove artificial nails. Check out any beauty supply stores in your area, where you can purchase the chemical. If asked, explain that you are a nail technician. If you don't look the part, say it's for someone else.

THC is readily dissolved in acetone and the extractions are more purified than isopropyl alcohol, ethanol or petroleum ethers. The resulting oils have none of the taste associated with some extractants, as very little of the non-psychoactive material is dissolved. Acetone is highly flammable and care needs to be taken as it evaporates rapidly, even at room temperature. Supplies of acetone from a beauty wholesaler will come in plastic bottles, which are fine, but larger amounts purchased for brush cleaning will be in aluminum containers. Store acetone away from any heat sources.

⚘ Acetone is highly flammable and precautions must be taken.

Acetone (CH₃ COCH₃)

Acetone is a colorless, flammable, organic solvent also called dimethyl ketone. It is prepared by the oxidization of isopropyl alcohol, heating calcium acetate or by the Hock method using benzene as its raw material. It boils at 133°F (56°C), which is a very low boiling point compared to water which boils at 212°F and alcohol at 173°F.

Simple Extraction

1. Take all your dried, cured leaf material and separate it from the plant stalks. Remove any seeds, as they taste bad. Mix smaller buds from the base of the plant in with the leaves and any trimmings from the manicuring process. Extractions made with bud material are two to three times more potent.
2. Super-dry the leaves and flowers to remove all traces of moisture. This is best done in a microwave oven. Place small amounts in at a time and heat for a few minutes. When sufficiently dried, the material should crumble between your fingers.
3. Place the super-dried leaves and flower material into a blender and reduce them to a fine powder. Then pass this powder through a flour sieve and into a large Pyrex bowl.

4. Pour acetone over the powdered plant material in the Pyrex bowl and ensure that it is well covered. Place a sheet of aluminum foil over the bowl to act as a lid and leave the solution for two days at a cool temperature. Store away from any naked flames.

5. After two days take the solution and pour it through a large funnel lined with a filter paper, such as those available in home brewing kits. Alternatively, use a coffee filter or a piece of silk. Collect the liquid and pour it into a container for the final stage.

6. This last stage requires a slow cooker. Slow cookers or crock-pots are readily available from household appliance retailers and are relatively inexpensive to buy. They consist of a ceramic pot and an electric heating unit. Set the slow cooker up outside where the acetone can be safely boiled off into the atmosphere. The fumes given off by this final process are extremely volatile. There must be no naked flames. Cook the acetone solution on the lowest heat setting until all of the solvent has been evaporated. The oil will remain in the bottom of the ceramic container.

Honey oil results from a frozen extraction.

Many marijuana connoisseurs enjoy honey hash oil for its strength and effect.

Once the acetone has evaporated, switch the cooker off, and while it is still warm scrape the oil from the base of the ceramic pot and store it in a glass container. You can get some useful glass containers from a hobby science kit or you can just use a cup. Acetone evaporates rapidly and it is possible to complete this process outdoors on a sunny day, but it can sometimes take days to evaporate a small amount. Don't try and speed up the process using microwaves or heaters. Acetone ignites easily. If you want more malleable oil, leave it suspended in a little solvent; you can then paint this onto cigarette papers and the acetone will evaporate away in seconds.

More Complex Extraction Techniques

The extraction process can be speeded up and made more cost effective by using an apparatus to allow you to heat the acetone solution, and to then collect it by distillation during the final stages. A working knowledge of chemistry is helpful.

The marijuana is prepared in the same way, powdered and covered with acetone, but instead of leaving it to stand for days the solution is heated gently in a specially designed reflux chamber placed in a large water container heated over an electric ring. The temperature of the water is checked with a heat resistant thermometer and kept at 133ºF (56ºC), which is the boiling point of the solvent. The refluxing is continued for three to four hours, depending on the quantities that are being extracted, and then the apparatus is allowed to cool. A condenser is fitted to the apparatus and the solution is heated to 133ºF (56ºC) once more. This causes the acetone to vaporize and rise into the distillation section where it can be cooled and collected in a separate vessel. The extracted oils are removed from the apparatus and stored. Alternatively, the oils can be further purified with laboratory grade filter papers to make Honey Oil, although this will lose you about half of the oil's weight and is only for the connoisseur.

Cannabinoids are the psychoactive compounds found in cannabis plants. They are collectively referred to as THC, but they also include CBN and CBD. CBN has been shown to increase the effect that THC has on the user, whereas CBD actually works as a blocking agent. It is possible to convert CBD into THC using a process known as isomerization, but this is best left to the experts. The process entails using sulfuric acid, which is a very aggressive chemical and difficult to obtain. Providing you have used good quality cannabis for your oil, there is no need to worry about CBD.

Making Hashish

THC is contained in multi cellular glandular hairs on the surface of the cannabis plant's leaves and flowers. These hairs are known as stalked capitate trichomes and appear as tiny, translucent mushroom-like structures that can be seen through a magnifying glass. Pure hashish, known as Cream or Skuff, is made by separating the resin-laden capitate trichomes and compressing them. The quality of your cream will depend on the method used to extract the glands. In its simplest form, the glands are collected by rubbing gently over the flowering females and then scraping the resinous deposits off your hands with a knife. The oil will contain some impurities but is composed mainly of trichome heads and stalks. This resin is placed between pieces of plastic wrap and compacted between the palms of your hands. You may already have experienced the sticky resin on your fingers when manicuring your buds.

Most commercially available hash is either silk-screen rubbed, which produces a high quality hash, or made from an oil extraction added to a very fine powder made from flower tops. This does not contain the high concentrations of THC that you find in cream, but that does not mean it is of poor quality. Most smokers find that cream is too potent for regular use. Preparing your own powdered flower tops and adding them to the oil you have previously extracted

Dinafem's California Hash Plant is one of the best plants to make great hash from.

from your crop can make reasonable hashish. The quality of the buds you use to make your powder will reflect on the strength or potency of your hashish.

Prepare the flower tops you are going to use by drying them slowly in a cool area to remove as much of the chlorophyll as possible. Some growers soak their buds for a few hours in cold water as this is supposed to extract a certain percentage of chlorophyll, but it is not necessary.

Once the flowers are cured, super-dry them in the same way as you would for an oil extraction, except that the final stage is to grind the material to a fine powder using a coffee grinder or mortar and pestle. If you have very resinous buds then this becomes more difficult, but using a pounding action rather than grinding will do the trick. The powder is then simply mixed with your extracted oil. It is better to have the oil slightly diluted with acetone to keep it malleable – the acetone will evaporate slowly at room temperature. Cover

You'll find yourself very popular if you've got a sizeable hash stash!

your hand with plastic wrap and then knead and roll the mixture into a ball. It is better to use a mold to shape the hash. The mold can be a simple wooden frame that is placed onto foil or plastic wrap and filled with the mixture. Cover the top with more plastic wrap and you can then roll and compress the hash with a rolling pin. You need to apply a lot of pressure while doing this. Many growers prefer to use a bench-mounted vice that can be hand tightened to give good compression to their hash. If you are preparing any quantity of hashish, you may want to construct a heavier press utilizing a car bottle jack.

Mixing equal quantities of powder and oil produces potent hashish. By adding one-part oil to two-parts powder you get a milder, less intense hash similar to Lebanese. By combining the stronger mix with the latex from Papaver somniferum, the opium poppy, you get something similar to Nepalese Temple Ball, although this should always be made with cream.

Because hash is so malleable you can find it pressed into fantastic shapes.

Some people that won't smoke bud are fanatic about hash!

Cream

Cream, also called Skuff, and made from compressed resin glands, is the most potent hashish you can make. There are a variety of methods to make cream other than rubbing the flower tops that a home producer can use. The best cream is made from the buds themselves but any bud trimmings and flower parts can be used. Fan leaves don't have any glands on their surface and are not suitable for use, but smaller leaves from around the flowers can be used. View your plant material through a magnifying glass before deciding if it is suitable. Don't confuse cystolith glands or unicellular hairs for stalked capitate trichomes. If there is no ball structure above the hair it is not a trichome gland. Flowers that are to be used in cream making must be cured in the same way as buds intended for smoking. Even though we do not require any of the plant material itself, cured flower heads make more potent hashish.

Silk Screening

You can purchase screens for this process that are actually made of polyester or saran. They consist of a fine mesh and are used in printing. Most art shops supply the screens. Choose one that has 124 threads per inch of screen (12XX used in SB4512, SB4514 and SB4699 Kits). The tighter the mesh, the greater the potency; however, there is a corresponding drop in volume produced. Alternatively, you can make a screen by stretching a fine silk stocking over a frame, but this is not very effective. The screen needs to be supported approximately 1" above a sheet of aluminum foil that acts as your collection plate for the trichome glands. The flowers are broken gently onto the surface of the screen and moved around the mesh using a plastic phone card. The more pressure you apply to the bud material, the more plant matter will fall through onto the foil. This will make a difference to the potency of the hash and it becomes harder to compress. You will not extract all of the trichomes with flat screening so the buds you have used can still be smoked (although they are not as potent.) Once you have collected the glands on the foil, remove your screen and using a phone card, scrape the deposits together to remove the newly formed cream. Compress it between your hands in plastic wrap. It is a very potent smoke and certainly unlike any commercial hashish. If you need to store it, keep it in a cool place in a light-proof container to preserve it. Do not freeze your cream.

Cheese Bubble and Shake

Shakers

These work by holding your flower tops in a small plastic container with a fine internal mesh. By shaking the container, the trichome glands are dislodged and collected. Shakers are not particularly efficient but will produce a reasonable amount of cream. Shakers can be purchased from specialist suppliers and are relatively inexpensive.

Food Processors

Resin glands, when placed into water, sink, whereas plant material that has been chopped and dried will float. In order to ensure that the glands are not too sticky to separate, this process is best carried out using very cold water. Fill your processor half way with buds or trimmings and then add all of the ice from an ice cube tray. Top the remainder up with cold water and blend for two to three minutes. You should end up with a green, ice water mix that you then pour through a large funnel into a clear glass or plastic jug. Line the funnel with a filter made from a silk screen with approximately 25 lines per inch of screen. This allows the glands to pass through, but traps the larger plant matter. You now need to remove the glands from the water, which is best done with a coffee filter or a piece of silk. The water will pass through, leaving the cream in the filter. The cream is then dried and compressed as before. It is not the purest of cream but it is certainly very potent.

Bubble Bags

Bubble bags are commercially available, and are also an ice water filtration system. This method combines the best of the screen and blender methods, using ice water to make the trichomes brittle, before straining the mix through the bag filters to increase the purity. The trichomes collected can then be compressed, and the Hashish made in this fashion is known as Bubble hash.

Bubble Bags are a fantastic way to create high quality hash.

The Bubble Bag method uses ice water and gives a very pure product.

Tumblers

Tumblers are mechanical separators that consist of a revolving drum with a silkscreen rim. The dried flowers are gently agitated as the drum slowly spins, allowing the glands to fall through the silkscreen to be collected at the base of the drum on foil. The secret lies in their slow rotation and they produce the purest cream you can make with no plant material contaminants. These machines are on sale in the Netherlands, but they are also cheap and easy to build yourself using the motor from a barbecue rotisserie to turn your drum. The drum itself is constructed from MDF (medium density fiberboard), available at most building supply stores. The MDF should not be more than $^3/_8$" thick. You need to cut two 16" circles from the board. Mark the circle with a piece of string pinned to the center, with your pencil tied to the end of it. It is best to use a jigsaw to cut the shape, and then round it off smooth with a file and sandpaper.

You now need a length of threaded bar that has a slightly larger diameter than the rotisserie spit shaft opening. This size can vary but is not a problem as you simply file the end of the bar square to fit the opening. Drill the centers of the two MDF discs you have cut to the same diameter as the threaded bar.

Mount the unit onto a small bench made from MDF board that has been cut into a 24 x 24" square. Then cut out a 20 x 8" section from the middle. This is where the wheel will rotate, with the rotisserie motor fixed to one side of the opening and a support mounted on the opposite side to hold the threaded axle. Mount the bench on sturdy legs that give the rotating drum clearance and allow you to catch the glands on foil below. The legs can be made from short sections of 2 x 4" timber. You will need to brace these with struts to keep them stable. Take one of the MDF discs and mark out an access panel close to the rim at least 6 x 6". Cut this out with a jigsaw. This is how you will place and remove your flower tops from the finished drum.

If you don't have the time to make your own, there are some great commercially available machines to do the job.

The opening is simply covered with a piece of acetate, or stiff plastic held on with duct tape. The buds are stripped of glands by the tumbling process and are usually discarded after use. The drum can be cleaned with a vacuum hose.

You now assemble the drum by passing the axle through the center holes in your discs. Hold the sides of the discs in position with nuts and large washers threaded onto the shaft and bolted either side. Leave a gap of 6" between the discs and fix 4 x ³/₄" wooden dowels around the inside edge to support the wheel structure and assist in the tumbling process by agitating the flowers as they rotate. The silkscreen mesh can now be stretched around the rim and held in position with a flexible strip of thin hardboard that is fixed to both rims with a hot glue gun and tacks. Glue any joins you make in the mesh with the glue gun. Place your newly assembled drum into the bench opening and then mount the rotisserie motor to one side attaching it to the axle shaft. The size and position of motors varies and you will need to do some fine-tuning at this stage to ensure that the axle, motor and opposite axle mounting are level and secure. Support the axle on the opposite side of the motor on a short piece of 2 x 4" timber with a groove cut into the top to sit the axle in. You can line this with a section of copper water pipe cut in half and glue-gunned into position. Ensure that your bench legs give you ample clearance, position your foil, and your machine is ready to go.

Fill the drum with flower tops and trimmings and then leave it to slowly rotate. The buds fall to the bottom of the drum as they are slowly tumbled. After 30 minutes you will have collected your first cream on the foil. Collect and compress it: it is the purest cream you can get. You now need to place a small rubber ball into the drum with your flower tops and then switch the machine back on again for at least an hour. The ball helps to agitate the buds. This process produces a lower grade of cream, but it is still exceptional. Once you have mastered this technique you can experiment with different size meshes to build your perfect cream maker.

Nepalese Temple Ball

Temple ball is prepared from a mixture of cream and the dried latex from the opium poppy. In the United States, it is illegal to grow or possess any part of opium poppy plants, except the seeds.

The opium poppy's botanical name is Papaver somniferum, meaning "sleep inducing". The history of this plant is unclear; some horticulturists believe it evolved naturally while others think it is a cultivar developed by man. Either way it is most likely to have evolved from Papaver setigerum, the wild

Hash can be processed into Nepalese temple balls for an interesting experience and a lasting high.

poppy that does contain small amounts of opium. There is another close relative of Papaver somniferum that also produces significant opium quantities, which is known by its botanical name Papaver bracteatum.

Papaver somniferum is an annual with a growth cycle of around 120 days. It is similar to cannabis in that it is photo-responsive and requires 12-hour light cycles to produce flowers. It can be successfully cultivated under HPS lamps indoors and thrives in hydroponic systems. Its nutrient requirements are similar to cannabis but it prefers an acidic medium. Organic crops of poppies should be started indoors. The seeds are tiny but generate quickly in a warm, moist environment. Use peat pots for germination, since poppies are notoriously difficult to transplant; they cannot tolerate any root damage. Peat pots degrade naturally once in the soil, allowing the delicate roots to grow through. Poppies are sown in early spring and need a sunny location with well-drained soil. The plant will reach a height of 3 to 5 feet and flowers in the autumn or in a 12-hour light cycle. Unlike cannabis, poppies are not dioecious. The buds all produce four large petals, with dark spots at the base that vary in color from white through to purple. The main stem and each tiller end in a single flower bud. As these flower buds develop, the ends of the penduncle and tillers extend and bend towards the ground, forming a distinctive hook shape. The young buds form upside down. As the bud matures the stems straighten upwards and within two days of becoming vertical the bud sepals open and the flower blooms.

The flowers only last for about four days and then the petals drop to expose a small round pod the size of a pea. This is the seedpod that will grow ovular in shape and narrow at the top as the seeds ripen and are eventually released through small holes that appear in the crown. When mature, the pod will measure between 2" and 3" in diameter. Two weeks after the petals drop you can harvest the latex. Opium latex is a complex organic substance composed of sugars, proteins, ammonia, latex, gum, wax, fat, water, acids and alkaloids. The alkaloids are a highly complex organic base of nitrogen, water and acids. The main alkaloids in opium latex are the following:

- Morphine
- Noscapene
- Papaverine
- Codeine
- Thebaine

The pod is cut with three sets of three incisions from the crown to the base of the pod. It is important that the cuts are of the correct depth. Incisions that are too deep will cause internal weeping of the latex that will kill the seed head. If the incisions are too shallow the pod will heal and latex will not flow out. The correct depth is 1.25 mm ($1/20$th of an inch) with a tolerance of 0.25 mm ($1/112$th of an inch). The traditional tool for harvesting opium is a three-blade instrument that allows you to cut each set in one action. You can use a craft knife to carry out this process but ensure it has a retractable blade that can be set to the correct depth.

The latex weeps from the cuts and first appears as a white malleable substance that oxidizes on contact with air and turns into a brown viscous gum. Scrape the brown gum off with a wet blade and dry it in the sun for several days until it takes on the consistency of soft wax and becomes raw opium. Once dried, the raw opium is stable. Over time, the opium slowly loses moisture and becomes more concentrated. You can expect to yield 70 mg per pod.

Raw opium typically contains about 7% plant material contaminants that are undesirable for smoking. A process known as cooking removes these contaminants. Dissolve the opium in boiling water then pass the water-opium solution through a fine filter to remove the plant material. Bring the liquid opium

This cereal is definitely not for kids.

solution back to the boil, and evaporate the water off, leaving a brown paste known as smoking opium. Allow this paste to slowly dry and harden. Then, powder the opium in a mortar and pestle or coffee grinder and add it to freshly made unpressed cream. Compress this mixture in your hands between pieces of plastic wrap. Temple ball is traditionally hand-rolled into small round balls.

Add 1 gram of opium to 7 parts of cream.

I have added this section because I feel it is relevant. It is up to you how you choose to use it but you must be aware that opium is an insidious, seductive and dangerous substance that causes dependence. It is not without reason that opium and its derivatives are known as "Nasty" in London slang.

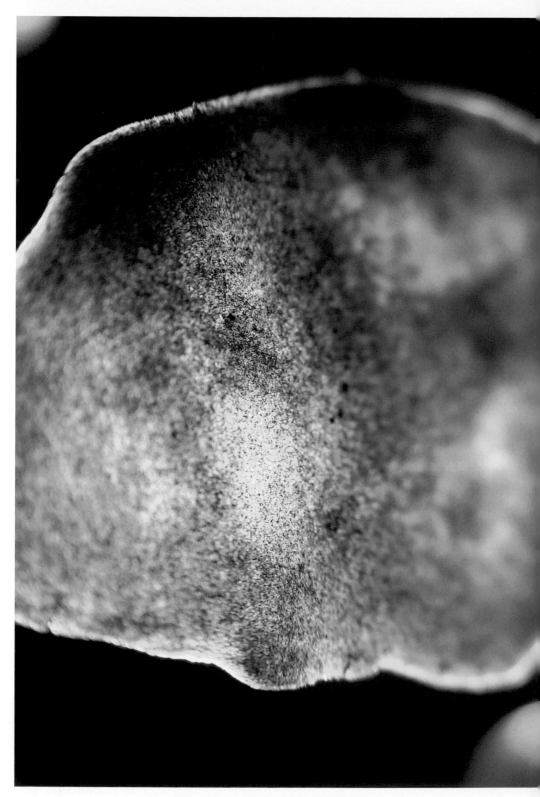

Hash can be beautiful as well as incredibly strong!

17. Enjoy!

One half of the world cannot understand the pleasures of the other.
Jane Austen. 1755-1817.

Cannabis bud, weed, resin and oil are generally smoked in hand-rolled cigarettes, either mixed with tobacco, herbs or on their own, known as Iytal. It can
also be smoked in small pipes called chillums or in larger water-cooled bongs.
Others prefer to heat cannabis on a hot knife and inhale the vapors through a
tube. In 500 B.C. the Greek writer Herodotus described the use of cannabis by
the Scythians who made sweat tents where cannabis seeds (and it is assumed
flowers) were thrown onto burning embers and the fumes inhaled. This would
have released large amounts of THC into the confined area, and it is hardly
surprising that Herodotus claimed users, "howled with pleasure." Marijuana

Pipes are a favorite method of smoking for many tokers, as the smoke is so clean.

can be used to make drinks such as Bhang lassi, while others make tinctures of cannabis by dissolving it in strong spirits. Tinctures can be used recreationally, and in herbal remedies to alleviate most of the illnesses described earlier. Many patients mix cannabis tinctures with herbal teas such as chamomile or rosehip, or alternatively it can be made into a convection for treating chest and breathing problems. In many countries it is traditional to cook with cannabis and it is added to a variety of dishes — this is a pleasant way to enjoy marijuana, but always remember that ingested cannabis is stronger and slightly hallucinogenic so only use small amounts.

Smoking Cannabis Vapors

Hand-rolled cigarettes, or joints, are usually made by joining two cigarette papers. The best way to do this is to overlap two skins slightly, and moisten the gum on the edge that is touching, then take a third paper and fold it in half with the gum outermost. Moisten the glue on both sides and then place it between the first two sheets and press them together, then slide out the folded paper and the gum will remain to secure your king-size papers. Others prefer to join three papers together with one stuck to the bottom and the third turned and gummed along the edge. The joint is then rolled in a slight cone shape that is fatter at the lit end, and a small tube of card is placed in the end

A traditional bone pipe from South Africa photographed by the experts at weed.co.za.

There are some gorgeously crafted pipes and bongs available worldwide, such as these beauties photographed by the guys at OGA Seeds.

This unique pipe from Russia has been hand-crafted from a cannabis sativa stem and blackwood, and is both beautiful as well as functional.

The breeders at OGA Seeds recommend quality pipes and bongs when smoking their bud.

These cobs from a weed.co.za member in Malawi show a traditional way of curing; weed is buried in the soil inside corn husks and dug up months later for a fantastic smoke!.

to act as a roach. It is better to leave out the roach and place the filter from a cigarette in the end to reduce the damage tobacco tars can do to your lungs.

The Tulip is a connoisseur's joint that is difficult to roll but consists of three papers joined to form a square. The cannabis and tobacco are mixed and rolled into a short fat cone in the papers and they are twisted at the end. A thin tube is then rolled from card and secured with cigarette papers and this is inserted into the opposite end of the bulb-shaped cone, and secured. The finished joint looks like a Dutch tulip flower. Pipes and chillums are made available specifically for smoking marijuana and these are worth investing in, alternatively tobacco pipes can be used. Small clay and cob pipes are excellent for smoking weed. There are a variety of specialized pipes available including one that resembles a credit card that can be discreetly carried. There are other designs available that incorporate small hash pipes in belt buckles and ball-point pens and these are ideal if you are away from home, but if you intend to travel abroad, leave them behind. Customs officers actively look for drug paraphernalia.

Bongs can be homemade from plastic bottles with a bowl and tube se-cured at the top. The bowl can be made from a socket set attachment with the plastic tube wedged into its base. Kitchen foil lines the inside of the socket attachment and is repeatedly perforated with a pin. Half-fill the bottle with water and then fix the bowl in place with heat-proofed mastic, ensuring the pipe extends into the water. Next make a small hole above the waterline and fix your smoking tube to it; ensure it is airtight with some clear mastic or Blue tack and you are ready to enjoy your water-cooled cannabis.

Cannabis fumes can be smoked in a vaporizer, which gives a cool and smooth taste that many smokers at first find strange. A large percentage of THC is destroyed in the burning process used to create the smoke in pipes and joints. Activation of THC acids called decarboxylation occurs at around 217.4°F (103°C) with vaporization taking place at around 392°F (200°C). Vaporizers gently heat the cannabis to a temperature where the cannabinoids evaporate. This is below the temperature that plant material will burn at, but still allows the vapors to be collected and inhaled. Vaporizers can be purchased from specialist suppliers and are a healthy way to enjoy cannabis, especially for medicinal users. Oil can be smoked in joints or chased off kitchen foil. A small amount is smeared on to the foil and then heated from underneath with a lighter, the resulting fumes are inhaled through a cardboard tube. Joints can be fitted into a hole made in the base of a cardboard tube. The end of the tube

Storing your bud properly is important; MMJars provide a great way to keep your stash tasty and potent.

is covered with the smoker's hand and the fumes are inhaled through the opposite opening. To increase the "hit" the smoker removes the hand and finds out why this method of smoking is called a Shotgun.

Those smokers who have yet to try a Bottle and Bucket or Gravity bong are missing a cannabis-smoking experience. A plastic bottle has the base cut away and a foil lid is pushed into the neck and perforated with a pin. The bottle is then gently pushed into a bucket of water then hash, weed or oil is placed into the foil bowl and lit. The bottle is then drawn slowly upwards and the resulting vacuum sucks the smoke into the bottle. When the bottle is full of rich, pungent cannabis smoke the foil bowl is removed and the smoker places their mouth over the bottle opening and then pushes the bottle back down into the water. This forces the smoke straight out of the bottle to be enjoyed by the rapidly stoned citizen.

Cannabis Tincture

THC can be dissolved into fats, milk, oil and alcohol but not water, so one way to enjoy a cannabis drink is to add it to your favorite spirit. Dry and powder your weed then place it into a container with an airtight lid. Soak it overnight in water to remove any impurities then drain and replace the water with spirit. Leave the mixture for at least a week before straining the liquid through a funnel lined with filter paper and pouring the mixture back into the spirit bottle. Most connoisseurs of cannabis tincture prefer to add it to brandy, fruit schnapps or liqueurs as the marijuana can have a bitter taste.

Cooking with Cannabis

Cannabis cooking is based on the principle that THC needs to be dissolved into either fat or oil. Once you have done this you can then use the extraction in your recipes. The most favored fat to use is butter or Ghee and the usual ratio for Hash butter is:

50 grams powdered flowers/hash + 500 grams of butter

Heat the butter gently to soften it, and then stir in your powder. It will take 20 to 30 minutes for the cannabis to dissolve into the butter so allow it to gently heat through, and stir occasionally. Cannabis oil or hash does not require as long. If you don't want any flower particles in the butter you can pass it through a sieve, muslin cloth or stocking. Alternatively, smaller amounts can be dissolved into vegetable oil heated in a teaspoon over a flame. This is useful

These baked goods from OGA Seeds will get you truly baked!

for making potent hash yogurt. Allow the oil to cool before mixing it into the yogurt pot. Non-alcoholic drinks can be made by simmering cannabis in milk for 30 minutes before straining. If you wish to add the milk to tea or coffee it needs to be fairly strong. It's a common misconception that tea can be made by pouring boiling water over cannabis flowers. THC does not dissolve in water.

Making cannabis butter is an easy way infuse your favorite recipes with quality pot like the experts at Red Star Farms.

Recipes you may wish to try

Breakfast Buds: A healthy start to the day.
Sprinkle two teaspoons of dried, powdered cannabis flowers onto one bowl of breakfast cereal. Add milk with yogurt, fruit or honey to taste.

Harrera. Traditional Moroccan soup served at the end of Ramadan.
Finely chop 1 onion, 1 celery stick, 1 parsnip and a small bunch of parsley. Cover the bottom of a large saucepan with half a centimeter (about 1/5") of olive oil and place on medium heat. Into this sprinkle two heaped tablespoons of pulverized hash or weed and stir for 10 minutes before adding the vegetables. Cook the vegetables in the oil then add about 1 quart of water, half a cup of

peas and 25 grams of fine noodles. Add paprika, salt and pepper to taste and allow it to simmer for 15 minutes. Remove from the heat and add two beaten eggs. Serve at once with sliced lemon.

Majoon. An Islamic delicacy.

Powder 1 cup of buds and add half a cup of chopped almonds, the same of dates and figs, a single tablespoon of honey and a teaspoon of ginger, then nutmeg and finally cinnamon. Dissolve the cannabis into a small amount of butter. Place all the ingredients into a saucepan of water and simmer for 10 minutes, stirring occasionally as it reduces. Turn off the heat and allow to cool slightly before adding a dash of orange juice then stir the mixture again before pouring it into a shallow baking tray to set. Cut the sweetmeat into cubes and serve.

Polm Chocolade Taart. A Dutch treat.

Melt 250 grams of butter over a low heat and add 25 grams of powdered polm, or you can use weed; stir gently for 20 minutes then pass it through a sieve to remove any plant material, reheat and add 200 grams of cooking chocolate and dissolve it into the butter. Next, gradually add 250 grams of sugar and mix well before adding four beaten eggs and 200 grams of flour; once again mix well. When the mixture is smooth add a further 100 grams of dark Dutch or Belgian chocolate and dissolve. Finally pour the mixture into a shallow baking tray and place in a moderate oven for 30 minutes. Allow to cool then slice and serve.

The results of a well-managed outdoor commerical grow.

18. Commerical Uses
of Cannabis

Forgive them father for they know not what they do!
Luke XXIII. 34.

This Mr. Nice facility is an exemplary commercial grow and will yield heavily for the lucky grower.

Cannabis sativa or hemp is grown as a bast or long fiber crop that is similar to flax. Humans have cultivated fiber hemp for thousands of years in a variety of different regions for its fibrous outer bark, its inner core (known as hurd) and its seeds. Archaeological evidence shows traces of hemp cultivation as early as 8,000 BC, with hemp textile production starting at the same point as the production of pottery. Hemp played a vital role in human development, providing clothing, fiber and animal feed. Where other fibers would have decayed rapidly in the saltwater spray, hemp was strong enough for sails, rope rigging and caulking, enabling humans to travel across oceans. The Romans used hemp ropes and sails produced in Gaul (France). Although hemp was not grown in Ancient Rome, Lucilius documented its use in 120 BC, and Pliny the Elder outlined its preparation and different grades in the first century AD. Henry the VIII's promotion of the cultivation of hemp in England to support the navy and the maritime supremacy of Elizabethan times caused demand to grow.

Farmers who grow hemp regularly lose part of their harvest to people who think commercial hemp can be used in the same way as marijuana. One misguided gang I met whilst in a European prison had hired three cube vans and spent an entire night stealing a sizeable portion of one unfortunate farmer's hemp crop, only to discover once it had dried that they had a storeroom full of compost and stalks.

Hemp is sown in the spring and is an extremely fast-growing crop — reaching heights of almost 12 ft in about 110 days — and requires no herbicides or pesticides. Hemp is such a rapidly developing plant that it requires granular fertilizers or manure to maintain its vigor.

Hemp strips the ground of nutrients but with careful management and

The huge, strong roots of this cannabis plant from No Mercy Supply help both anchor it into the ground and control erosion.

If these hemp seeds from South Africa's weed.co.za were used properly many problems in the world could be alleviated.

This cat is playing in a woven hemp basket.

good soil preparation each season, crops can be grown continuously on the same land. The strong roots help to anchor the soil and control erosion.

Fiber hemp is planted in dense rows to encourage tall, upright growth and this method of planting ensures that very little foliage is produced. As the plants mature, the leafy tops form a dense canopy that blocks out light and chokes weed growth, leaving the field in good condition for the following season. Fiber hemp is usually harvested before the onset of flowering to ensure optimum fiber quality. After harvest, the foliage is turned back into the soil; this process returns nutrients to the fields and that means less fertilizer is required the following season.

Fiber hemp differs from cannabis that has been bred for its psychoactive THC content. Marijuana varieties have up to 50 times the THC content of hemp varieties. Good marijuana plants contain around 15% THC, and some skunk varieties contain much higher levels. In contrast, fiber hemp varieties typically contains less than 0.3% THC.

Throughout history, hemp has provided humans with the strongest natural fibers available. Although traditionally used to make ropes and cloth, up until 1883 almost 90% of the world's paper was made from hemp fiber. Hemp paper lasts several times longer than wood pulp papers yet 95% of the world's paper is still made from trees as a direct result of the prohibition of cannabis cultivation. Hemp yields more than four times as much sustainable pulp per acre as timber. Each ton of paper made from hemp saves 12 mature trees and processing hemp uses less acids than processing wood pulp, thereby reducing pollution. Prohibition of cannabis cultivation has led to the destruction of thousands of acres of forests every year, purely to make wood pulp for paper.

If we were to stop using trees for paper production, we would still be destroying our rainforests for timber to be used in the construction industry. The majority of our concrete buildings require formwork to provide molds for the wet concrete, which are traditionally constructed from plywood. Hemp stalks can be chipped and processed into fiberboards that actually perform better than marine-ply and can be reused. In France, a hemp product called Isochanvre has been used as a replacement for concrete in construction and, although one seventh of the weight of concrete, it has greater shock resistance.

Hemp pulp and fiber also offer a biodegradable alternative to plastic for many uses and can be polymerized without the use of petroleum. Advancements and innovation in hemp products and uses are restricted by prohibition. For example, hemp is perfect for the production of biomass fuel that is cleaner than fossil fuels, contains no sulfur, and can provide petroleum and methane that could meet all of our industrial and transportation needs. Cars could quite easily be adapted to run on cannabis fuels. Hemp oils can be used as a replacement for synthetic solvents. Prohibition prevents this and contributes to world pollution.

Hemp seeds were traditionally used to make a high protein seed cake for animal feed. They are more nutritious than Soya and far more digestible, causing less gas production in the gut. Hemp seeds could provide a complete source of vegetable protein for humans. The seeds contain about 30% oil by volume that can be extracted and used in cooking. Prohibition deprives us of a good supply of nutritious vegetable protein that contains high levels of edestin and albumin.

Fabrics made from hemp are stronger, more durable, have higher insulation properties and are more absorbent and longer lasting than cotton. Hemp fiber holds its shape like polyester, but breathes in the same way as expensive man-made materials such as Gortex. It can be spun into a fine silk-like fiber or woven into coarse sacking such as burlap.

This rug has been hand-woven from hemp and will be incredibly durable.

Hemp is one of the most versatile and durable materials we have, and, if used to its full potential, it could drastically reduce the effects of pollution and deforestation on our planet. Despite its potential, however, our elected governments largely prohibit hemp use because people enjoy the marijuana plant's intoxicating effects.

It is a strange world we make for ourselves.

Redd Cross from Genetics Gone Madd helps break up phlegm in the lungs,
making it a great strain for those with cystic fibrosis.

19. Medicinal Cannabis

Truth can never be told so as to be understood,
and not be believed.
William Blake. 1757-1827.

Medical marijuana is still criticized by many, despite its many health benefits and proven effects.

Cannabis was highly valued in ancient medicine and its use can be traced back to the early classical physicians, Discorides and Galen, who reported that it relieved a wide variety of medical disorders. In the famous Chinese pharmacopoeia text The Pen T'sao Kang Mu, written in 100 CE but dating back to the Emperor Shen-Nung (2000 BCE) the compiler Li Shih Chen referred to works from previous authors who for centuries regarded hemp seed as both a food and medicine. Once ripened and mature the cannabis seed contains a rich, translucent oil high in amino and unsaturated fatty acids, which are classified as 90% unsaturated. The seeds typically contain around 30% protein, which is rated as one of the most complete forms of protein available from plants containing albumen, and globulin edestin, which is similar to globulin, found in blood plasma. Globulin is vital in maintaining a healthy immune system. There are 45 essential nutrients that humans cannot manufacture: 21 minerals, 13 vitamins, 8 amino acids and 2 Essential Fatty Acids. No one food source has them all but hemp seed has all eight amino acids and the oil pressed from the hemp seed is one of the best known sources of the two Essential Fatty Acids; Omega 3 AIpha-Linolenic Acid and Omega 6 Liholeic Acid. Today cannabis use is principally recreational, and the medical community remains cautious over its value as a medicine, primarily due to the prohibition argument. Divisions also exist within the medical cannabis lobby, with many protesting that people exploit the campaign with little interest in helping medical users. The medicinal use of cannabis is seen by many as a back door to legalization and attracts individuals with purely commercial interests who see the moral high ground as a good way of promoting themselves or their business interests.

Scientific data within the medical debate is also commonly misrepresented, although both sides are in agreement that cannabis is a powerful drug with differing effects. Dried cannabis plants vary in dosage, depending on the variety and growing conditions, therefore it is difficult to quantify dried and cured cannabis in the same way that regulators oversee other medications. The well-known psychological effects of cannabis use are a sense of well-being or euphoria, increased talkativeness and laughter, alternating with periods of introspective dreaminess, lethargy and sleepiness. Although many medical users consider these as undesirable side effects, mood enhancement, anxiety reduction and mild sedation can be useful for some patients.

Cannabis has no potential for overdose; however, inexperienced or chronic users can experience acute, adverse reactions to large doses. Anxiety and paranoia are the most common; others include panic, agoraphobia, depression, dysphoria, depersonalization, delusions, illusions and hallucinations. The reactions don't last long, yet 17% of surveyed marijuana smokers reported experience of at least one of these symptoms. Cannabis use can also cause rapid heartbeat (tachycardia) in humans, 20 to 100% above normal. The increase in heart rate is highest in the first 20 minutes after smoking then decreases rapidly, depending on dose. In contrast, chronic oral ingestion of cannabis reduces the heart rate in humans. A change in heart rate and blood pressure can present serious problems for some patients, but cannabis has no proven long-term health risks associated with its use and has no serious potential for dependency. However, withdrawal symptoms have been observed. In one study, subjects

MMJars are designed to keep medical marijuana as fresh as possible, so it's ready when you need it.

were given very high doses of oral THC: 180 to 210 mg per day for 10 to 20 days, (equivalent to smoking 9 to 10, 2% THC cigarettes per day). Once cannabis use stopped, the subjects were irritable and suffered mild insomnia, runny nose, sweating and decreased appetite. The withdrawal symptoms lasted for around four days yet there was no associated craving for the drug, unlike cocaine, opiates, alcohol and tobacco. Cannabis users should avoid joints due to the carcinogenic effect tobacco has on the human body. In addition, tobacco smoke contains many other harmful additives including sulfur and ammonia. Those who like to smoke joints should use a cigarette filter instead of a roach and medical users are advised to use vaporizers or cook with it. Disorders that cannabis can alleviate are:

AIDS
The body has no defense against Acquired Immune Deficiency Syndrome because the complex virus attacks the very cells that help to fight disease. Symptoms can include weight loss, fever, exhaustion and swollen glands. Patients suffer infections to their lungs, skin, nervous and digestive systems along with cancerous tumors and cannabis helps to alleviate these symptoms and relieve pain. Some HIV carriers never go on to develop full-blown AIDS — this is helped by a healthy, stress-free lifestyle coupled with a positive mental outlook. Sufferers report a feeling of well-being and contentment from marijuana use.

Gage Green Genetics' Grape Stomper is a fantastic sleep aid for those with insomnia.

Alzheimer's Disease

Sufferers experience a gradual mental degeneration late in life and cannabis has been shown to slow down the rate of deterioration in some patients. It is thought to reduce users' risks of developing the disease.

Arthritis

There are more than 100 different types of arthritis that all involve some disorder of the joints. The two most common are osteo and rheumatoid arthritis, and women are more susceptible than men. Patients suffer pain, swelling and deformation of their hips, knees, spines and hands, muscles are weakened, and tissues, tendons and ligaments become inflamed. Cannabis use eases the pain and discomfort of these attacks and slows the deformation process.

Asthma

Asthma attacks occur when inflammation or muscular spasms cause the bronchial passage of the lungs to contract, making breathing difficult. Other symptoms are coughing, wheezing, increased pulse rate and in some cases the patient will go blue in the face. Mostly the patient is panic stricken and pale. 85% of asthma sufferers can alleviate their symptoms by smoking marijuana.

Dinafem's Moby Dick strain stimulates the appetite, and is fantastic for patients going through chemotherapy or suffering from anorexia.

Cancerous Tumors

These are proliferations of swollen tissue. The use of cannabis can help in the control of many benign and cancerous tumors and alleviate the nausea associated with chemotherapy treatment.

Cystic Fibrosis

This is caused by an inherited genetic disorder that starts when two genes fail to function. Symptoms are disruption of the exocrine glands that affect the pancreas, intestine, bronchial and sweat glands. Breathing and digestion are impaired by mucus. Cannabis is a local analgesic and will relieve symptoms of Cystic Fibrosis.

Dementia

Moderate cannabis use is thought to delay the onset of dementia in elderly patients, but is not recommended for those with cardiovascular problems.

Depression

Cannabis has been successfully used to treat depression and is less habit-forming than antidepressant drugs available for prescription. Cannabis has a euphoric effect on the nervous system.

Northern Light Special from Spliff Seeds is said to help patients suffering from chronic pain.

Emphysema

This is a gradual deterioration of the lungs caused by heavy cigarette smoking and pollution. It occurs when the lungs' tiny air sacs become distended and rupture. This makes the lungs less elastic and inefficient, and as a result the heart has to work harder to pump blood through the system, which leads to heart attacks and heart failure. Symptoms include breathlessness and blue lips. Research has shown that cannabis smoke inhaled into the lungs can relieve the symptoms associated with emphysema as it causes an expansion of the bronchi and bronchioles, leading to higher oxygenation.

Epilepsy

People who have epilepsy suffer from periodic convulsions or fits in which they lose consciousness for either a few seconds or several minutes. The two most common are Grand Mal (or tonic-clonic seizure) and Petit Mal (or absence seizure). Grand Mal usually affects adults who can froth at the mouth, fall and writhe uncontrollably on the ground, and suffer injuries as a result. Petit Mal affects young children and teenagers. They can be so brief that the sufferer is unaware they've had a fit, as they only lose consciousness for a few seconds. In 60% of all epilepsy cases cannabis would have a positive effect on the sufferer. The extract of cannabis has been proven to be more effective than prescription drugs in reducing the frequency of epileptic seizures.

Glaucoma

Cannabis is one of the most effective treatments for glaucoma, an eye disorder caused by an increase of intraocular pressure. This condition can lead to complete loss of sight. Marijuana can help 90% of glaucoma sufferers, as its effect on intraocular pressure is three times as high as prescription drugs, without any of the side effects.

Herpes

This is caused by the cold sore virus. Once contracted it lives in the central nervous system and attacks the genital regions of both men and women. There is no cure for herpes and patients will continue to suffer attacks for life, however the severity diminishes with time. THC has been proven to kill the herpes virus when it comes into contact with it. This is not a cure but sufferers report reduced recurrences of attacks when using marijuana. A topical application of THC can reduce the healing time for herpes blisters.

High Blood Pressure

Blood pressure affects the rate at which the heart has to work. Abnormally high blood pressure is known as hypertension and usually affects middle-aged men. Cannabis extends the arteries and causes a reduction in pressure.

Insomnia

This is the chronic inability to sleep and can range from occasional nights of sleeplessness to regular, prolonged periods. Sufferers have found that cannabis ingested an hour before sleep has a less stupefying effect than prescription drugs, gives the user a better quality of sleep and has no hangover, residual drowsiness or potential for dependency.

Low Libido

Cannabis is a natural aphrodisiac and while it has no proven effect on male impotence it can greatly assist patients who are suffering from low libido.

Migraines

This is one of the most common ailments of the nervous system that causes recurrent headaches and other symptoms such as numbness or weakness in one side of the body. The first sign of an attack can be visual disturbance, such as bright spots or jagged lines before the eyes followed by a severe one-sided headache. Migraines stem from a convulsive narrowing of the arteries. The consumption of marijuana eases attacks by reversing this effect.

Multiple Sclerosis

This is a disorder that results from damage to the nerve fibers in the central nervous system. Like electric wire with no insulation, affected fibers cannot function properly. Symptoms can vary from a lack of coordination to slurred speech and incontinence. The muscular spasms and twitches associated with multiple sclerosis can be significantly reduced through cannabis use.

Muscular Cramping

Cannabis when smoked or used in a topical ointment is one of the best morphine-free antispasmodics available.

Nausea

Cannabis can be used to treat nausea, especially with patients who are undergoing chemotherapy treatments. It also acts as an appetizer stimulant with patients who don't have an interest in food; this is helpful in treating patients with eating disorders as well as those with pancreatic and intestinal problems.

Pain

After nausea and vomiting, chronic pain is the condition cited most as a medicinal use for marijuana. Research has shown cannabinoids to be beneficial in the control of pain. Cannabinoids can be used alone or combined with opiates.

Using a variety of different strains can be a great idea for medicinal patients.

Taleggio from AlphaKronik Genes can help IBS, Crohn's Disease, lupus and muscular dystrophy.

Post Traumatic Stress Disorder

Cannabis can be used in the treatment of traumatic stress sufferers who report benefits from using it to treat psychological symptoms such as depression, anger and rage. Cannabis has a euphoric effect on the body and has no hangover or potential for dependency as with some prescription drugs.

Schizophrenia

In a recent study, schizophrenic patients were found to prefer marijuana to other available drugs, including alcohol and cocaine, which were found to be used less frequently than average. The reasons for this are unknown, but schizophrenics may be able to obtain some relief from moderate marijuana use. People with schizophrenia are more likely to suffer adverse psychiatric effects from chronic cannabis use.

Tourette Syndrome

In extreme cases this psychiatric disorder causes uncontrollable spitting, shouting and swearing. It is very distressing for sufferers, who are otherwise perfectly normal. Researchers have discovered that cannabis use reduces the compulsion to behave in socially inappropriate ways.

Cannabis has grown wild in the mountains of several countries for thousands of years.

20. Cannabis History, Religion, and Prohibition

> To see what is right and not to do it is want of courage.
> *Confucius.*

Cannabis is by far the most widely used illegal drug in the world. Several million people have tried it at least once: even former U.S. president Bill Clinton admitted to trying cannabis once or twice while studying in England, but claimed he didn't like it and did not inhale. Arnorld Schwarzenegger, the governor of California, is more forthright about his cannabis use and claims he did inhale. Cannabis use causes no lasting physical or psychological damage and there is no evidence to suggest that it leads to experimentation with other drugs. However, there is some recent evidence of mild physical dependence in "frequent chronic users."

The anthropologist Weston La Barre speculates that cannabis use reaches as far back as the Mesolithic (Middle Stone Age) period when apart from being a source of food and fiber, it was also used as part of a religio-shamanic complex. Nearly two pounds of green cannabis plant material was discovered in a 2,700-year-old grave excavated at the Yanghai Tombs near Turpan, China. It was found lightly pounded in a wooden bowl contained within a leather basket near the head of a blue-eyed Caucasian man who had died when he was around 45 years of age. Professor Ethan Russo stated that the individual was buried with an unusual number of high-value, rare items, which included a make-up bag, bridles, pots, archery equipment and a kongou harp. He is believed to have been a shaman from the Gushi people, who spoke a now-extinct language called Tocharian that was similar to Celtic. Cannabis, throughout recorded history, has obviously played an important cultural, industrial, religious and medical role. Presented here is a brief glimpse into the history of the cannabis plant as a social, industrial, recreational, and medical phenomenon.

Historic Cannabis

The Scythians
The oldest saddle ever found was of Scythian origin, and was made from hemp

This Asian landrace plant is a great example of the plants that grow wild in that region.

fiber. Their skilled horsemanship allowed them to travel long distances and in so doing they spread their knowledge of cannabis throughout the ancient world, and they are documented as having settled extensively throughout Europe, the Mediterranean, Central Asia, and what is now Russia. The Scythians also provide us with some of the earliest evidence of people using hemp smoke as a psychoactive stimulant; various pipes and hemp residue have been unearthed in their tombs, and Greek historian Herodotus wrote describing Scythian funeral rites:

They make a booth by fixing in the ground three sticks inclined towards one another and stretching around them woollen felts, which they arrange so as to fit as close as possible: inside the booth a dish is placed upon the ground, into which they put a number of red-hot stones, and then add some hemp seed.

Ancient China

The earliest written record of hemp usage comes from the oldest known Neolithic cultures in China, the Yang-Shao and the Ta-Wen-Kou, which appeared along the Yellow River valley about 6,500 years ago. In the early classics of the Chou dynasty, written over 3000 years ago, mention is made of a prehistoric culture based on fishing and hunting, a culture without written language but which kept records by tying knots in hemp cord. Hemp was used extensively by these early peoples for cloth, cordage, ropes, twine, bowstrings, fish netting, medicine, and its seeds were a valuable food source.

Hemp paper is said to have been invented in China around 105 CE during the Han Dynasty and the reign of Emperor Ho-Ti, and they kept the discovery a guarded secret until the ninth century CE when the Arabs learned the process and its use spread. Hemp paper was lightweight, durable and, above all, cheap to produce, and to this day hemp paper is far superior to any other.

Ancient Japan

Hemp was used in Ancient Japan for driving away evil spirits and traditional purification rites. Shinto priests used a Gohei that was a short staff with hemp fibers on one end. Believing that evil and purity cannot co-exist, the priest waves the Gohei, symbolizing purity, above a person's head to drive the evil spirit away. Hemp was worn during formal and religious ceremonies because of its traditional connotation with purity; however, as in China, hemp did not become popular as a recreational drug.

The Ancient Greeks and Romans

Whilst the Greeks and Romans may not generally have taken cannabis for intoxication purposes, there are indications that they were aware of the psychoactive effects of the drug. Pliny the Elder at the time of his death in 79 CE left behind 160 manuscripts that included his work entitled Natural History, which accounted tales of fauna and wildlife from around the empire. Pliny had very little to record about cannabis, but he noted:

The fibers of the plant, made superb rope. Juice extracted from the cannabis seed was used for extracting worms from the ears, or any insect that may have entered them. While the seeds render men impotent, they were beneficial in alleviating gout and similar maladies.

The Roman Empire consumed huge quantities of hemp fiber much of which was imported from the Babylonian city of Sura. Cannabis was not a major crop in early Italy but the seed was a common food. Emperor Nero's surgeon, Dioscorides, a Greek physician who traveled with the Roman army, famously praised cannabis for making the stoutest cords and for its medicinal properties. There is evidence that by the 2nd century BCE Romans were cultivating hemp around Palestine and Mesopotamia and as the Roman empire expanded so did its hemp production. Hemp was also being grown in Southern Greece at around the same time.

Ancient Egypt

Traces of cannabis have been detected in Egyptian mummies and pollen found on the mummy of Ramses II has been identified as originating from the hemp plant. Fragments of hemp fiber were discovered in the tomb of Amenhotep IV and the ancient Egyptian word for hemp also occurs in the Pyramid Texts, in connection with rope making.

Ancient India

Cannabis assumes an important role within a religious context in India, where it plays an important part in both meditation and rituals. Legend has it that the first cannabis plant sprouted in the Himalayas and the plant is of great significance in Tibet Region of China. Cannabis was actually introduced into Jamaica by Asian Indian workers migrating to farm the sugar plantations after the abolition of slaveryand Jamaicans still use the Indian name for cannabis: ganja.

A South Indian strain from Autofem Seeds.

Kandahar is a classic Afghani strain, and one that has become much respected in the cannabis world.

The Vikings

The Vikings were a fierce seafaring race originating from Norway, Sweden and Denmark who traded extensively with Byzantium, Persia and India. In the ninth century, there were active trade routes both eastwards through Russia and westwards along the European coasts and waterways. The Vikings were also ruthless raiders and pirates. They raided the coasts, rivers and inland cities of Western Europe as far as Seville, which was attacked by the Norse in 844 CE.

Archeological Viking remains were discovered in a large Norwegian burial mound at the Oseberg farm near Tønsberg. The burial contained a large Viking ship and the remains of two female skeletons dating from 834 CE. The scale of the site suggests that this was a burial of very high status. Numerous grave goods were recovered including a piece of hemp cloth that is thought to have been part of a sail. Four hemp seeds were discovered, one contained in a small leather pouch. It is believed these seeds played a symbolic role, and the small number used would perhaps indicate their value to the Viking people.

South, Central and North America

Cannabis is said to have been introduced into South America in 1545 by the Spanish and some believe the Mexican word marijuana is of Christian origin, Maria (Mary) and Juan (John) being the names of Jesus' mother and disciple. Although the British had introduced hemp to the newly established Jacobean colonies of Virginia by 1611, they called male cannabis plants Carl and females Fimble hemp. The word "marijuana" was adopted by Americans in the 1900s when they were introduced to new drug varieties by migrating Mexican laborers in the South West.

Medieval Europe

Cannabis was readily available in 16th and 17th century Europe. Shakespeare wrote of "Invention in a noted weed" (Sonnet 76). His sonnets are full of riddles, but include references to the effect of substances distilled from flowers: But flowers are distilled, though they with winter meet, leese but their show; their substance still lives sweet. (Sonnet 5). Traces of cannabis have been discovered in Elizabethan clay pipes and there is a high probability that William Shakespeare had experience of cannabis use.

Traditional European folk remedies list cannabis as a tonic, antispasmodic, analgesic, sedative and anodyne, seeds were given to teething infants and preparations of the plant were used to treat conditions ranging from snake bites to gonorrhea. The 11th century Anglo-Saxon Herbarium specifically rec-

Autofem's Macho Mexicano is a fantastic strain from Mexico used as breeding stock for many great strains.

ommends haenep (old English for hemp) in the treatment of breast pain, and by 1588 Tudor herbalists in England grew 85% of their own drug plants, listing 'water of hempe' as a treatment for fevers in The Vertuous Boke of Distillacioun (Andrewes).

Medieval Arabic Medicine

Medieval Arab doctors considered cannabis a useful medicine, calling it Kannab, and approved of its use for medicinal and therapeutic purposes. In the 14th century the Islamic scholar Az-Zarkashi spoke of "the permissibility of its use for medical purposes if it is established that it is beneficial." It has served as a medicine in the Arab world for at least six thousand years. Rhazes, a skilled 9th century Islamic physician, prescribed it widely for ailments ranging from coughs to skin complaints. The earlier physicians, Hippocrates, Dioscorides and Galen, all used medicinal preparations of cannabis and their text books had been translated by Arab scholars. This knowledge was passed to the Islamic world and cannabis was seen as an important part of the physician's apothecary.

Autofem's Sativa Ecuatorial grows well in the hottest regions of the world.

Cannabis and Religion

Ancient Egypt

Cannabis was an ingredient in the ancient incense and perfume of the Pharaohs, known as kyphi, which was used as an offering to the Gods. As the sun set worshippers would burn this fragrant preparation as an offering to the Sun God, Ra (who created cannabis) praying for his return the following morning. The God Ra was later merged with the god Amun to become Amun-Ra (Amen-Ra) and to this day Christian prayer is ended with 'Amen.'

Judeo-Christianity

Sula Benet, an etymologist from the Institute of Anthropological Sciences in Warsaw, Poland, established the first evidence of the Hebrew use of cannabis in 1936. The word cannabis was thought to be of Scythian origin, but Benet demonstrated that it has a much earlier origin and appears several times throughout the Old Testament. In 1980, the Hebrew University in Israel confirmed the interpretation of kaneh-bosm as cannabis. As with the Ancient Egyptians, cannabis incense was assigned magical powers by the Israelites who burned it in golden bowls placed at the altar and in hand-held censers.

Religions of India

There are four books of the Vedas, the four seminal books of the Hindu faith that were written in Vedic, an early form of Sanskrit around 1100 BCE. According to the Vedas, the Lord Shiva brought cannabis down from the Himalayas for the pleasure of humankind. The gods had stirred the oceans from Mount Mandara (thought to be Everest) and a drop of celestial nectar or amrita fell on the Earth. From this drop was created the first hemp plant and it was named sacred grass or indracanna (food of the gods).

In Hindu mythology, amrita means immortality and early legend maintains that the angel of humankind lived in the leaves of the cannabis plant. It is said that when evil spirits tried to possess the plant the Gods vanquished them and cannabis acquired the name vijaya, meaning victory. According to the fourth book of the Vedas, the Atharva Veda, cannabis is one of the five sacred plants that also includes Holy basil, the most sacred of plants, and san dalwood that is used in incense and the paste applied as a dot on the forehead between the eyes. The Vedas state that through cannabis use one can commune with Shiva, known in Hindu scripture as the destroyer of the world, following Brahma the creator and Vishnu the preserver. After Shiva destroys the world, Brahma once again recreates it in a never-ending cycle of death and rebirth.

Ethiopian Zion Coptic Church

The Ethiopian Zion Coptic Church is a contemporary Jamaican religious movement which considers cannabis sacred and for the communion of saints, the forgiveness of sins and for the resurrection of humankind. Their teachings follow those of the Bible. Interestingly, some church elders claim their beliefs traveled with slaves from Africa to the Caribbean, denying the Hindu influence as being so profound.

This is swazi hand-rolled charas, a type of hand-rolled hash popular in several parts of the world, especially with the members at weed.co.za.

Rastafarianism

The Rastafarian movement is another contemporary religious group that accepts Jesus Christ and Haile Selassie I, the former Emperor of Ethiopia, as incarnations of Jah (God). Haile Selassie is seen as the returned messiah. Other aspects of Rastafarianism include the spiritual use of cannabis, a rejection of western society, which they call Babylon, pride in their African heritage and belief in the words of modern day activists such as Marcus Garvey who is considered a prophet. Like the Zion Coptic Church, many Rastas profess that the cannabis plant was brought to the Caribbean from Africa with the first slaves years prior to any Indian influence.

Cannabis is known as: Healing of the nation; Iley; Ganja; Lambs Bread or Herb to the Rastafarians and its use is primarily considered a spiritual act to accompany Bible study and an integral part of 'reasoning sessions.' They see cannabis as allowing the user to discover truth within the scriptures and it is believed to burn corruption from a believer's heart. It is seen as a sacrament that cleanses both body and mind, intensifies consciousness, gives pleasure and peacefulness and brings users closer to Jah. Many believers see the illegality of cannabis as evidence of the persecution of Rastafarians. They reason that cannabis is a substance that opens people's minds to the truth, which they believe Babylon clearly does not want.

Sensi Seeds' Jamaican Pearl is a great example of Caribbean genetics.

Different climates bring out some beautiful colorings, as seen in Himalaya Blue Diesel from Short Stuff Seeds.

Roman Catholicism

The Roman Catholic Church has regularly campaigned against cannabis use with publications and Papal edicts claiming that it leads to criminality and violence. There is unsurprisingly a serious conflict between the Papal edicts released to prohibit cannabis use and the undeniable role cannabis played in early Christian worship. The Roman Catholic Church makes no distinction between cannabis and other narcotics, yet symbolically uses a known addictive substance like alcohol (wine) in its religious rituals.

Sufis

In contrast to mainstream Islamic beliefs, a group of Muslims maintained the Old Testament's shamanic heritage and were called Sufis. They had a mystical approach to worship and believed enlightenment came through a state of altered consciousness. To the Sufis hashish was a sacred portal through which they could communicate with the divine prophet 'Khizr.' According to legend, Haydar, the founder of Sufism, discovered the hemp plant in the Persian mountains. Amazed at how the plant lifted his spirit he sent his disciples back to collect it and it became an integral part of Sufi worship. Other versions of the story replace the Persian mountains with the desert.

Throughout history, cannabis has been associated with dissenters and undesirables by the conformist mainstream within certain societies, and orthodox Muslims openly despised the Sufis.

The experts at Russia's Original Seeds strive to document every aspect of landrace cannabis strains. Here we see them measuring seeds from a landrace plant from the Himachal Pradesh region of Northern India.

Cannabis Prohibition

In the United States, the city of El Paso's governing council calculated that marijuana prohibition would be a convenient way of controlling the unpopular Mexicans who came there to work. So, in 1914 they passed the 'El Paso Ordinance Act of 1914,' banning cannabis in the state. The new marijuana laws gave police added power to arrest and harass migrant workers and to this day arrests for marijuana offences are more likely to occur on non-white racial groups.

Cannabis was also arriving in American port cities, transported by West Indian sailors who called it ganja. In New Orleans it became known as muggles, tea or reefer in the popular jazz clubs where it was consumed. However, its use was once again associated with unpopular ethnic minorities and became a focal point for racist politicians. Marijuana's migration North was inevitable and prompted the formation of the Federal Narcotics Bureau headed by the right wing, evangelical extremist Harry J. Anslinger, who began an orchestrated campaign of propaganda and misinformation regarding cannabis use and its effects. The newspapers ran sensational headlines with graphic accounts of violent crime, madness and murder caused by reefer use. Anslinger himself gave press and radio interviews:

...Parents beware! Your children, homeward bound from school, are being introduced to a new danger in the form of the drug cigarette, "marijuana." A Chicago woman, watching her daughter die as an indirect result of smoking marijuana told officers at least fifty of the girl's young friends were slaves to this narcotic...

Anslinger's tireless campaign against cannabis use continued unabated and on June 14th 1937 the Marijuana Tax Act was passed in the United States, effectively making cannabis illegal. Anslinger's behavior was both bizarre and sinister, and when scientists began to dispute his claims regarding the effects of cannabis use and presented him with the evidence from various trials, he destroyed the documents and discredited the experts. By 1961 Anslinger had gained sufficient power and influence to insist the United Nations follow American drug policies and 100 member states were coerced into signing an agreement virtually outlawing cannabis worldwide. It remains illegal in most countries to this day; however, prohibition has little to do with any concerns

As probition continues on, documenting our knowledge of this plant becomes more and more vital.

This strain from weed.co.za is growing well outdoors in Africa.

for the cannabis users' health. Contradicting Anslinger, a United Kingdom House of Lords committee concluded:

The acute toxicity of cannabis and the cannabinoids is very low: no one has ever died as a direct and immediate cons equence of medical or recreational use.

The absurdity of the prohibition of cannabis is best demonstrated in the Netherlands. Although possession of marijuana for personal use is permitted and it is possible to purchase small amounts from licensed coffee shops, in one 12-month period, 92,145 pounds of hashish were seized by the Amsterdam police and destroyed. Dutch law as it stands both encourages the smuggling of marijuana to supply the coffee shops and wastes police resources in attempting to stop it. Despite decriminalization it is estimated that there are only between 220,000 and 400,000 regular cannabis users in Holland.

Prisons worldwide are full of people serving sentences for cannabis-related offences. The resources spent by our respective governments for marijuana policing policies are huge and ultimately it is the taxpayers that fund them. This ancient plant has benefited humankind throughout history yet the campaign to legalize its use is still met with furious opposition from politicians and law enforcement agencies alike.

The same ignorance and prejudice is repeated time and again. On my last prison sentence for producing cannabis, I was made to complete three separate courses designed to address my offending behavior, as I refused to accept that there were any victims in my case. The prison officials continually blocked my attempts to be moved to a lower security prison until I had completed the courses. I heard the same flawed arguments over and over again, from people who I am sure were well intentioned, but just stupid. I still maintain that the only victims of my cannabis production were the skunk connoisseurs of London, who lost one of their best suppliers when I was imprisoned.

There are thousands of medical marijuana users throughout the world who have found that cannabis relieves disorders ranging from asthma to cancerous tumors. It is a disgrace that most of these people are denied relief because of unjust and repressive laws. People are still being jailed for growing cannabis plants in the 21st century.

POTTED HISTORY

2700 B.C. First instance of cannabis use is recorded.

1500 B.C. Scythians cultivate cannabis and use it to weave fine hemp cloth.

1200 - 800 B.C. Cannabis is mentioned in the Hindu sacred text Atharvaveda.

700 - 300 B.C. Scythian tribes leave cannabis seeds as offerings.

It's difficult to believe that there is such a fuss over such an organic plant.

500 B.C. Hemp is introduced into Northern Europe by the Scythians.

500 - 100 B.C. Hemp spreads throughout northern Europe.

430 B.C. Herodotus reports on use of cannabis.

100 B.C. - 0 Cannabis is mentioned in the herbal Pen Tsíao Ching.

400 A.D. Cannabis is cultivated in England for the first time in East Anglia at a place called Old Buckenham Mere.

500 - 600 A.D. The Jewish Talmud mentions Cannabis.

1231 Hashish introduced to Iraq.

1271 - 1295 Journeys of Marco Polo in which he reports using hashish.

1378 Turkish Ottoman Emir Soudoun Scheikhouni issues first edict against hashish.

1494. Hemp paper-making begins in England.

1563 Queen Elizabeth I, passes a law requiring all landowners with over 60 acres to grow cannabis crops or face a £5 fine.

1776 United States declaration of independence is drafted on cannabis paper.

1798 Napoleon declares a total prohibition among soldiers returning to France.

1842 Queen Victoria's personal physician prescribes cannabis for her menstrual cramps claiming it to be "one of the most valuable medicines we possess."

1843 Le Club des Hachichins, or Hashish Eater's Club, established in Paris.

1850 Hashish appears in Greece.

1856 British tax ganja and charas trade in India.

1875 Cultivation for hashish introduced to Greece.

1877 Kerr reports on Indian ganja and charas trade.

1884 The British Raj in India conduct one of the first studies into cannabis use and conclude it is harmless and helpful.

1893-1894 155,000 to 177,000 lbs of hashish legally imported into India from Central Asia each year.

1901 A Royal commission concludes that cannabis is relatively harmless and not worth prohibiting

1912 Cannabis control is raised at the first International Opium Conference.

1915 Cannabis begins to be prohibited for non-medical use in the US. In California (1915), Texas (1919), Louisiana (1924), and New York (1927).

1928 Cannabis is made illegal in Britain following the passing of the dangerous drugs act 1925.

Isn't it crazy that a simple plant like this beauty from Project Skunkenstein can cause so much fuss?

21. Questions & Answers

The scientist is not a person who gives the right answers,
he is one who asks the right questions.
Claude Lévi-Strauss. 1908-2009.

The Cannabis Plant

What are the differences between Cannabis indica and Cannabis sativa strains?
Cannabis sativa is an herbaceous annual, meaning that it is an herb-like flowering plant that completes its life cycle in one season and develops seeds to propagate the next generation. It grows from 3 to 9 feet high with a sturdy erect branched stem. The leaves are alternate or opposite, on long stalks (petioles), with linear serrated leaves tapering to a point. The flowers form in clusters. The seeds are rounding, ovate and slightly flattened. The plant is thought to originate from Central Asia but is naturalized in North America, Brazil, and Europe.

Although the botanical classification of cannabis is Cannabis sativa, there are actually three distinct varieties of cannabis grown for their psychoactive properties. These are:

- Cannabis sativa
- Cannabis indica
- Cannabis ruderalis

Cannabis sativa plants are characterized by long, thin leaves and loose flower clusters. These plants originate from equatorial regions where the growing season has relatively even photoperiods, resulting in day and night cycles that are almost the same length year round. This means sativa varieties from these equatorial regions can complete their vegetative growth stage under a 12-hour light regime. The flowering is only triggered in the plant after it has thoroughly completed vegetative growth. However, this is impractical for indoor growers as growth is slower than under an 18-hour-day period and flower induction takes longer. Equatorial Cannabis sativa plants evolved in regions

Auto Blue Kush from Autofem seeds is a great autoflowering indica-dominant strain.

where the growing season is much hotter than Central Asian regions and as a consequence these plants are not as resistant to mold attacks. The buds of the Cannabis sativa plants give the user more of a high than those of indica strains.

Cannabis indica plants are characterized by broad maple-like leaves and tight bud formations. These plants originate from northern India and the area formally known as Persia. The growing conditions in the mountainous regions of Asia can be demanding for vegetation and Cannabis indica plants have evolved into a hardy variety that matures early and generally shows moderate resistance to mold. Mature plants yield heavy resinous flowers and are ideal for indoor cultivation due to their shorter size and high THC production. The buds of a Cannabis indica plant tend to have a more sedative effect on the user.

Cannabis ruderalis is a variety native to Eastern Europe and Russia. Its cold and harsh growing environment has produced a tough, hardy plant characterized by early flowering. Cannabis ruderalis plants tend to yield less than sativa or indica varieties. However, when hybridized with indica they produce a tough, mold-resisitant, and early flowering outdoor plant.

Hybrid varieties have been developed that combine the best traits of all three varieties and are readily available for cultivators to choose from.

This plant is in the vegetative stage and is exhibiting very healthy growth.

How long is the cannabis growth cycle?

Cannabis is photosensitive and produces a hormone called phytochrome that enables it to measure the amount of daylight the plant is receiving. During a natural growing season outdoors, plants receive longer periods of daylight during the spring and summer months and shorter periods during the end of the season. As cannabis is an annual (meaning that it completes its life cycle in one season) it knows as daylight decreases it needs to prepare seeds for the next generation. Consequently, flowering is triggered when the cannabis plants measure light levels of 12 hours or less. In a natural outdoor growing cycle plants will germinate in spring and die back as winter approaches. However, indoor cultivators can manipulate the plant growth cycle by controlling the day lengths within the grow room. Flowering can be induced after as little as 2 weeks' vegetative growth, and interestingly, there is no difference in potency between a young plant that has been forced into flower and a mature plant that has completed a natural vegetative growth cycle. The younger, smaller plant will, however, yield less.

Cannabis plants that have flowered do not necessarily have to die and can be regenerated by cutting the plant back hard and placing it back into a vegetative light regime of between 18 and 24 hours. The plant will assume that it has survived the winter and begin vegetative growth again. Plants can be regenerated several times with no significant loss of yield or potency.

What is the difference between annual and perennial plants?
An annual plant is one that germinates, grows, reproduces and dies within a year. Perennial plants return year after year, growing in size and stature until they reach their full maturity. Although they have a longer life span, many perennials lose their vigor after 3 or 4 years. Although cannabis is an annual it can be made to exhibit perennial traits by careful manipulation of the light cycle.

Which varieties are best suited for indoor cultivation?
Pure Cannabis sativa varieties grow too tall for successful indoor cultivation. Although pruning can reduce the size and shape, pure Cannabis sativa strains are better suited for outdoor cultivation. Pure strains of both Cannabis indica and Cannabis ruderalis are ideal for indoor cultivation and favored by many growers. There are hybrid plants available that combine the traits of all three varieties, and providing there is a good balance between Cannabis sativa and the other two varieties, these sativas can make a useful addition to indoor plant genetics. If you have access to the Internet you can research the characteristics of the different strains available and select the one most suited to your requirements.

The genetic history of plants and their growing patterns dictate whether they are best grown indoors or outdoors. This Critical Mass from Mr. Nice is enjoying this outdoor grow!

As this Biddy's Sister plant from Magus Genetics shows, the extra room given the plants when growing outside can be well worth it!

Is it better to grow indoors or outdoors?

Indoor growing is the only way to ensure consistent year-round crops that can easily be forced into flower at a few weeks old. Although outdoor crops can be forced into flower by covering them to reduce the daylight hours, this is often impractical with large numbers of plants, making growers dependent upon the natural growth cycle, which will only allow one crop per season. There are also security implications to be considered when growing outdoors. Cannabis is illegal and law enforcement agencies, bandits, and herbaceous mammals alike will target your plants. Although there are also security risks when growing indoors, these can be minimized. Indoor growers are also not at the mercy of the elements. Many outdoor crops are lost due to adverse weather conditions, particularly heavy precipitation at harvest time. On the other hand, if you do have a suitable area in which to grow a successful outdoor crop you will be rewarded with large plants that will yield significantly more than indoor plants.

What is the difference between male and female cannabis plants?

Only the female cannabis plant produces buds and any significant quantities of psychoactive material (THC). Cannabis is dioecious, which means that plants

When it comes to sexing your plants, look for preflowers like these ones on a Diesel male.

are either male or female. In order to determine the sex of individual plants you will need to induce flowering. Either the whole plant must be flowered or cuttings must be taken and flowered separately. Female flowers are identified by small pairs of tiny white hairs extending from the top of the calyx. These are known as pistils and their function is to catch pollen and channel it into the ovule for fertilization. Sexual reproduction is carried out by the female flower in the ovaries at the base of the pistils. These ovaries contain female germ cells. Male plants develop small clusters of white flowers that release pollen before dropping from the plant. Male plants can be identified by clusters of tiny green balls, which will eventually develop into flowers.

Genetically unstable hermaphrodite plants do occur. These plants will have both male and female characteristics and can self-fertilize. If you have a plant displaying both sex traits it is likely to be a hermaphrodite plant and should be removed from your crop immediately.

How do I ensure an all-female crop?
The most commonly used technique to ensure an all-female crop is to take

cuttings or clones from a known female that has been positively identified by the flowering of a test cutting. The offspring from this female will be an exact genetic copy of the mother plant. Plants grown from seed can be allowed to develop for a few weeks and then placed into flower under a 12-hour light regime. Once the seedlings have indicated gender they can be reverted to a vegetative state and grown on.

What are feminized seeds?

Feminized seeds are available from specialized breeders and have either been treated or bred to produce all-female crops from seed without the need to grow mother plants and take clones. In my experience some of these plants will develop into hermaphrodites. Having said that, feminized seeds will cut down on the time required to start your crop, as you don't need to grow and identify your mother plants. Many growers start a feminized crop while growing on their mother plants and then revert to cuttings once the mothers have been identified.

What are the most common mistakes made by novice growers?

One of the most common mistakes made by novice growers is overwatering. You should only water your plants when the top two inches of compost becomes dry to the touch. For organic growers this is usually twice a week. For hydroponic growers using a system such as flood and drain you will need to water with nutrient solution at least twice a day. Start your fertilizing with a solution diluted at 25% of the manufacturer's recommended strength and work your way up to full strength as the plant develops. If your organic plants show any signs of overfertilization leach the medium with fresh water and cut back on your fertilizing. As a precaution, leach the plants with pure water every 2 to 4 weeks.

Is it possible to grow bonsai cannabis plants?

Bonsai is the Japanese art of growing and maintaining miniature trees. Although this may include hardwood perennials, cannabis is a soft-wooded annual. This makes it difficult to create a bonsai tree in the true sense of the word. However, bonsai types can be produced from cannabis plants. To bonsai a cannabis plant you simply restrict development of the plant in a vegetative growth cycle by trimming roots and leaf growth until the required effect is achieved. The plant can then be flowered under a 12-hour light regime or used as a mother plant.

Getting Started

Where can I get seeds?
Don't use seeds collected from imported marijuana that you may have purchased from dealers. These tend to be unviable and are of indeterminate breeding. The best place to buy viable seeds is online from the many reputable dealers who specialize in cannabis seeds. These are generally sold in bags of ten and delivered by regular mail. Obviously there are security implications to consider so never have seeds sent to your home address. Instead, arrange to have them delivered to someone trustworthy who is not involved in growing.

How long do seeds remain viable?
If seeds are stored in cool and dry conditions they will have a shelf life of about five years. It is possible to seal and freeze them, extending their life for up to ten years, but the germination ratio will be compromised.

What is the best way to germinate my seeds?
There are several ways to germinate seeds. The simplest method is to place seeds into small pots containing either compost or hydroponic medium and water

There are many seed companies and distributors online, but be sure to research each one before you choose to buy from them.

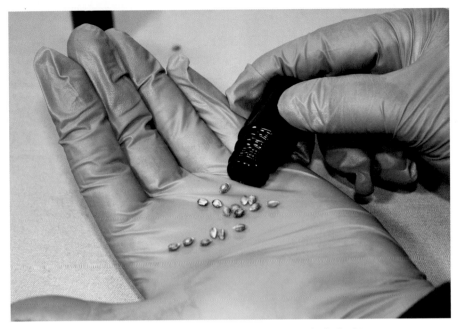

Store these safely before you plan to germinate - MMJars are made specifically for this purpose.

them. Plant seeds just below the surface ensuring that they are lightly covered. It is not necessary to place them in a dark area. Keep them moist and subject them to at least 18 hours of uninterrupted daylight at around 80°F. Some growers like to soak the seeds in a jar of water, which can be effective. Place the jar in a warm dark place and check the seeds regularly, and as soon as they begin to sprout remove them from the jar and place into your chosen medium.

Why are my seedlings stretching?
This is generally due to insufficient light levels; the seedlings are stretching to reach the light. Plants will also stretch when subjected to conditions of high humidity so ensure humidity remains at an even 50%.

What problems could I encounter in germinating seeds?
Ensure that all equipment used is clean and sterile as seedlings are susceptible to a fungal infection called damping off. This fungal disease attacks young seedlings and clones causing stem rot at the base. Overwatering is one of the main causes of damping off. Providing you maintain an optimum growing environment for your seedlings, you should find they develop without too many problems. Cannabis is a hardy plant.

What is the best method for obtaining clones?

Choose a vigorous mother plant that has been positively identified as a female by the flowering of a test cutting. Select a healthy lower branch and remove this from the mother using a sharp blade or sterilized scissors. Scissors can pinch the plant tissue as you cut but this doesn't seem to affect the strike rate of cuttings. Dip the cutting into a rooting gel and place it into your chosen medium. As the cutting has no roots you will need to keep her in a humid environment and this is best achieved using a propagator. The cuttings should be misted with a spray mister during the early stages of development. Your cutting should root within two weeks, after which it can be treated as a young plant. Some growers simply place the fresh cutting into a jar of water and this is called water cloning, but in my experience fewer cuttings strike with this method.

Keeping a mother plant will give you a constant supply of clones. You can also be sure of their quality this way.

Scarring the cut site of your clones can increase strike rate. Be sure to use rooting powder or gel as well.

What is scarification and how does it improve the strike rate of cuttings?
The stem of your fresh cutting can be scarified to increase the surface area available for root development and thereby increase your clone's strike rate. Take a sharp razor blade and cut your clone at a 45° angle to expose more of the stem. Next, using the edge of your razor blade gently scrape the surface tissue of the stem starting at the 45° cut and going up one inch of the stem. Do this until you can clearly see the internal tissue layers. This process will give your young clones a greater advantage during rooting.

Does the moon effect the germination of cannabis?
Planting according to the phases of the moon is a tradition that goes back centuries; it also has a basis in scientific fact. The moon has four phases or quarters that last seven days each. The first two quarters are during the waxing (increasing light), between the new and the full moon. The third and fourth quarters are after the full moon, when the light is waning (decreasing light). The earth is in a large gravitational field, influenced by both the sun and moon. The ocean tides are highest at the time of the new and the full moon, when the sun and moon are aligned with the earth. In the same way that the moon pulls the tides, it also pulls water in the soil, causing moisture to rise and encouraging plant

germination and growth. The highest amount of moisture is available at the time of the full moon and seed germination is improved, producing stronger, more vigorous plants. Cannabis seeds will germinate at any time of the year providing you supply them with the correct environmental conditions, but a growing number of cultivators will only start their seeds at this time of the month, especially those growing organically.

Which is better, hydro or organic cultivation?
For novice growers, organic cultivation using compost mixes is far more forgiving and requires far less equipment to set up. Hydroponic growing does ensure your plants receive optimum nutrition levels but it won't make your buds any more potent than compost mixes. Hydro should only be attempted after you have had a few successful compost crops. There is now a growing movement

These plants are growing in relatively small pots in a hydro system but will be fantastic yielders.

against hydroponic cannabis buds as there is some question as to whether all of the chemicals used in nutrient feeds are totally removed from plant tissue once dried. As cannabis is uniquely smoked there could be health implications caused by smoking this residue.

Nutrients can help to make sure your plants have all they need for optimal growth.

What is the best pot size for indoor cultivation?

Square plastic pots of 6 inches depth and width are ideal for most indoor crops. Square pots allow you to pack the plants closely together during the early stages of development. Some organic growers like to use bigger pots indoors and any pot designed for tomato cultivation can be utilized. If space is at a premium then start young plants in smaller containers and pot on as they develop.

Can I plant seeds directly into the soil outdoors?

Seeds can be planted directly into the soil outdoors but this is both wasteful and inefficient. It is far better to start seedlings in a compost mix indoors. Once they have developed into healthy young plants they can be transplanted to the outdoor grow area. As we have seen, many growers like to sex their seedlings by forcing them into flower and then reverting them to vegetative growth once gender has been identified to ensure an all female crop, and this is best done indoors.

What does N-P-K mean on fertilizers?

N-P-K refers to the nitrogen, phosphorous, and potassium levels contained in the fertilizer. These are commonly referred to as the major elements, along with calcium, magnesium, and sulfur. They are the major causative compounds in plant growth. A fertilizer labeled 30-10-10 should have nitrogen content of 30%, phosphorous content of 10%, and potassium content of 10%. In practice some fertilizers can have up to a total of 80% nitrogen content and still be accurately labeled. They could also have any combination of phosphorous and potassium adding up to 100% as long as it has at least the minimum listed. Try to use a fertilizer, such as Botanicare, which gives the elemental concentration after dilution, as these are more accurate.

How does cannabis make use of carbon dioxide?
Plants use carbon dioxide during the process of photosynthesis. During the early stages of plant development on earth, carbon dioxide was available in much higher concentrations than we find in the atmosphere today. Plants have not lost the ability to utilize these higher levels of carbon dioxide so by adding supplemental CO_2 growers can increase their harvests by up to 100%. Plants growing in a CO_2 enriched space develop thicker stems and produce higher yields.

What is the most effective way of adding additional carbon dioxide (CO_2)?
The most effective method is to use gas cylinders controlled by a timer and regulator. The cylinders can be purchased or hired from hydroponic stores or welding suppliers. They are also used in bars to pump beer. There are security implications in purchasing and refilling these cylinders and CO2 is not essential for good growth. Many growers are content to vent their plants with fresh air containing normal levels of carbon dioxide; these levels are unfortunately increasing yearly with global warming and everyone should be attempting to cut back on their CO_2 emissions. Having said that, America is producing so many toxic emissions due to the American government's continual refusal to sign the Kyoto agreement or its successors that it is unlikely cannabis growers will make much difference by not releasing CO_2 into the atmosphere, and a well-run system will only vent when the carbon dioxide has been expended.

Other methods that can be used include yeast fermentation and vinegar dripping onto baking soda. These are more effective in grow cabinets than in larger grow rooms.

What is the optimum temperature for cannabis plants?
Daytime temperature (without supplemental CO_2) should be 70-80°F.

If you are adding CO_2 then it can rise to between 80-90°F.

In the last two weeks of flowering the daytime temperature should be kept between 70-80°F.

Night temperatures should be kept above 60°F to prevent stress, stimulate hormones, and reduce stem elongation.

This Skunk plant from OGA seeds is just 4 weeks into flower and looking great.

Be inventive in your set up, like this grower.

What is the ideal humidity for cannabis?

Try and maintain grow room humidity at around 50% during vegetative growth and allow this to drop as low as 30% during flowering to prevent mold attacks on the buds.

How do I identify hard water?

Usually you will find that soap fails to produce lather in hard water. There will also be a buildup of lime deposit in your kettle. If you are not sure you can always ask your water supplier and they can send you a full analysis, which will include a reading for bicarbonates. Any water sample containing more than 150mg/liter of bicarbonates (HCO_3) is termed hard. You can also take a sample of your water to a local hydroponic store. They can arrange a full analysis through the nutrient manufacturers; this will include advice as to the best solution for your water. Hard water usually has a high pH and the bicarbonates need to be neutralized before the pH will come down. The hydroponic grower will usually add phosphoric acid (H_3PO_4) to lower the pH. Normally this is very effective, but if the water is hard it will take a large quantity of acid to neutralize the bicarbonates and lower the pH.

What parameters should I run my hydro system on?

For most hydroponic setups you need to adhere to the following parameters:
- pH 5.1-5.9 (5.2 optimal)
- TDS 500-1000ppm / EC .75-1.5
- Temperature 68-78°F, (75°F optimal)

What are herbal teas?

Herbal teas are feeds made from plant-based extracts such as stinging nettle, horsetail, comfrey, and clover. A common method is to stuff a barrel about three-quarters full of fresh green plant material, then top off the barrel with tepid water. The tea is allowed to ferment at ambient temperatures for up to 10 days. The finished product is then strained and diluted in portions of 1:10 or 1:5 and used as a foliar spray or soil drench. Herbal teas provide a supply of soluble nutrients as well as bioactive plant compounds for organic cannabis cultivation.

Eva Female Seeds have exposed this Papa's Candy plant to plenty of light and will get a great yield from her.

Lights should be kept fairly close to the top of seedlings, otherwise the seedlings will stretch to reach the light.

What are the optimum indoor light levels for cannabis?
As a general rule of thumb you will require at least 50 watts of HID lighting per square foot of grow area.

What does PAR mean?
PAR stands for Photosynthetic Available Radiation and differs from lumens in that it is not a direct measure of energy. It is the standard measure of light available for photosynthesis and is expressed in photons. Photosynthesis takes place as plants absorb these photons. PAR measures lamp output between 400 and 700 nm (nanometers).

What's the best light to use, metal halides or high pressure sodium?
MH lights produce a more natural light and some growers like to use them for vegetative growth and rooting cuttings but they are not as efficient as HPS lamps. HPS lamps can be used for both vegetative growth and flowering, providing light in the correct spectrum for both and emitting significantly more light, and so are a better option. HPS lamps produce less light in the blue spectrum and so are not suitable for rooting clones, but you can use cheaper fluorescent lamps to root cuttings.

Reflective materials on the walls of your grow room will ensure optimal use of the available light and greatly benefit your plants.

What is a switchable ballast?

If you do decide to use MH lamps along with sodium, then a switchable ballast allows you to run a standard halide or sodium bulb from one ballast; you just insert the appropriate lamp and set the switch to the correct operating setting.

Can I grow using fluorescent lighting?

Fluorescent lamps have a reduced output compared to high intensity discharge lamps but can be used to grow a crop through all stages of growth, from the cutting stage through to flowering. In order to gain maximum output from the lamps plants are kept close to the bulbs, almost touching the glass. Yields are less when using fluorescents but they are cheap to purchase and run. I have seen a commercial setup based entirely around fluorescents and although it required a large number of smaller plants kept close to the lamps it still was a very productive system. Change the bulbs regularly to maintain lumen output.

How far should the lights be from the plants?

As a general guide:
- Fluorescent tubes: tips of leaves can be almost touching the fluorescent tubes
- 400-watt halide: 2 feet away from seedlings and 1 foot away from developed plants
- 1,000-watt halide: 4 feet away from seedlings and 2 feet away from developed plants

What's the difference between watts and lumens?

Watts are the standard unit of power. 1 joule of energy per second corresponds to a power of 1 watt. Lumens are the measure of light intensity and are relative to but different from wattage and based on what the human eye can see, rather than what a plant uses for photosynthesis. Indoor cannabis gardens require between 3,000 and 9,000 lumens per square foot.

What is the best reflector or hood to use?

Try and get a decent hood with a dimpled, anodized surface. I really like the Adjust-A-Wing reflector; its simple design provides good light distribution and heat dissipation. If you want to try an air-cooled reflector then try building a cool tube from an adapted vase or hurricane lamp. Just put aluminum foil on the back to act as an improvised reflector.

How can I stop unwanted odors in my garden?

Cannabis produces distinctive odors during both vegetative growth and flowering. These odors can easily be controlled both within the grow room and around your external venting. Ionizers have some effect on controlling odors in smaller setups, and work by emitting negative ions into the grow area. Air purifiers that combine powerful ion emissions with multistage, odor-absorbing carbon filters can be purchased and are ideal for smaller grow rooms.

Ozone generators can also be used to remove odors from your grow area and they are effective; however, many growers avoid them due to the health risk that ozone (O_3) can pose. Ozone molecules quickly break down once released, typically within 30 seconds; however, once the odors have been destroyed O_3 can easily build up in the room, so only consider using one when other methods prove to be ineffective. Repeated exposure to ozone may cause permanent damage to the lungs. Even when ozone is present in low levels, inhaling it triggers a variety of health problems including chest pains, coughing, nausea, throat irritation, and congestion. It also can worsen bronchitis, heart disease, emphysema, and asthma, and reduce lung capacity.

Carbon filters are by far the safest and most effective way to eliminate odors from your exhaust vents. Carbon filters are readily available in good hydroponic stores or you can build one yourself using activated carbon that is sold in aquarium supply shops. Although carbon filters are effective for up to 12 months, make sure that you replace them every 6 months or so to ensure maximum efficiency.

How can I harvest a crop every two weeks?
It is possible to crop every two weeks by using a rotation system that staggers your harvest. By introducing plants into the flowering room at two-week intervals you will have a selection of plants ready for harvest at the same rate. To feed this system you will require a separate vegetative area that contains your mother plants and clones. This area is also used to grow out the young plants for a minimum of two weeks before placing them in the flowering area. This system was initially developed in the Netherlands and called the Sea of Green technique. Although this originally began as a commercial technique it can be scaled down for hobby growers and can involve placing as little as one plant into the flowering area every two weeks.

Vegetative Growth

How much daylight do cannabis plants require to stay in vegetative growth?
Cannabis plants require at least 18 hours of uninterrupted daylight to remain in the vegetative state. This best mimics the spring and summer months, although cannabis can be given 24 hours of uninterrupted light as there is no requirement for it to sleep. The benefit of increased growth developed during a 24-hour light regime needs to be off set against electricity costs.

This Hero Seeds Zombie Rasta plant came from feminized seeds which will only give female plants.

How long should I leave my plants in vegetative growth?
There is no limit on how long cannabis plants can remain in the vegetative growth stage; mother plants can be kept for years under an 18-hour light regime. The minimum you should leave your plants in vegetative growth before forcing them into flower is 2 weeks and this can work well on a rotation setup, however plants that have had a longer vegetative growth period develop thicker stems and will yield more. Vegetative growth periods of 4 to 6 weeks produce sturdier plants.

Can you determine sex during vegetative growth?
It is difficult to accurately determine gender during vegetative growth; however, when grown from seed, cannabis plants will produce what are known as preflowers and these generally appear above the fourth node around the third to fifth week of vegetative growth. The female preflower is pear-shaped and produces a pair of pistils located at the node between the stipule and emerging branch. Preflowers are tiny and a jeweler's loupe or magnifying glass is required

to positively identify them. Some varieties will produce taller, thinner male plants that can be spotted during vegetative growth, but this is not an accurate way to identify gender.

Do I need to prune during vegetative growth?
Indoor growers will need to do a certain amount of pruning during vegetative growth to shape the plant and make optimum use of the space and light levels. It is advisable to pinch out some of the growing tips, especially if you are growing in a closet or confined space. Two new grow tips will be produced from the pruned site, however many growers prefer to keep the main cola intact and just prune the side shoots. If you have room to allow your indoor plants to develop then you can reduce the pruning. Some growers like to remove large fan leaves, but don't strip the plant right back as the fan leaves act as energy-producing factories for further development and excessive leaf stripping can slow growth and reduce yields.

Which nutrients are required during vegetative growth?
Cannabis requires high amounts of nitrogen (N) during vegetative growth. High amounts of nitrogen promote vigorous vegetative growth, firm stem development and increased protein synthesis. Fertilizers with an N-P-K of 30-15-15 are ideal for vegetative growth.

Flowering

What triggers flowering in cannabis plants?
Cannabis is an annual plant so as winter approaches it needs to reproduce before dying back. The seeds it drops will be the next generation of plants. As we have seen, cannabis produces a hormone called phytochrome that measures the amount of daylight the plant is receiving. Once the daylight levels reach the critical 12 hours daylight / 12 hours darkness, flowering is triggered. This can be recreated indoors by adjusting the light cycles, or by covering plants outdoors.

What causes hermaphrodite plants?
Hermaphrodite plants are genetically unstable and will exhibit both male and female flowers. These plants are undesirable, as they will self-seed and pollinate the other plants with unstable genes. Hermaphrodites are genetically determined and naturally form flowers of both sexes given normal growing conditions. However it is possible that genes other than the sex chromosomes can modify cannabis gender. Hermaphrodite plants can sometimes randomly

Watch out for the preflowers on your plants so that you can identify the males and females, and are aware that they are entering the flowering stage.

No Mercy Supply studies hermaphroditism in plants like this in order to create better, more reliable strains.

appear within your crop. They are usually faster maturing than the other plants and form both male and female flowers simultaneously. Cannabis sativa strains from equatorial regions tend to produce more hermaphrodite plants than Cannabis indica.

Many environmental factors can cause hermaphrodite plants: under artificial light the length of the photoperiod can influence cannabis sexing in genetically susceptible plants. Low light intensity, photoperiod, UV, low temperatures, severe pruning, nutrient problems, age, and a combination of chemicals can all trigger hermaphrodites.

Do cannabis plants require any special nutrients during flowering?
During flowering cannabis requires less nitrogen and higher amounts of phosphorus, which promotes blooming and flower production. Fertilizers with an N-P-K of 15-30-30 are ideal.

Does pH effect flowering?
The pH level will affect all aspects of cannabis growth. pH is a measurement of acidity or alkalinity. On a scale of 1 to 14, neutral is 7. The ideal pH range for cannabis is 6.5 in soil and 5.5 in hydroponic solutions, so ensure that you maintain a correct balance within your medium at all times.

How can I increase my yields?
Ensure that you provide your plants with an optimum growing environment at all times. Any fluctuation will affect plant growth and subsequent yields. In addition to providing optimum growing conditions you may wish to consider supplementing the environment with additional carbon dioxide as described earlier. You may also want to try supplementary feeding with seaweed extract and/or other commercially available growth enhancers.

Polyploidy is basically a genetic mutation within plants that can produce abnormally high yields. Continual and severe defoliation can trigger polyploidy in cannabis plants or it can be chemically induced using colchicine. If you wish to treat your plants with colchicine be aware that it is toxic and should be handled with care.

What is secondary budding?
Secondary budding involves reverting a flowering cannabis plant back into vegetative growth to elongate the bud sites before returning the plants to a flowering light regime. If you wish to try this, take a plant that has been flower-

Some plants exhibit beautiful colorings in response to temperatures as well as different types of light, such as this High Level plant from Eva Female Seeds.

ing for 4 to 5 weeks and place it under 24 hours of continuous daylight. After 4 weeks, return it to flowering. You can expect a 25% increase in yield using this technique.

How does UV light affect flowering?
Cannabis produces more of the psychoactive chemicals (THC) in response to receiving high levels of ultra violet light. Some growers add UV light to budding plants to reproduce this effect. If you wish to try this, divide plant exposure into three 10-minute sessions per 12-hour period.

Harvest

How can I tell when to harvest?
Cannabis plants require around 8 weeks to reach maturity. By carefully examining the individual pistils on maturing buds you can gauge when to harvest. When one-third of the pistils have turned brown you can harvest and the resultant buds will give you more of a high. If you require a heavier, more lethargic effect, harvest when three-quarters of the pistils have turned brown.

Do I have to harvest the whole plant at the same time?
Some growers prefer to selectively harvest their plants by removing the ripe top buds and allowing the lower branches to continue to flower and mature. This works particularly well on outdoor crops but can also be applied indoors.

These beautiful plants are almost ready for harvest.

How can I harvest outdoor plants earlier?
Outdoor plants can be forced to flower at any time by covering the entire plant with a light-excluding membrane. This requires you to maintain a 12-hour flowering regime, which is time consuming. If you wish to try this, don't use polythene as a cover unless you can guarantee it won't come into contact with the plant as it sweats the plant and encourages fungal growth, which can ruin your harvest.

What is the best way to dry my harvested buds?
The best way to dry buds is by hanging individual branches on a line in a darkened room. Ensure that you don't apply too much heat to the drying buds as this can result in a much harsher smoke. Cannabis that has been slowly dried and allowed to cure produces a much sweeter harvest. Correctly dried and cured cannabis contains around 15% moisture. Below 10%, the buds will crumble and over 15%, the marijuana will sweat and decay when packaged.

How do I manicure my buds after harvest?
Manicuring is the process of cleaning and trimming your buds so they appear presentable, and removing leaf material with low THC percentages. This material is used for hash making or cooking although many people still value the leaves as a lighter smoking mix. The most important tool you will need is a pair of sharp scissors; you can use small pruning shears available at most gardening stores. If you are manicuring a lot of buds, get a pair that has a spring-loaded squeeze grip rather than finger and thumb holes, as trimming for long periods cramps your hands. Your blades will also clog up with sticky resin, which slows the job down, so use rubbing alcohol or vegetable oil to keep them clean. The resin should be collected and saved as it makes good handrolled hash similar to charas. Charas is a hand rolled hashish that originates from India. They collect the resin by hand, rubbing the flowering buds just before harvest time and forming it into balls that are later flattened. A single-edge razor blade or craft knife is also useful, as is an old newspaper to protect your work surface and catch any smaller leaves and buds that you trim. Some growers like to manicure over a glass table in order to collect the resin glands that will fall off the buds during trimming; these are scraped up with the single-edge razor.

Most growers like to manicure when the buds are dried but you can trim them wet and this is less destructive to the finished product. Trimming when the buds are very dry and brittle knocks off a lot of resin glands. Whichever method you choose, hold the bud firmly and trim and pluck out all the leaf material. The finished bud can then be stored.

Manicuring buds will leave you with a great looking stash, so good you can't keep your hands off it!

How can I store buds without losing potency?
If you wish to store buds for any length of time it is vital that you remove as much moisture as possible from them to prevent decay. Buds that are left to cure actually increase in taste and potency, as anyone who has left cannabis for over 6 months will testify. I prefer to leave them in a cool, dark place, sealed in a mason-type jar, however some growers like to refrigerate their harvest and this works well. Be careful when freezing, as you can damage the stalked, capitate, trichome glands as they become brittle during the freezing process.

What is the easiest way to make hashish?
The easiest way is to make charis by rubbing your fingers over ripe cannabis buds, similar to the way resin collects on your fingers during manicuring. This hash is simple to make but can contain plant leaf material and other contaminants. If you wish to make a purer form of hashish you need to soak your dried and powdered bud material in acetone. Acetone is readily available from fiberglass suppliers, who use it to clean their tools. The plant material is soaked overnight in the acetone, a process that dissolves the cannabinoids. The acetone solution is then strained to remove the plant material and the acetone is boiled off leaving pure cannabis oil. Acetone has a relatively low boiling point and one

There are many ways to make hash - try all of them and find whichever suits you best.

of the best ways to evaporate it is in a slow cooker. As acetone is highly flammable, this process is best done outdoors. Many growers are content to just use the oil which can be smeared onto cigarette papers and smoked, or the oil can be mixed with more powdered bud material and kneaded into a round ball of hashish. There are other methods for removing cannabinoids from cannabis plant material, such as silk screening and tumbling. One of the simplest methods is to place your dried and powdered buds into a large glass Pyrex bowl. The powder is then gently swirled around as if you're panning for gold. The scuff containing the cannabis resin glands will separate and adhere to the upper part of the bowl, where it can be scraped off and collected using your fingers.

How do you make cannabis capsules?
The cannabis needs to be dried and ground to a fine consistency in a coffee grinder. Pour the ground cannabis into a small bowl and add enough olive oil to the concentrate so that the cannabis powder adheres. Use this mixture to fill the capsules, obtainable from homeopathic pharmacies, several of which are available online, if you have access to the Internet. They will also be able to supply you with a manual capper that allows you to fill several capsules at a time. The manual capper holds one piece of the cap, making filling easier. Capsules

come in several sizes; choose a smaller size as they are easier to swallow and you can control the dosage with greater accuracy. Keep refrigerated. For long-term storage, place the capsules in a container and keep frozen.

Troubleshooting

What is the most effective treatment for spider mites?
Spider mites are the most serious pest you will encounter in the grow room. Spider mites are not insects but are more closely related to spiders (arachnids). They actually resemble ticks and many growers refer to them as plant lice. Mites have four pairs of legs, no antennae and a single, oval body region. Spider mites are tiny, being less than 1/50th of an inch (0.4mm) long when adults, with tiny mouth parts modified for piercing individual plant cells and sucking out the fluid. This results in tiny yellow or white speckles on the leaves. When several feeding spots occur near each other, the foliage takes on a yellowed or bronzed appearance. Heavily infested cannabis plants will be covered in fine webs, the leaves will be discolored, and mites and their eggs will infest the underside of leaves.

All spider mites go through the same stages of development. Adult females lay eggs on their host plants, and the eggs hatch into the first stage, called larvae. Larvae are round-bodied and have only three pairs of legs. The larvae feed for a few days, seek a protected spot, and then molt into the first nymphal stage. The first nymph now has four pairs of legs. The first nymphs feed a few days, rest, and molt into the second nymph. The second nymphs feed, rest, and molt into the adult stage. The males are usually the size of the second nymph and have pointed abdomens. The females have rounded abdomens and are the largest of all the mites.

Biological Control - Predators
There are numerous insects such as lacewings and ladybugs that prey on spider mites. However, the most commonly sold predators are other types of mites. Predatory mites can be purchased and released onto infested plants. Predatory mites commonly sold via mail order are:
- Galendromus occidentalis
- Phytoseiulus persimilis
- Mesoseiulus longipes
- Neoseiulus californicus

If predators are used, do not apply pesticides or insecticides that will kill them.

Most problems will show themselves first on the leaves, so make sure you can recognise any change in the leaf shape or color.

Cultural Control - Water Jet
Using a jet of water from a handheld spray bottle is an organic way of controlling spider mites and does not kill any predators you may have released. Place the plants into your bath or sink and blast the undersides of all the leaves with a fine jet of water from the handheld sprayer.

Chemical Control - Soft Pesticides
Most spider mites can be controlled with insecticidal oils such as neem oil, and soaps, both horticultural oil and dormant oil, can be used. Remember that mites are very tiny and soaps and oils work by contact only. Therefore, thorough coverage of the plant is necessary for good control. Once again, remove the plants from the growing environment and spray them in the bath or sink area.

Chemical Control - Miticides
Spider mites are usually not killed by regular insecticides, so be sure to check the pesticide label to see if miticide is present. Pesticides claiming to be for mite suppression are usually weak miticides and will not perform well. It is important to remember that your cannabis is intended for human consumption, so only use chemicals that are recommended for fruit and vegetable crops and be cautious in your administration.

This Buddha's Sister plant from Soma Seeds has been kept pest and disease free and is giving great rewards.

Over-the-counter pesticides:
- dicofol (Kelthane)
- acephate (Orthene)
- dimethoate (Cygon)
- chlorpyrifos (Dursban)
- diazinon, disulfoton (Di-syston)
- malathion

Restricted-use pesticides available only to licensed applicators:
- avermectin (Avid)
- bifenthrin (Talstar)
- dienochlor (Pentac)
- fenbutatin-oxide (Vendex)
- fluvalinate (Mavrik)
- oxamyl (Vydate)
- oxydemeton-methyl (Metasystox-R)
- oxythioquinox (Morestan)
- propargite (Omite)

Treatments for Pest Problems

Active Ingredient:	Trade Name(s):	Observations:
Acephate.	Orthene,certain Isotox formulations.	Insecticide with some effectiveness against spider mites. Systemic.
Bifenthrin.	Talstar, others.	Insecticide with good miticide activity.
Dimethoate.	Cygon.	Insecticide with fair miticidal activity. Few food crop registrations. Systemic.
Dicofol.	Kelthane.	Selective miticide labeled for some food crops in addition to ornamental plants. Some reduced activity at higher temperatures.
Horticultural Oils.	Sunspray, others.	Used at the summer oil rate (2%), oils are perhaps the most effective miticide available.
Sulfur.	Various.	Generally sold in dust formulation for control of various fungal diseases and some mites on some ornamental and vegetable crops.

What is the most effective treatment for botrytis (gray mold)?
Gray mold will attack young seedlings and cuttings causing damping off. Gray mold also attacks the stems of mature cannabis plants and during flowering, affects the large resinous buds. The treatment for all fungal infection starts with good prevention; carefully control humidity in your grow room and don't allow plants to become waterlogged. If your grow does suffer from fungal infection

isolate the infected plant, cut out all the infected plant material, and spray with a fungicidal spray. Remember plants are destined for human consumption and systemics can remain in the plant tissue after harvest.

Systemic fungicides that treat gray mold include:
- Griseofulvin
- Carbaryl
- Funginux
- Vitavax

Nonsystemic fungicides include:
- Bordeaux Mixture
- Cheshunt Compound

Why has plant growth slowed in my room?
Slow growth generally indicates that you are not providing the optimum growing environment for your cannabis plants. It could be you are overwatering; water that is not absorbed and remains in the soil quickly turns stagnant and plants rapidly use up any oxygen it contains. This will slowly suffocate the plant roots, preventing oxygen uptake and ultimately causing root rot.

It could mean that the pH is too high or too low. Cannabis plants are unable to absorb nutrients in adequate quantities if pH is outside of the recommended parameters. Adding too much of a nutrient (overfeeding) can lock up one or more of these nutrients, rendering them chemically unavailable to the plant. Nutrient lock-up will occur at extreme pH ranges—under 5.0, and over 7.0.

Although your plant may be receiving light, it may be you are not delivering 50 watts per square foot. Furthermore, light that does not contain enough red spectrum (too much blue) can have a negative effect on plant growth, with different light frequencies affecting different photosynthetic processes.

Plant metabolism will decrease at low temperatures. Chemical reactions within the plant will take longer. Optimum plant growth often requires close temperature regulation and differences in daytime and nighttime temps should not be extreme, as this difference may shock the plant.

Miscellaneous

Is it safe to smoke cannabis?
No. You're better off to vaporize, use a water pipe, or eat it! Like those in to-

bacco, cannabis tars are rich in carcinogenic compounds known as polycyclic aromatic hydrocarbons, which are a prime culprit in smoking-related cancers. However, cannabinoids themselves are not carcinogenic. An obvious way to protect smokers' health is therefore to minimize the content of smoke tars relative to cannabinoids. Smoking cannabis in vaporizers or water-cooled pipes significantly reduces the amount of tar you inhale. Vaporizers have been proven to completely eliminate three measured toxins—benzene, a known carcinogen, plus toluene and naphthalene.

Smoking cannabis in tobacco joints is proven to be even more harmful to your health. Aside from the main carcinogenic agents produced when you smoke cannabis in joints, long-term inhalation of tobacco smoke exposes your body to powerful chemicals that can cause cancer and cell mutations. Thirty percent of all cancer deaths can be attributed to smoking tobacco.

Cancers other than lung cancer that are linked to smoking include:

• cervical cancer
• cancers of the mouth, lips and throat
• pancreatic cancer
• bladder cancer
• kidney cancer
• stomach cancer
• liver cancer
• leukemia

Cigarettes are only about 40% tobacco, and 60% other additives. Tobacco smoke from cigarettes contains over 4,000 chemical compounds and breathable, suspended particles. These include ammonia, arsenic, benzene, cadmium, carbon monoxide, formaldehyde, lead, mercury, naphthalene, urethane and a variety of nitrosamines. There are also radioactive chemicals in tobacco smoke, like polonium-210. Formaldehyde, ammonia, urethane, and naphthalene are contained in household products and manufacturers of these cleaning products are forced to include labels on them telling you to avoid inhaling them.

Many seemingly innocuous additives such as cocoa also have more sinister effects. For example, cocoa when burned in a cigarette produces bromide gas that dilates the airways of the lung, and increases the body's ability to absorb nicotine. Menthol is also suspected of enabling the smoker to inhale more easily by numbing the throat. Addition of ammonia compounds speed the delivery of nicotine to smokers by raising the alkalinity of tobacco smoke. These compounds also distort the measurement of tar in cigarettes, giving lower readings than would actually be inhaled by the smoker. Other chemicals, such as acetal-dehyde and pyridine act to strengthen nicotine's impact on the brain and central nervous system. I used to know a Dutch girl whose father was head of a seriously well-known tobacco company; he wasn't a salesman or business guru, he was a qualified chemist. Use a vaporizer or water pipe to smoke your cannabis; they are far safer than tobacco joints.

> vaporizer = 0.10mg tar per inhalation
> water pipe = 1.75mg tar per inhalation
> cigarette = 4.00mg tar per inhalation

Research carried out in the United States suggests that nicotine may be much more addictive than originally thought. According to one study, people can become addicted to nicotine in just a few days and after just a handful of cigarettes. If you are addicted to tobacco smoke and use this as the delivery method for cannabis you can use a filter on your joints instead of a roach, although recent studies have shown that filters are actually fairly ineffective at reducing tar levels and can trap cannabinoids, making the joint less potent. Heavy cannabis joint smokers who do use filters claim they cough less, but this is purely anecdotal.

According to doctors at The Southend Hospital in England, who studied 2,000 lung cancer patients, women are more likely to develop severe non-operable forms of lung cancer than men. Lung cancer has overtaken breast cancer as the biggest killer of women in Britain. However, scientists now believe women who take aspirin on a regular basis cut their risk of developing the most common type of lung cancer by more than half. The study, involving more than 14,000 women, suggested the drug's anti-inflammatory effects reduce the chances of developing any form of lung cancer by a third. However, not smoking is still the best protection against the disease.

How can I avoid leaving footprints when I surf the Internet?
The best way to surf anonymously is to use what is known as a proxy server. This basically acts as a shield between you and the Internet and only shows the proxy server's IP address, not yours. If you do an Internet search for proxy servers you will find them. There is no charge for using the service. If you are concerned about data you have downloaded and stored on your computer then a program such as Evidence Eliminator will clean up any tracks you have left on your hard drive.

These Trainwreck plants from 420Clones.com are being grown under LEDs in a DWC system. LEDs use very little electricity, making them ideal for stealth growers.

Do power companies report high usage of electricity to the police?
Not generally. Their primary concern is to their shareholders so unless you are using ridiculous amounts of electricity you should not have a problem. If the police contact the power company about your usage, be under no illusion: they will not respect your privacy and/or the data protection act. They will give detailed records of all your power consumption and even supply an expert witness in the event of any possible court case.

What happens if I'm arrested?
The following advice is produced by the American Civil Liberties Union but

is pretty much standard advice for most democratic countries. Guidelines for searches carried out without a warrant are related to the United States and are different for Canada and other countries.

1. What you say to the police is always important. What you say can be used against you, and it can give the police an excuse to arrest you, especially if you insult a police officer.
2. You don't have to answer a police officer's questions, but you must show your driver's license and registration when stopped in a car. In other situations, you can't legally be arrested for refusing to identify yourself to a police officer.
3. You don't have to consent to any search of yourself, your car, or your house. If you do consent to a search, it can affect your rights later in court. If the police say they have a search warrant, ask to see it.
4. Do not interfere with, or obstruct the police - you can be arrested for it.

IF YOU ARE STOPPED FOR QUESTIONING

1. It is not a crime to refuse to answer questions, but refusing to answer can make the police suspicious about you. You can't be arrested merely for refusing to identify yourself on the street.
2. Police may pat down your clothing if they suspect a concealed weapon. Don't physically resist, but make it clear that you don't consent to any further search.
3. Ask whether or not you are under arrest. If you are, you have a right to know why.
4. Don't insult the police officer or run away, even if you believe what is happening is unreasonable. That could lead to your arrest.

IF YOU ARE STOPPED IN YOUR CAR

1. Upon request, show them your driver's license, registration, and proof of insurance. In certain cases, your car can be searched without a warrant as long as the police have probable cause. To protect yourself later, you should make it clear that you do not consent to a search. It is not lawful for police to arrest you simply for refusing to consent to a search.
2. If you're given a ticket, you should sign it; otherwise you can be arrested. You can always fight the case in court later.
3. If you're suspected of drunk driving and refuse to take a blood, urine, or breath test, your driver's license may be suspended.

IF YOU ARE ARRESTED OR TAKEN TO A POLICE STATION

1. You have the right to remain silent and to talk to a lawyer before you talk to the police. Tell the police nothing except your name and address. Don't give any explanations, excuses, or stories. You can make your defense later, in court, based on what you and your lawyer decide is best.

2. Ask to see a lawyer immediately. If you can't pay for a lawyer, you have a right to a free one, and should ask the police how the lawyer can be contacted. Don't say anything without a lawyer being present.

3. Within a reasonable time after your arrest, or booking, you have the right to make a local phone call: to a lawyer, a bail bondsman, a relative or any other person. The police may not listen to the call to the lawyer.

4. Sometimes you can be released without bail, or have bail lowered. Have your lawyer ask the judge about this possibility. You must be taken before the judge on the next court day after arrest.

5. Do not make any decisions in your case until you have talked with a lawyer.

IN YOUR HOME

1. If the police knock and ask to enter your home, you don't have to admit them unless they have a warrant signed by a judge.

2. However, in some emergency situations such as a person screaming for help inside, or if the police are chasing someone, officers are allowed to enter and search your home without a warrant.

3. If you are arrested, the police can search you and the area close by. If you are in a building, "close by" usually means just the room you are in.

We all recognize the need for effective law enforcement, but we should also understand our own rights and responsibilities.

(Produced by the American Civil Liberties Union.)

Pink Plant from Eva Female Seeds is excellent for medical patients because of its reliability and high quality.

22. And Finally

There are a lot of psychopaths in prison,
unfortunately most are on the staff.
Craig Charles.

In a truly free society there should be no laws to protect citizens from themselves. If an individual wants to grow and use cannabis plants then he or she should be free to do so: it is their choice. It seems incredible that by choosing to grow cannabis, individuals will be prosecuted by the state. In most of Europe, there is a tolerance of recreational cannabis use, and a person arrested for the first time with a small amount of personal marijuana will usually be cautioned and have the drug confiscated. Cultivators are generally prosecuted, which results in confiscation of the equipment and a fine or imprisonment (or both). If a person is shown to have benefited from dealing in cannabis the prosecution will attempt to seize their assets. Serious cultivators should keep nothing on paper and only keep small amounts of money in the bank.

If You Are Arrested
The usual procedure is that the police are made aware that an individual is cultivating or dealing in marijuana. The senior officer makes an evaluation as to the scale of the enquiry. The response will be calculated based on this evaluation. If it is suspected that the individual is growing a small amount for their own consumption, the police will decide to raid the premises where they believe cultivation is taking place.

If, after the evaluation by a senior officer, they decide that you are producing or dealing in cannabis on a larger scale, then the next stage will be to put you under observation to assess the scale of your operation and to build a picture of you and your associates. Whatever happens, the arrest will probably be the first you know about the operation against you. Raids often take place first thing in the morning, unless there are exceptional circumstances. You will be awakened by loud hammering on your front door or the sound of the door being forcibly removed. If you want some good advice, buy a dog. My English

Unfortunately a raid on your grow space will probably end in your babies being destroyed.

bull terrier once held off an entire section of officers from the tactical firearms unit who tried to storm my back garden. All you could see was a row of black baseball caps peeking over the fence at her.

But be warned, the majority of these officers are failed Rambos who have found a way to live out their fantasies, and they are dangerous. They will use CS gas against your dogs, which is very distressing. The gas attacks moist areas of the body and dogs will convulse and howl in agony. They gassed my friend's Staffordshire bulls through the letterbox, before smashing down his door to search for cannabis. Once they have gained access to your property they will arrest you. By this stage, they are in a state of excitement; they can't help it, so just stay calm. The arresting officer will explain that you are under arrest and say why. Do not say anything at this stage. A search of your premises will then take place at which you may or may not be present. Just say nothing.

You will then be taken to a police station where you will be processed and searched. Ask to speak to a lawyer, and do not say anything else. After processing you will be put in a cell with a thin, plastic-covered mattress. Lie on the mattress and try to sleep. Even though this is the last thing on your mind, it gives you an opportunity to collect your thoughts. Police procedure is to check on the prisoner in custody and report this to the investigating officers. They hate it when you are relaxed and asleep. Do not say or do anything until you have spoken to your lawyer. It is always better to say nothing and argue that you were confused or fearful in the police station. You may want to make a statement to the police in which case you must never tell the truth or give information on anyone. Play down any cultivation you have been involved in and any profits that you have made. The police are interested in figures and will provide their own experts to say that you have benefited from ridiculous amounts. Don't worry about this either, the first thing any competent barrister or lawyer will do is commission an independent forensic expert to examine the evidence in your case. The police will try to trick you into admitting to supplying cannabis to others. If you have been arrested with a small amount,

If you're lucky enough to be a certified grower, you may never face these problems.

The best way to avoid being found out is to be stealthy with your grow and keep your mouth shut.

maintain that it was for your own personal use and you never intended to pass it on to another person, even as a gift.

After being interviewed by the investigating officers, you will either be released on police bail or charged with the offences. Being charged with an offence does not preclude you from police bail, but if the offence is deemed serious enough you will be remanded in custody. A remand in custody means that you will appear before a local magistrate the next day. They sanction the decision the police have already made. You are then taken to a local prison where you will enter the reception area, be processed, assigned a wing and once again locked in a cell. Imprisonment is not to be feared. It allows you time to think and prepare your defense, but please, never discuss your case with anyone except your legal advisors or co-accused, and even then be careful. The authorities regularly use other inmates as informants and there have been many cases where inmates have given evidence against fellow prisoners in exchange for lighter sentences.

To the police, information is a valuable commodity and they are prepared to trade for it. All of the defendants in my case were approached and offered deals; the only one who claimed not to have been asked had already taken the deal. I told them nothing; it's not what I'm about. You choose certain paths in

Ultra Jax from Alpine Seeds is a well-respected strain in Europe where many countries allow people to grow cannabis legally.

life and must take responsibility for your choices. Unfortunately, there are weak individuals who fail to grasp this concept. Even the police despise them and that is saying something when you consider how corrupt, racist and dishonest some officers are. British detectives took $7,000 in cash from my partner's house on our last arrest. They thought he wouldn't declare it but it was legal money from his shop. When his lawyer demanded its return they denied ever seizing it and threatened his wife with prosecution. The money is still missing. While I was in prison, four London drug-squad detectives wearing hoods were arrested in the early hours of the morning breaking into a lockup garage to steal a consignment of cannabis that had been stored there by dealers. They hadn't known that the area was under surveillance by another police squad.

Even if you have been caught in possession of large amounts of cannabis, do not give up. Think your case through. Are there likely to have been informants in the case? If so, do you have an idea as to who they might be? Police procedure is to protect informants at all costs, they must do this or no other informants will come forward, and this is to the defendant's advantage.

A defense of duress exists in most countries. If the defendant can convince a jury that at the time the offence was committed the accused was in fear of his or her life and only acting because they were threatened by another person or persons, then the accused is not guilty of that offence. It can suit the defense to say that the offence was only committed because the informant threatened the defendant who, as a result of this threat, was in fear for their life. This defense allows your lawyer or barrister to call and cross-examine the informant in open court. The prosecution cannot allow this because they know that if your legal team asks the witness if he or she is a police informant, they must answer truthfully or perjure themselves. Prosecution counsel will drop a case rather than disclose the identity of any informants.

If you have no idea who the informants are, and have no defense, then a guilty plea can earn you a certain discount off your sentence for saving the court time and money. Ensure that your legal team plays down the sums of money involved and have their own forensic scientists back this up. This is where any statement you may have made can be useful, especially if the police have only found equipment and not plants, as you can claim what you like. The judge in my case remarked that if the court was to believe what I was saying, it would appear I had lost $14,000 since starting cultivating. At one point he lost all composure and shouted "Liar" at my co-accused.

If you suffer from any of the illnesses that cannabis can alleviate be sure to mention them in court and if you don't have any, develop one. When you enter a plea of "not guilty" it means you then have to face a trial before a jury. You will be represented by a lawyer or barrister who will argue your case before the court and cross-examine witnesses on your behalf. It is entirely possible for defendants to represent themselves in court but doing so is not advised unless you are competent with legal procedures.

A defendant is under no obligation to give evidence during the trial itself and I know of cases where barristers have advised their clients not to do so. This is invariably a mistake, as juries tend to assume that if you will not answer the prosecution's questions you have something to hide. It is important to appear in the dock and to tell your side of the story. The prosecutor will use a variety of techniques to show you to be a liar before turning to the jury and claiming that they should believe nothing you have said.

Important Hints for When You're Being Cross Examined

Do not allow the prosecutor to rush you through questions to confuse you. Keep asking them to repeat the question to allow you time to think. Say, "I am sorry I did not hear/understand you, can you repeat the question, please?" This frustrates their efforts. Always pause and think before answering.

Do not allow the prosecutor to draw you into any arguments and don't

Perhaps someday in the near future companies like Alpine Seeds will be allowed to set up in North America, and we'll be able to grow phenomenal plants like these legally.

lose your temper. Consistently deny all the allegations with a firm but polite: "No, that simply is not true." It is very difficult for a prosecutor to unsettle you if you adopt this approach.

If you cannot remember a specific fact or detail then say so, and only give facts and details that you are sure of. Believe any facts you are giving them.

If a prosecutor continues to go over points you have answered, turn to the judge and say, "Your honor, I've answered this question several times." The judge won't like it but will direct the prosecutor to move on.

Don't spend your time planning answers to specific questions that may or may not be asked. You know the direction your defense is to go, so always answer the prosecution's points with this in mind. Stay focused and stay strong.

> L'homme est né libre, et partout il est dans les fers.
> Man is born free, and everywhere he is in chains.
> *Jean-Jacques Rousseau. 1712-1778.*

This Cannaberry plant from Allele Seeds Research has been pollinated and is ready to pop!

Glossary

I was reading the dictionary. I thought it was a poem about everything.
Steven Wright.

Acetone: Solvent chemical used in the extraction of oil from cannabis plants.

Ballast: Used to control HID lights. Can be housed in the light unit itself, as with Poot horticultural lamps, or as a separate remote unit connected by a cable.

Bhang: A drink made from cannabis.

Botrytis: A fungal infection that attacks plants. Is easily identified by a gray fluffy growth on the affected part. Particularly damaging during flowering and will ruin a crop (See Troubleshooting Pests and Fungi).

Capillary Action: Refers to the tendency of liquid to be drawn up or through a plant or a material.

CF: The ability of a liquid to conduct a current. Used to measure the amount of dissolved nutrients in a solution.

Chillum: A small pipe used to smoke cannabis.

Chlorophyll: The green coloring matter of plants.

Chlorosis: The name given to the condition whereby a plant appears pale and has thin leaves and stems. Caused by insufficient light levels.

Colchicine: A chemical found in crocus plants used to induce polyploidy in cannabis.

Cytokinins: Hormones found in sea plants.

Defoliation: Process in which leaves are stripped from a healthy growing plant to induce shock and polyploidy that can increase yields.

Dioecious: Term for species that have separate male and female plants.

Dronabidol: The name given to synthesized THC.

Ethylene: Naturally occurring gas given off by ripening vegetables and fruit.

Feminized: The process in which seeds are treated to produce more females than males.

Hashish: Pressed extract of cannabis.

Hermaphrodites: Plants that develop both male and female flowers.

HPS: High pressure sodium lights used in indoor cannabis cultivation.

Humidity: The measurement of water held in the atmosphere.

Humus: The term used to describe decayed living matter in the soil.

Hygrometer: Instrument used to measure the humidity of an area.

Hypocotyl: The name given to the stem that emerges from the seed case and pushes up towards the light.

Internode: The point on the plant where side shoots develop.

Iytal: Term for a cigarette consisting of cannabis weed without tobacco.

Manicuring: Trimming the leaves from around the dried cannabis flowers.

Marijuana: Mexican word used to describe cannabis.

Marinol: See Dronabidol.

MH: Metal Halide lights used in indoor cultivation.

Moraceae: The family to which the cannabis plant belongs. Hemp is classified as Cannabis sativa.

NPK: Used to classify fertilizer by its nutrient content.

Papaver somniferum: Latin name for the opium poppy.

pH: A measurement of acidity or alkalinity.

Phytochrome: A light-sensitive hormone responsible for regulating the growing and flowering stages of the cannabis plant. Flowering is induced when the phytochrome reaches critical levels in the plant.

Pistils: The term used to describe the thin white hairs that emerge from the female pods on the female cannabis plants when they flower.

Polyploid: Genetic mutations in plant species.

Resin: See Hashish.

Sinsemilla: Mexican word meaning "seedless," used to refer to a crop of female cannabis flowers that have been cultivated without being pollinated. Sinsemilla marijuana is more potent than seeded crops.

THC: Tetrahydrocannabinol is the psychoactive ingredient found in cannabis.

Tincture: A medicinal solution of a drug in alcohol.

Transpiration: A process in which evaporation takes place on the surface of the plant leaves, causing water to be drawn up through the plant by capillary action.

Vaporizer: Pipe that gently heats the cannabis without burning, to release fumes of THC.

Vermiculite: Lightweight, inert growing medium.

Resources

Cannabis Websites and Forums:
Breedbay.co.uk
Cannabis.co.za
Grubbycup.org
Icmag.com
Originalseeds.org
SinsemillaWorks.com
Skunkmagazine.com
Weed.co.za
Weedworld.co.uk

Further Reading:
Cannabis Indica: The Essential Guide to the World's Finest Marijuana Strains, by S.T. Oner, Green Candy Press, 2011
Ed Rosenthal's Marijuana Grower's Handbook, Quick American, 2010
Hashish by Robert Connell Clarke, Red Eye Press, 1998
Marijuana: A Grower's Lot by Kog, Green Grass Publishing, 1999
Marijuana Horticulture by Jorge Cervantes, Van Patten Publishing, 2006
Mr. Nice, by Howard Marks, Canongate, 2003
The Cannabis Grow Bible, 2nd Edition, by Greg Green, Green Candy Press, 2010

Seed Breeders and Companies:
420Clones: 420clones.com
Allele Seeds Research: Alleleseedsresearch.org
AlphaKronik Genes: Facebook.com/Alphakronik-Genes
Alpine Seeds: Alpine-seeds.net
Apothecary Genetics: Apothecarygenetics.com
ASG Seeds: Asgseeds.com

Autofem Seeds: Autofem.com
BC Bud Depot: Bcbuddepot.com
Bomba Seeds: Bombaseeds.com
Cabin Fever Seed Breeders: Cannacollective.co.uk
Ch9 Female Seeds: Ch9femaleseeds.com
Delta 9 Labs: Delta9labs.com
Dinafem Seeds: Dinafem.org
Dr. Atomic Seedbank: Dratomicseedbank.com
Dr. Canem & Company: Facebook.com/drcanem
Dr. Greenthumb Seeds: Drgreenthumb.com
Dr. Underground: Drunderground.com
Dutch Passion Seeds: Dutch-passion.nl
Eva Female Seeds: Evaseeds.com
Finest Medicinal Seeds. Finestmedicinalseeds.com
Gage Green Genetics: Gagegreen.org
Genetics Gone Madd: Facebook.com/GeneticsGoneMad
Hero Seeds: Heroseeds.com
Holy Smoke Seeds: Puresativa.com
Homegrown Fantaseeds: Homegrown-fantaseeds.com
Karmaceuticals LLC: Facebook.com/Karmaceuticals
Kiwiseeds: Kiwiseeds.com
Magus Genetics: Seriousseeds.com
Mandala Seeds: Mandalaseeds.com
Mosca Seeds: Seedsman.com
Mr. Nice Seeds: Mrnice.nl
No Mercy Supply: Nomercy.nl
OGA Seeds: Ogas.ca
OG Genetics: Oggenetics.com
Paradise Seeds: Paradise-seeds.com
Peak Seeds BC: Peakseedsbc.com
Pitt Bully Seeds: Pittbully.com
PureBred Growers: Purebredgrowers.com
Red Star Farm: Redstar420.com
Riot Seeds: Riotseeds.nl
Sensi Seeds: Sensiseeds.com
Short Stuff Seeds: Shortstuffseeds.com
Sinsemilla Nursery: Mmjclones.org (Grow consultations offered as well.)
Soma Seeds: Somaseeds.nl

Spliff Seeds: Spliff.nl
The Joint Doctor: Jointdoctordirect.net
TH Seeds: Thseeds.com

Cannabis Gear:
Bubblebag.com – Creator of Bubble Bags
Bcnorthernlights.com – Grow cabinets
Hydrofarm.com – Large hydroponics company
Hydrohuts.com – Hydroponic grow boxes
Hydroplexonline.com – Manufacturer of the Spinner
Ledgrowlight.com – Growl LED lights
Mmjars.com – Medical storage jars
Stealthgrow.com – LED lighting
Trimpro.ca – Trimmers and harvest supplies

Index

and ultra violet light, 51, 160, 303

The Joint Doctor
  Lowryder, 146, 193
thrips, 204
timers, 52–53
tobacco
  health risks, 253, 313–14
tomato plants
  nutritional requirements, 76
ton of skunk, 187–90
Total Dissolved Solids (TDS), 105–6
transplanting, 94
  clones, 95
treetop cultivation, 184–85
triacontanol, 102
trichomes, 7, 223, 227
troubleshooting, 308–12
  fungus and fungal diseases, 212–15
  growth problems, 113–15, 287
  hydroponic systems, 113–15
  insects, 203–7
  pH levels, 105
  spider mites, 203, 204, 209, 308–10
  viruses, 216
tube systems, 129, 132, 134
tumblers, 229–30, 307
tungsten halogen lamps, 51

ultra violet light, 51, 160, 303

vaporizers, 239

vegetative growth stage
  gender identification, 299–300, 301
  humidity levels, 293
  length of, 299
  light cycles, 4, 298
  metal halide lights (MH), 46
  NPK ratios, 96
  nutrient solutions, 96, 301
  pruning, 301
  Sea of Green (SOG), 148, 151
vents and ventilation
  compact cultivation, 140
  fan size, to determine, 53
  generators, 33
  odor control, 14, 24–25, 297–98
  pantyhose filters, 203
vermiculite, 15, 78
  for starting seeds, 89, 118
viruses, 216

water
  aquarium water, 84
  in compost, 75
  hard water, 107, 293
  overwatering, 312
  pH levels, 70
  tap water, 102, 107
  temperature, 12
watering systems
  capillary watering, 122
  drip irrigation systems, 130–31
  organic cultivation, 102–3
  outdoor cultivation, 180
  tube systems, 129, 132, 134
  wick systems, 121, 124